SECRETS AND SYMPATHY

SECRETS AND SYMPATHY

Forms of Disclosure in Hawthorne's Novels

Gordon Hutner

The University of Georgia Press

Athens and London

© 1988 by the University of Georgia Press
Athens, Georgia 30602
All rights reserved
Designed by Mary Mendell
Set in Trump Medieval
The paper in this book meets the guidelines for
permanence and durability of the Committee on
Production Guidelines for Book Longevity of the
Council on Library Resources.
Printed in the United States of America
92 91 90 89 88   5 4 3 2 1

Library of Congress Cataloging in Publication Data
Hutner, Gordon. Secrets and sympathy: forms of
disclosure in Hawthorne's novels / Gordon Hutner.
p.   cm.   Bibliography: p.   Includes index.
ISBN 0-8203-0992-3 (alk. paper)
1. Hawthorne, Nathaniel, 1804–1864—Criticism
and interpretation. 2. Secrecy in literature. 3.
Sympathy in literature. 4. James, Henry, 1843–
1916—Criticism and interpretation. I. Title.
PS1892.S42H88 1988
813'.3—dc19   87-20583
CIP
British Library Cataloging in Publication Data
available

To my mother and to the memory of my father,
who first instructed me in sympathy

CONTENTS

ACKNOWLEDGMENTS

I wish to express my gratitude to the Graduate School of the University of Wisconsin for its financial support during two summers. I would also like to thank several of my colleagues at Wisconsin, including William Andrews, E. N. Feltskog, William T. Lenehan, and Joseph Wiesenfarth, for their helpful advice. Most especially, I would like to thank Sargent Bush and Jeffrey Steele for their patience and their cogent criticism of this manuscript. It is also a pleasure to acknowledge the indispensable aid of Kathleen Diffley of the University of Iowa; her incisive suggestions helped me to see my book. Over the years, I have incurred debts to Alan Howard of the University of Virginia and Perry Lentz of Kenyon College for their vigorous scrutiny of these pages. Both have led me to grasp my ideas and to refine their expression. Kathleen Dauck and Mary Ann Ford are expert typists who provided diligent and good-humored support in preparing this manuscript.

My greatest debt—it should be no secret—is to David Levin of the University of Virginia. He first encouraged my interest in Hawthorne and gave many hours of his time in directing this project from its inception through its completion. His example of a scholar's generosity, rigor, and kindness is more than any student could hope to find.

INTRODUCTION

A recent biographer of Hawthorne closes his account with a story that Julian Hawthorne tells of a visit to his father's friend, Herman Melville. The novelist remarked to Julian that "Hawthorne had all his life concealed some great secret, which would, were it known, explain all the mysteries of his career."[1] Let us resolve, from the beginning of this study of secrets and Hawthorne's major romances, that this alleged "great secret" cannot be ascertained. The relinquishment of any search for a key to the relation between the author's life and works enables us instead to examine the functions that secrets perform in the texts and thus to develop a rhetoric of secrecy out of Hawthorne's conception. For the consequences of secrets, and the narrative method of simultaneously concealing and revealing them, are fundamental to Hawthorne's view of the life of the mind, the life of society, and the life of the text. The haunting sense that some central mystery needs to be disclosed but is often deferred and sometimes withheld is one of the most distinguishing features of Hawthorne's fiction. A Hawthorne novel will often seem immersed in this mystery, enveloped by a secret which the author struggles or refuses to articulate, at least until the close, to give meaning and motive to plot events. So the desire to define an implied relation between the circumstances of Hawthorne's biography and the operations within any one of his novels can distract readers from understanding the general concerns that secrets raise in this writer's oeuvre. In a sense, this argument commences with the wish to respect Hawthorne's notorious personal privacy: even as I mean, in places, to examine Hawthorne's secretly veiled way of talking about himself in his works, the primary interest of this analysis is to study the presence of secrets—their purposes, effects, and themes—in those works, so that we may come to know Hawthorne's achievement even better than we already do. Throughout, I focus on the questions that have alerted the attention of previous readers—the relation between "The Custom-House" and *The Scarlet Letter*, the problem of the ending in *The House of the Seven Gables*, the point of view in *The Blithedale Romance*, the interest of withheld information in *The Marble Faun*—in order to develop a paradigm for reading Hawthorne.

The idea of the mysterious in Hawthorne's works is so readily available that it will be to the point to suggest immediately that the interests of this study are not at all biographical or psychological, though as a matter of course, basic facts and credible postulations will necessarily be brought to bear on a wider concern for broadening the issues that secrets create in Hawthorne's romance narratives. A study of secrets in Hawthorne's novels does not seek to rediscover or rehabilitate this nineteenth-century author's place in our national literary history. It seeks instead to explore the implications of the ways in which this writer saw himself writing, why and how he meant to make secret what readers want to demystify. Many inquiries into Hawthorne's fiction sooner or later concentrate on some debt that the novels pay to the author's private life, and many readers have offered deft, provocative explanations of how the fiction is enlivened this way. In fact, one of the most recent students of this subject titles his report of the correspondence between incest themes and little-known events in the family history *Hawthorne's Secret*, while others have researched equally compelling versions of the implied relation between the life and the fiction.[2] The question of how and why Hawthorne brings himself into his texts has fascinated his interpreters, so much so that, for all of six decades' warning to trust the tale rather than the teller, the image of a brooding Hawthorne still hovers over scholarly discussion. Yet the romantic notion that the further study of his personality will provide a key is unnecessarily limiting. The search for some "great secret" really substitutes one discourse of reading for another rather than meeting the discourse Hawthorne actually establishes, one that has proven so remarkably supple that it has accommodated as sweeping a range of interpretation as any other American novelist's. Only the much more prolific Faulkner and James invite as many and as variously specialized ways of reading as Hawthorne, whose rhetoric has opened itself to a host of critical allegories.[3] Moreover, one personality theme or version of Hawthorne's world view will illuminate some issues while blinding interpreters to others that another theme helps to justify. I argue that secrecy, the positing of the unsaid as a vital feature of novelistic discourse, creates a manifold rhetoric for interpreting Hawthorne's romance art. The conviction guiding the close readings offered here in explication of Hawthorne's major works is that secrets in narrative serve not only biographical and psychoanalytic themes or stylistic values, but they also function to clarify issues of genre, of history and culture, along with conditions of reception. My study does not aspire to be either a phenomenology or archaeology of the secret, but it will demonstrate, through several points of emphasis, how fundamental for Hawthorne is the reader's responsiveness to the critical mass that secrecy generates.

Secret is a portentous, "complex" word for Hawthorne, and he uses it frequently and variously in his writings, especially after 1849.[4] He favors it because it signifies the whole range of qualities we now so readily associate with his epistemological interests—mystery, ambiguity, privacy—and characteristic expression—the implied, equivocal, obfuscated. He invokes it elusively; no single value can always be assigned. A secret may mean what exists but is not disclosed or what is hidden but which eventually can be revealed. It may also mean that which the reader should know but which the writer pointedly refuses to say or cannot express. A secret may be something the reader does not know, while the author does, or something some characters know but which readers are not yet entitled, and may never be, to learn. A secret may be rea-

sonably ascertained, yet it can also be left maddeningly indeterminate. Some can be verified positively, while others, like the presence and origins of the *A* on Dimmesdale's breast, cannot. A secret,
like Hilda's knowledge of murder, may not warrant the drama it
infuses; others, like Coverdale's "foolish little secret" of love, do
not explain the stories they have prompted. However obscure or
plain, secrets so predominate Hawthorne's plots, settings, characters, and style that each romance ultimately turns on a secret,
sometimes several: What would *The Scarlet Letter* be if Hester
named her lover in the second chapter? How would *Seven Gables*
be changed if the truth behind Maule's Curse were known earlier?
What would happen in *The Blithedale Romance* if Coverdale could
easily learn his friends' "secrets" or could readily share his own?
What would *The Marble Faun* be about if the identity of Miriam's
model were immediately available or if she could confess her "horrible secret" to Kenyon? Rather than point to the tenuousness of
any plot that depends on crucial yet withheld information to stimulate its unfolding, these questions call to mind the centrality of
secrets in Hawthorne's romances and his habitual insistence on
the secret as a basic fact of experience.

   In these broad respects, Hawthorne's exploiting of a secret to propel his plots is linked to one of narrative's fundamental features,
the covert communicating of special knowledge or sacred wisdom
through the telling of a tale, which, in turn, suggests an implied
message that the careful interpreter is supposed to recover.[5] Not
only does this function apply to Hawthorne's concern to impart
moral instruction, but also does it give his romance art the resonance of "magical narratives," connecting the force of Hawthorne's
historically operative consciousness and socially motivated rhetoric with the illusion of an even eternal and transcultural power.[6]
Secrets, by their very nature, appeal to this pregnancy of transcendent possibilities, since those who have and keep a secret believe in
its power to sustain, by granting identity, or to destroy, if only in
the attenuated form of risking shame.[7] Thus, not at all surprisingly, the secret, signifying latent meanings, proves invaluable to
the conventions and assumptions of fiction, as may be suggested in
the plethora of novels, stories, plays, and films that use the word in

their titles. Indeed, Julian Hawthorne aptly intuited his father's commitment to the secret as a privileged interest for fiction when he published some of Hawthorne's unfinished manuscripts as *Dr. Grimshawe's Secret*.

Devoted as they are to treatments of secrets, Hawthorne's novels ambivalently participate in the prevailing novelistic convention of mimetic narrative that the revealing of a secret will illuminate the plot events or confirm the writer's sense that the troubled world of experience has been edifyingly rectified. Although each of Hawthorne's novels ends with a revelation or confession, each ends somewhat inconclusively, offering resolutions of less certainty than they can be argued to perpetrate. The qualified exposure of the *A* on Dimmesdale's chest is exemplary, since no revelation—even at its most naked—is clear and complete for Hawthorne. It remains an open question whether the secrets told finish the proceedings appropriately, like the "secret spring" in *Seven Gables*, or if they conclude the plot at all. Even the short stories which would seem to hinge on the revelation of a secret—the meaning of a black veil, the truth behind Dr. Heidegger's experiment or of Goodman Brown's experience, the nature of the bosom serpent—demonstrate that the secrets finally affixed do not answer the several kinds of questions Hawthorne's tales raise and elaborate, as if to suggest that our understanding is destined only to be always partial. The novels may be more compromised by a narrative logic centered on the enacting or elucidating of a mystery that is never satisfyingly brought to a conclusion. When secrets are told, they seem inadequate, or their revelation is aborted, foreclosed, even negated, as we see in *The Marble Faun*. Conceivably, Hawthorne might have added the kind of epilogue that he attaches to his last novel to any of its predecessors: the author imagining whether he should tell all he knows, holding out the possibility that there is still more to tell, or whether he should leave the reader, as he does, in a chronically frustrated state of merely relative certainty.

Hawthorne is famous for this frustration, appearing coy in his unwillingness, or incapacity, to make his meaning explicit yet seductively complex in the qualifications he provides. The studied evasiveness of his style—the ambiguous alternatives, subtle distinctions, ironic contradictions—contributes to producing the effect of secrecy as an animating, ineluctable condition for his fictions. The style itself reinforces this conviction and submits the reader to a world where certainty, especially moral and psychological knowledge, is impossible or, at best, problematic. The frustration that some find oppressive and the gratification that others find rewarding in reading Hawthorne come out of the density of this style, especially for its expression of the artist's reluctance to make bald the issues he sets before the reader, withholding the key he has indicated that readers need. In this way, Hawthorne presents an example of the author as enjoying a special status as the knower of secrets, even as he also is ready to disavow knowing or to deny the interest of those secrets. Why Hawthorne assumes this position is a question to be addressed directly, but this dual process of promising and deferring disclosure lends his rhetoric its characteristic tension. Out of these dually competing narrative directions, Hawthorne makes secrets "narratable," for they provide the very atmosphere in which actions take on meaning, characters exist, in his fiction.[8] Readers are to become absorbed in the general and pervasive life of secrets, where mystery is enshrined as inescapable. Discovering the unknown or unknowable, the unsaid or unsayable, constitutes the very interest of the characters' experience and the narrative's activity. For the distinguishing of whether the unknown can be learned and whether the unsaid can be disclosed become the very questions that a Hawthorne romance finally investigates.

How Hawthorne's fiction instructs his readers in grasping secrets is fundamental to any rhetoric or thematics of secrecy. Only the right kind of response will bring readers properly to appreciate and seize the ways in which Hawthorne renders secrets—of the psyche, of the social life, of the cultural mind. The response that Hawthorne most wishes to excite is one of "apprehensive sympathy," as he describes in the preface to *The Marble Faun*, the faculty that he asks his ideal reader to exert. This sympathy yields the instinctive, spiritual, even visceral response that confirms what Hawthorne cannot, will not, or dares not articulate, the secrets buried in his texts. Sympathy, like the secret, is scarcely a new value in reading Hawthorne, yet the ways in which the words are linked together, and the implications of their conjoining, secure an integrated understanding of his major romances.[9]

Like *secret*, "sympathy" is also the kind of "vague rich intimate" word that opens itself to several kinds of analysis: rhetorical and moral, to be sure, but also epistemological, social, and, as A. N. Kaul and Harold Kaplan suggest, political.[10] The conjunction of these key words is habitual in Hawthorne's prose and signifies a paradigm that Hawthorne himself implies. As he writes to Sophia in a well-known letter concerning his refusal to tell his mother and sisters of his marriage:

> Thou wilt not think that it is caprice or stubbornness that has made me hitherto resist thy wishes. Neither, I think, is it a love of secrecy and darkness. I am glad to think that God sees through my heart; and if any angel has power to penetrate into it, he is welcome to know everything that is there. Yes; and so may any mortal, who is capable of full sympathy and therefore worthy to come into my depths. But he must find his own way there. I can neither guide him nor enlighten him. It is this involuntary reserve, I suppose, that has given the objectivity to my writing. And when people think that I am pouring myself out in a tale or essay, I am merely telling what is common to human nature, not what is peculiar to myself. I sympathize with them—not they with me.[11]

Rarely is Hawthorne so explicit about his personality, his art, and their relation. In his mind, the necessity of keeping secrets, his "involuntary reserve," is to be met in love and reading through the sensitive penetration that makes one "worthy to come into [his] depths." This reserve in his imaginative writing also obeys the "tacit law" in his family that "our deepest heart-concernments are not to be spoken of," a stricture that results in an "incapacity of free communion."[12] Here Hawthorne instructs Sophia in how to love him and also introduces her into how to be a member of his family, how to communicate by giving and taking hints from the implied or the obscure. The passage, in fact, follows a description of how unrewarding is his explicit talk of his beloved to others, as if to offer her an example of how the "deepest heart-concernments" can only be dissembled, since they risk being voided or trivialized by "free communion." Such talk can capture "nothing of thine inner and essential self," he says, and by implication can communicate nothing of his own essential self. Whether Hawthorne derives his premises for a rhetoric of secrecy from formative family experience is, of course, less the point than the myth he is creating here, the fiction he lives and writes by. He posits that his reserve is not a love of secrecy for its own sake, but a manner of communication that stipulates how others must come into his sphere, that is, through sympathetic penetration. His powers of sympathy with the common lot of humanity give him access to the secrets of all, and for others to know him, they must extend their own capacities, not rely on any guidance from the author.

In teaching Sophia how to love him in "full sympathy," Hawthorne provides the occasion for readers to see how he means to be read. Perhaps as a further defense against self-revelation—his "pouring" himself out in his works—he denies any personal content, a tactic that will prove central to *The Scarlet Letter*. Instead, he insists that he gives nothing "peculiar" of himself, only what is "common to human nature." Here we may observe Hawthorne's characteristic posture of keeping his personal relation to his creations secret, and he does this, paradoxically, by claiming that his psychological interests are general. We may even detect a further reserve in his emphatic distancing of himself from his readers. He is fully capable of sympathy, but readers, we see, must earn the sympathy that they feel with the aloof author, that he can only be intruded upon by those who are worthy, so that what is "peculiar" to himself will not be violated. Thus does the need for expressing secrets call for a corresponding intuition, one that is both perceptive and compassionate.

In this letter, and throughout the canon, these complex words appear in the same context, especially when Hawthorne couples a value for the untold with a call for a special intuition. Hawthorne's characteristic sense is that a secret may be culled or guessed, without having to be exposed, by someone in sympathy. For Hawthorne, sympathy imparts a Romantic ideal of communication; it predicates an understanding that passes beyond words. In this regard, it is an emotional state that takes on the burden of a moral and social imperative. Aside from being a privileged value for communication, sympathy is most of all the condition for any effective rhetorical relation, connecting in ever-tauter terms the reader as the friend or gentle person an author can address.[13] Through sympathy, a reader can become the sharer of the secrets that are embedded in the text, can become the "unseen brother of the soul," as Hawthorne idealizes this relation in the preface to *The Marble Faun.*

Hawthorne's narrative procedures are calculated to win the reader's more thorough engagement, a heightening and strengthening of the capacity for sympathy, even as Hawthorne protests that he "can neither guide" the reader "nor enlighten him." Through such techniques as the formula of alternatives, multivalent symbols, interpolated tales, and blocked disclosures, a reader's curiosity, Hawthorne hoped, will be raised, intensified to the point that it more nearly matches the writer's apprehensiveness or conviction of a secret's power. Especially is the reader encouraged to lay aside initial assumptions, alter premises, question preliminary responses; then the reader is more prepared either to submit to the example of sympathy that a character, like Phoebe or Hilda, provides or to improve upon the ones that other characters, like Coverdale or Kenyon, present. Sooner or later, each novel gives a wrong application of sympathy, and its deleterious effects, which readers can use to test their own sympathetic powers and which they may eventually overturn. Thus even as Hawthorne avers that he cannot explicitly bring another party into his own depths, the whole elaborate process of inference that he sets before the reader is geared to making the reader's sympathy that much finer. In this way, readers are brought to an enlarged understanding of the "objectivity" that Hawthorne prides himself on as "merely telling what is common to human nature" and are led to find their own secrets.

Here we may observe how Hawthorne wraps himself in mystification, using this moral philosophy to justify and defend his own peculiar reserve. The special call for sympathy can mask an idealized vision of union, one that Hawthorne could involve himself in if he chooses, but one which he finally forbears to join. The latent hostility—indeed, the antipathy—implied in this relation goes beyond Hawthorne's asking of another party to include oneself in a communion that the writer himself declines. In Hawthorne's version, it is up to others to find their way into his heart; if anything, he will block their efforts, obstruct their view. The writer constructs a rhetorical situation in which the reader must call upon reserves of sympathy, must extend beyond the confines of the self, in order to meet the author, while with monumental detachment, the writer refuses to submit to the same leveling, even democratizing expenditures. Readers who do so may even win the writer's contempt rather than approbation, for they are participating in an activity he has bid them to enter but from which he withdraws. Yet this attitude is recommended to the reader as a worthy one in the name of a moral faculty, a vagueness of motive in which Hawthorne may take refuge.

This vagueness, the reader comes to see, is purposeful insofar as one may imagine grasping Hawthorne's meanings, although the author wants to keep them elusive. The play of possible meanings within a phrase, the senses suggested, and the doubts incurred lead the reader to surmise that a secret is being expressed and that its import can be known. At this, Hawthorne demurs and suggests that whatever secrets are to be learned are of the most general cast, applying for all, even as they may seem to bear some personal stamp, which to some extent, of course, they do. Notoriously is this frustrated and frustrating interaction the very subject and scene of "The Minister's Black Veil," which is a tale as much about a community of interpreters' failure to respond to a publicly displayed secret as it is of the Reverend Mr. Hooper's obsession.[14] The secret that the veil signifies is never individualized, though several possibilities are raised. Instead, at the close, the secret of Parson Hooper's veil, and his reasons for donning this peculiar habiliment, is understood as a distinctly general one, that "on every visage a Black Veil," with each member of the community concealing a sinful secret. Like the story's parishioners, readers are invited to make the very gesture that the veil simultaneously demands and denies. Instead of bringing together a community in the recognition of its sins, the parson's strategies only show the limitations of his community's sympathy, the value ascribed only to the parson's beloved Elizabeth but upon which she is forbidden to act. Similarly, Hawthorne's rhetorical strategies divide a reader's attention, so that the personal peculiarity of a secret is subordinated to a seem- ingly objectified account of what is human nature.

The special value that Hawthorne attributes to the reader's sym- pathy is cloudy and notably problematic. No doubt, Hawthorne's conviction results from his college instruction in the eighteenth- century Scottish philosophers, an interest that he later expanded during the twelve-year indenture to his art. Among the many intel- lectual pursuits of that period of intensive study was his reading of Adam Smith, who made systematic the notion of sympathy as a moral principle. Furthermore, Hawthorne's interest in sympathy as a rhetorical value may well have been improved by his reading of Thomas Carlyle, who characterized this power of response as the primary attribute of a critic.[15] More likely than not, however, the underlying strength of Hawthorne's sense of sympathy was neither personally constructed nor intellectually achieved, but derived from a cultural norm shared by the learned and unlearned alike. Sympathy was so prized during the late eighteenth and nineteenth centuries that its popularity as a value for enhanced personal com- munication was formidable, a term used more for its resonance than its definition. Since Lord Kames, sympathy had worked so forcefully as a key word that its effects still may be perceived in hermeneutic and psychoanalytic traditions.[16] Nor was Hawthorne alone among American writers in cherishing the moral and critical dimensions of elective affinity. The word appears again and again in Emerson, Whitman, Melville, Fuller, and Thoreau, though none of these writers use it quite so tellingly as Hawthorne does for combining moral, social, and rhetorical characteristics. So popular was sympathy as a moral and social concept that it invited both an elaboration and attack during the second half of the century. The pragmatist sociologist Charles Horton Cooley would use it as the cornerstone for his doctrine of complicity, while Clemens has Huck Finn satirize the inauthenticity of the abused term and its reformist application when Pap has his hour of salvation: "The old man said that what a man wanted that was down, was sympathy;

and the judge said it was so; so they cried again."[17] Cultural by-word that it became, when Henry James criticizes Hawthorne's indulgent overuse of *sympathy*, the younger writer's irritation is so patent that he may have been annoyed as much with the general habit of New England mind, long muddled by casual talk about superior communication and understanding, as with his predecessor's apparent intellectual laziness.[18]

The particular uses that Hawthorne finds for sympathy are manifold. Sometimes the word suggests a simple value for simple intuition; at other moments it is weighted to mean a rarefied state of exchange where secrets can be expressed, even without one or both parties becoming conscious of the negotiation. Whether the senses that Hawthorne discovers are the Romantic sacralizing of personal union or the dimmer belief that the possibilities of articulating the deepest "heart-concernments" are futile, he reserves this term, at the least, as a substitute for any precise sense of the temperament and conditions facilitating the act of inference. If the word is used consistently at all in Hawthorne's writing, it applies to the capacity to learn, through a faculty more acute than rational intellection, an incisiveness based on a moral conviction. For sympathy readies one to hear or to share in another's confession of secrets; it eases the nervousness of having secrets brought to light. In addition, sympathy reminds one who keeps yet wishes to tell a secret that someone else exists who can appreciate what may need to be left unsaid. In this, we may also understand how sympathy is supposed to take both parties, listener and teller or writer and reader, out of the confines of the self.

Rather than readers who, unbidden, understand all, Hawthorne means to create an audience that is gently skeptical, though compassionately disposed, and warily willing to enter the qualified intimacy that the writer counts upon.[19] Anything in excess of this skepticism could lead the reader to suspend sympathy's critical dimension, for too complete a sympathy leads to the reader's blind acceptance and thus to the limitation of the reader's powers to go beyond the self and the writer's purposes in exercising those powers. For Hawthorne, sympathy must be "apprehensive," a quality of restlessness that allows readers a happier, if inexplicit, communion with the writer's mind than any simplistic, undifferentiated view of Hawthorne's motives or a text's meanings. Such sympathy preserves a necessary distance, as if the writer were warning his readers against appropriating what belongs to the author. So even as Hawthorne may seem to follow a conventional sense of addressing readers as potential friends, he also wants to uphold an important difference, perhaps out of a fear of having his text subsumed by a reader, of having his work removed from his execution and authority. Moreover, his anxiety over the reader's tendency to violate a text may come out of the apparent fear of having his "peculiar" or private life ferreted out of the universal traits he describes. Here Hawthorne embraces a Romantic value for communication only to modify it, or so he makes the gesture in the preface to the reissued *Twice-Told Tales* of 1851, where he describes his early stories as imperfectly successful attempts to enter an "intercourse with the world" and announces his desire for the state of rhetorical intimacy by renouncing any claim to its possibility. This inversion reveals a characteristic double bind, one that his narrative method of eliciting sympathy imitates and that is reproduced in the romances through a structure of ambivalence.

The specific uses that Hawthorne finds for "sympathy" are to be found in the ways he connects it to the learning of a secret. In the conclusion of this study, I will suggest how Hawthorne serves as a precursor for a nineteenth-century tradition exemplified in the career of Henry James, but throughout this analysis lies the assumption that Hawthorne's invoking of readers' sympathy as the response he believed necessary for the completing of his works also supplies a narrative logic for the century's characteristic mode of intellectual inquiry. Not only does the learning and telling of secrets lie near the very center of Romantic Prometheanism, but also is sympathy, for the critical Hawthorne, the enabling power of response to a world newly being seen as mysterious, filled with hidden sources of knowledge. The probing of mystery, the learning of secrets, emerges either as the positivist, scientific endeavor or the characteristic reaction to a social life grown increasingly complex and challenging, as Richard Sennett argues in *The Fall of Public Man*.[20] Sympathy marks the human effort to establish and verify meanings in a world no longer illuminated by Divine Revelation. Sympathy sanctions a spirit of inquiry, one which comes from the close, though not complete, identification with another. Through sympathy, the secret purposes of others can be discerned, corroborated, and met, without being made explicit. In the less than perfect union it is supposed to create, sympathy allows neither party to risk a vacating of the self or of having the self violated. Yet to the extent that sympathetic apprehension keeps the unsaid intact, it also participates in the mystification that it is intended to penetrate. Thus, paradoxically, sympathy confirms the necessity for keeping secrets by offering a heart-knowledge—based on conjecture—in place of a more radical and thoroughgoing skepticism. In this, Hawthorne retreats from the thunderous NO! that Melville ascribes to his vision, seeking refuge instead in the value of the human heart's "sanctity."

The means by which sympathy is to bring one into sensitive understanding of secrets is given its most detailed treatment when Hawthorne defines his relation to his public in "The Custom-House." In the sketch, he makes into doctrine, through myriad qualifications, veilings, and dissemblings, the dynamic relation between secrets and sympathy, a rhetoric that *The Scarlet Letter* transforms into psychological, moral, and cultural analysis. Again in *The House of the Seven Gables*, Hawthorne finds the correspondence between the terms irresistible and portrays their connection, especially in scenes and images of story telling and representation. In *The Blithedale Romance*, the conjunction of these terms appears only occasionally, whereas their implications stand as the novel's predominant subject. Hawthorne returns, in *The Marble Faun*, to the sustained and consistent coupling of the words to the effect of bringing together the novel's subject and Hawthorne's meditation on aesthetics. While there may be some biographical schema to observe in these shifts, these potent words in Hawthorne's vocabulary would surely have come to the author's pen without ado, much less calculation. Their immediate availability recommends them to the writer's attention—and ours. It may be that the circumstances of writing his first mature romance encouraged Hawthorne to inquire more deeply into the demands of both his rhetoric and his subject, just as he was perhaps more supremely conscious than ever before of his relation to his work and the possibility of exposure. When Hawthorne comes to write the *Seven Gables*, having seen how his personal sense of history could be turned into a romance, he may have turned to a more rigorous consideration of the requirements of the genre he had so recently taken up. Similarly, in *Blithedale*, Hawthorne seems most interested in the relation between a novel's responsiveness to the society that creates its subject matter. In *The Marble Faun*, all these issues combine to make Hawthorne confront, as his subject, the transmission and reception of art. I will address these concerns as they arise in order to demonstrate how the relation between secrets and sympathy elucidates such fundamental categories of literary study as the work as an expression of a writer's oeuvre, of genre and its changes, of a socially observable model for interpretation, and of the rhetorical relation between writer and reader. My method will be to study how these four romances treat these issues in ways that Hawthorne's contemporaneous readers could recognize, that the author's modern interpreters have analyzed, and that contemporary readers can see as reflecting their own theoretical concerns.

Other writers invoke sympathy for one reason or another, just as other writers assign special meanings or develop interests for treating the secret, but Hawthorne brings these terms together in ways that especially serve our understanding of his romance fiction. While this consideration of Hawthorne's rhetoric of secrecy will provide new responses to some traditional questions in the study of Hawthorne's major romances, my purpose in bringing these readings together is to contribute to a norm for reading Hawthorne. The following chapters observe how secrets begin with the self and then echo, in the text that writer and reader share, in the culture to which they both belong, and in the revelatory nature of art that has drawn them together in the first place. Each chapter, in its turn, takes up the progress of these concerns, as the focus of each chapter moves from issues of biography and psychology, to the constitutive features of the novel, to milieu, and to response. Thus the relation between secrets and sympathy can be submitted to a broad range of critical approaches and can help to illuminate the array of critical responses that Hawthorne's novels continue to inspire.

CHAPTER ONE

Secrets and Sympathy in *The Scarlet Letter*

A famous passage near the close of *The Scarlet Letter* makes emblematic the implied rhetoric of Hawthorne's simultaneous revealing and concealing of secrets. Illustrative as it is, we can only infer from Hawthorne's description of Dimmesdale's Election Sermon how readers are meant to be instructed in sympathy, just as readers also infer how the parson's personal experience stimulates his larger assessment of the colony's destiny.[1] In observing Hester's response to her beleaguered lover's finest public hour, readers may take a lesson in apprehending the particular power of Hawthorne's narrative, for Hester, even more than the rest of the rapt audience, listens "with such intentness, and sympathized so intimately" that she perceives the underlying personal passion of the minister's rhetoric. Even if she could not distinguish the words themselves, the "sermon had throughout a meaning for her." Her attention, Hawthorne tells us, is necessarily diverted from the literal meanings—the "grosser medium"—for those would have only "clogged the spiritual sense" and thwarted her intimate response. As an interpreter, she can hear the oration, "muffled as the sound was"; so keenly does she attend to the parson's tone of voice rather than to his words that she is moved to identify herself with that voice, "having caught the low undertone" and "then ascended with it . . . through progressive gradations of sweetness and power." Its volume seems "to envelop her with an atmosphere of awe and solemn grandeur," but it is not the "majestic" timbre alone that confers upon Dimmesdale's voice its imperial command. Instead, there was forever in it an "essential plaintiveness," a modulation equally compelling:

> A loud or low expression of anguish,—the whisper, or the shriek, as it might be conceived, of suffering humanity, that touched a sensibility in every bosom! At times this deep strain of pathos was all that could be heard, and scarcely heard, sighing amid a desolate silence. But even when the minister's voice grew high and commanding,—when it gushed irrepressibly upward,—when it assumed its utmost breadth and power, so overfilling the church as to burst its way through the solid walls, and diffuse itself in the open air,—still, if the auditor listened intently, and for the purpose, he could detect the same cry of pain. What was it? The complaint of a human heart, sorrow-laden, perchance guilty, telling its secret, whether of guilt or sorrow, to the great heart of mankind; beseeching its sympathy or forgiveness,—at every moment,—in each accent,—and never in vain! It was this profound and continual undertone that gave the clergyman his most appropriate power.[2]

This "expression of anguish," a secret's beseeching of sympathy, provides the tonal complement for Hawthorne's methodical indirection. The catch in the throat, understood as the murmuring of the heart, expresses the presence of a secret, makes manifest the unsaid. Similarly, this scene of expression and response indicates how Hawthorne exploits the "profound and continual undertone" throughout the novel, and he begins by masking, with his genial wit, the "deep strain of pathos" embedded in "The Custom-House." There the defensively confessional character of Hawthorne's humorous account muffles the "cry of pain" that resounds in the whisper or the shriek of a secret's exhorting of sympathy.

■ Convinced that his new book would "weary very many people and disgust some," Hawthorne added a preface, in part to balance the romance's gloomy proceedings with the warmth of his clever wit. The tone of the sketch delighted some readers and angered others, who doubted the propriety of the author's mocking assessment of his recent dismissal as the Surveyor of Customs at Salem. Of course, the satire gave Hawthorne the chance to clear his name after an embarrassing political squabble, but more important, the sketch allowed him to conjoin the story of private guilt publicly displayed with his own sense of secret crime and punishment.[3] This connection between the characters' fortunes and a writer's purposes has been so cogent that critics have long sought to explain the romance's achievement, and its haunting intensity, through some biographical rationale.[4]

None of his other romances prompted Hawthorne to meditate so elaborately upon its production or his personal relation to his work. Only once before, in the preface to *Mosses From an Old Manse*, did he introduce a work with so extended a narrative, nor would he ever again. The richness of his relation to *The Scarlet Letter* may be observed in the widely diverse explanations to which "The Custom-House" gives rise, especially in the historical and psychological parallels that readers have discovered.[5] I argue, however, that the sketch and the romance are unified in ways Hawthorne did not avow but which can be discerned in the rhetoric of secrecy that they share. That relation is established in the ways both communicate secrets—dually mystifying the literal reality yet exposing and illuminating a secret's presence. Both the sketch and the romance adopt narrative strategies that elicit the reader's sympathetic response to a secret destined to remain indeterminate. Moreover, these strategies—of displacement, of inference—suggest the range of associations that Hawthorne counts on his readers to make and disclose how the character of a secret can be observed.

The interest of these narrative procedures, it should be stressed, is not so much the ultimate naming of a secret weighing upon Hawthorne or, even, as an older criticism would have it, the elucidating of a projected psychology that structures his novel. Instead, *The Scarlet Letter* demonstrates how that which cannot be said urges its unfolding, makes itself narratable.[6] For Hawthorne, a secret does this substantially through the response it inspires. In this public dimension of response lies the discovery of a secret's dual aspect—its psychological intensity and social range. The narrative that a secret generates becomes a dialectic of public and private meanings, the tone of which emerges out of anxieties over exposure or confession. *The Scarlet Letter* exemplifies this sociological significance of a secret insofar as the novel creates a "mode of realization" for the "individual's capacity or inclination to keep [a secret] to himself, in his resistance or weakness in the face of tempting betrayal." The tension that results between private and public narration not only registers the tone, but it also creates, according to Georg Simmel, a "counterplay" between concealment and revelation, out of which "spring nuances and fates of human interaction that permeate it entirely."[7]

In fact, Hawthorne doubles his sense of this counterplay when he introduces his novel about the public history of private lives with his private history of public life, "The Custom-House." This connection between Hawthorne's personal record and his characters' experience is held to be so intimate that one critic includes the novel with the sketch in a study of autobiography as a narrative form. While Hawthorne's "autobiography could not simply describe his public self, therefore, neither could it simply express his private self," writes William Spengemann. "It would have to display the private self in symbols that common sense could comprehend. At the same time, it would have to make the public self receptive to the heart's secret truths, no matter how unpalatable they might seem."[8] Calling the novel an autobiography, however, only adds to the confusion that Hawthorne so teasingly creates in the sketch devoted to his recent experiences as surveyor and preserves an arbitrary distinction between private and public domains.[9]

In Hawthorne's account, it is not so much that he lies about his attitude toward the post he had lost. He observes the truth about those circumstances, but he also suggests how it may be learned. The "manly" author (as his friend Bridge remembered him) represents the "firing" in a way that would quell his anger and ease his discomfort over having his good name trampled in the "public prints" during the controversy that surrounded the case.[10] Ousted from office as a routine of political patronage, Hawthorne schemed to keep his sinecure in spite of his professed ambivalence for the position. As much as he found the job to be enervating, he needed the financial security of a steady appointment. During the ensuing imbroglio over whether to help Salem's distinguished author, Hawthorne enlisted the support of Whigs and Democrats alike, who testified in a vigorous letter campaign to the virtue of extending his tenure. Hawthorne's suit was eventually frustrated by Whig politicos who alleged, perhaps by exaggerating questionable evidence, that while in office Hawthorne had tacitly approved of petty graft among his subordinates by doing nothing to stop a common (apparently traditional) practice of thievery. Hawthorne's enemies, led by Dr. Charles Upham, further claimed that the writer had permitted his name to be used for political purposes, even if Hawthorne contended that he was above such machinations.

At these disclosures Hawthorne's friends, their own reputations risked, could do little but withdraw their support and recall their letters. The increased public attention, once these misdemeanors were charged, humiliated Hawthorne all the more. Stephen Nissenbaum has argued that the sketch hides the truth about Hawthorne's dismissal and treats the novelist's conduct in terms that he, and his friends, preferred to believe. The sketch, for Nissenbaum, falsifies the actual Hawthorne: an artist in unflattering financial straits who worsened his predicament by trying to disguise his role in a political squabble and who rendered his guilt in the fanciful character of feigned detachment. Although Hawthorne assuredly was not the conniving partisan his enemies painted, neither was he the "political innocent pictured by his friends." According to this historian's carefully qualified account, Hawthorne "never wanted to dirty his hands, and he was generally able to avoid doing so," but "by trying to appear better than he actually was . . . he ended up looking worse." Nissenbaum pursues the implications of the artist's flattering self-description and explains that while the author plants the clue that "Nathaniel Hawthorne and the Surveyor were not quite the same person," this confusion of identities was, finally, "little more than a facade behind which his real self would remain, at best, dim." The preface, one may say, occupies a "neutral territory" where the Actual and the Imaginary meet, even as the romancer, animated he says by an "autobiographical impulse," professes to tell the truth.[11]

One need not accept all of this historian's lessons to see that the dominant strategy of the preface is obfuscation rather than confession.[12] As strong as the desire for self-justification may be, the author stipulates, from the outset, that a writer who addresses his public ought to "keep the inmost Me behind its veil. To this extent and within these limits," according to Hawthorne, may an author be "autobiographical, without violating either the reader's rights or his own."[13] As a policy for confession, these strictures are, at best, misleading, yet they are also of a piece with the novel's famous moral: "Be true! Be true! Be true! Show freely to the world, if not your worst, yet some trait whereby the worst may be inferred!" (260).

In aligning himself against the confessional mode, Hawthorne exploits the situation and insists on a special note of reserve. The author explains that his remarks do not require the "perfect sympathy" of a closest friend; instead, a confession can be hinted at to a listener who is both "kind and apprehensive," the writer entrusting himself to a reader of genial skepticism rather than one of ready acceptance. Yet no sooner does Hawthorne ask that this "kind and apprehensive" friend respond to his circumspect admissions than he avers how his real interests are not confessional at all but consist of "offering proofs of the authenticity of the narrative therein contained," that his real purpose in speaking of himself is his "desire to put myself in my true position as editor, or very little more. . . . this, and no other, is my reason for assuming a personal relation with the public" (4). Certainly, the reader is expected to share in the humor of Hawthorne's ironic qualifications, the playful modesty of his announced intentions, the whimsical treatment of a novelist's conventional disavowing of fiction's fictive nature, and even, perhaps, his tricky pun on "assuming" (as in feigning). Hawthorne's insistence on being the mere editor, however, wears after a while, and the reader begins to wonder why Hawthorne takes so much pleasure in persistently making this joke throughout the sketch. Nor does the reader yet know that Hawthorne first takes up this "true position" only at the very end of the novel.

The secret is that Hester and Dimmesdale's story and his own are intimately related, the chronicle of their ordeal a virtual transcription of the passions aroused through the recent embarrassments that well may have seemed traumatic to Hawthorne.[14] In his pose as "editor," he needed only to delete the personal details, leaving but traces in the narrative record and echoes in the voice that provide Hawthorne's most memorable romance with much of its force. It may be that Hawthorne never once saw this relation or, at least, not with the identifying passion that Flaubert invested in his adulteress. Yet as he read the novel on separate occasions to his wife, they both felt its highly charged quality. Once, when he read aloud the concluding chapters and, again, when he read from the proofs, Sophia was overcome by the experience, and Hawthorne himself was brought to tears.[15]

This deeply felt relation to the story of Hester's humiliating victimage and Dimmesdale's tale of anguished degradation may help to explain the furious burst of energy that produced *The Scarlet Letter.* Much has been made of the hectic composition in which Hawthorne was immersed: once he was freed from the stultifying life of a bureaucrat, writing may have seemed redemptive. It might also be that financial need now pushed him on. In addition, intensely as he may have felt such pressures, his anxieties were certainly increased by his mother's fatal illness during that bleak season.[16] Whatever the intimacy between Hawthorne's emotional circumstances and the romance he wrote, such relations are perhaps indefinable. Still, at the moment Hawthorne first adopts his role as editor, he also offers the dictum for being indirectly "true," which many readers have understood as summarizing the novel's moral vision of the relation between the private self and public expression and, I suggest, its narrative assumptions too: Hawthorne's call to show only the evidence whereby the "worst"—perhaps an untellable or indeterminate secret—may be inferred. In his editorial stance, Hawthorne could revise all the evidence the readers need to make this inference, just as he could pretend to strike from the record or could embellish upon that which too closely expresses what he would not or could not make explicit.

The psychology of this procedure is as much apparent in the preface as it is in the novel. About the suffering his situation caused him, Hawthorne could joke freely. But in a letter to his wife's brother-in-law, Horace Mann, Hawthorne addresses the cause of suffering much more seriously, even vitriolically. There he vows that a "man who should know better," Upham, his antagonist, will not go unpunished: "I will do my best to kill and scalp him in the public prints; and I think I shall succeed."[17] Hawthorne here recurs to the construction "public prints," as if to pay back in kind the scene of grief he wants to cause through the means that he himself suffered. The target for Hawthorne's revenge is not the lethargic, avuncular Customs Official from the sketch (as Nissenbaum rightly observes), but Chillingworth, the relentless if perhaps impotent investigator who scorns the privacy and "sanctity" of another human heart to see his distorted idea of justice served—a physician who ought to know better. Even more important than the figure for Hawthorne's vendetta is how the author conceives of his ideal revenge. Not only must this be a public act of writing, but also must Hawthorne's victim feel the same extent of punishment: to "kill and scalp" doubtless speaks more of an angrily impatient imagination than it does of any literal savagery Hawthorne means to inflict. Rather than the conventional expression of Indian triumph, scalping occurs to Hawthorne as a punishment worthy of the fearful injury he has felt. Thus he may controvert his sense of being violated by appropriating an uncivilized, brutish power to torture his tormentor. For the fear of being scalped, which Hawthorne would apparently like to instill in Dr. Upham, is an especially worthy punishment for a "decapitated surveyor" to impose, since such a fear, as Freud describes it, is a version of the fear of being beheaded.[18]

Angry as Hawthorne was in this threatened revenge, his image of punishment reminds the reader of "The Custom-House" of the image by which Hawthorne lightheartedly compares his political offenses to those of the *ancien régime*, which ended only at the guillotine. Indeed, Hawthorne's jokes about losing his head dominate the sketch's closing pages. Certainly, the guillotine image would have been a popular convention: The Reign of Terror was still sufficiently a part of anyone's political consciousness, and there was even a reference to the guillotine in a letter to a Boston newspaper earlier that summer. Furthermore, when Hawthorne returned from his last day at the office, he asked his wife—as his son records—whether she noticed anything missing, whereupon he informed her that he had lost one of his heads.[19] While one must be careful not to credit Julian's memory too highly (he was only three at the time of the conversation), the idea of losing one's job as tantamount to losing one's head may well have been a favorite joke in the family. But it wasn't merely a joke for Hawthorne. He so consistently coupled his firing with decapitation that he called a portrait for which he sat, soon after completing *The Scarlet Letter*, the image of "the very head that was cut off!" In fact, the portrait was the first one ever to please him, having captured his "bedevilled melancholy," and he lamented that it could not be used for *The Scarlet Letter*'s frontispiece, though later it served that purpose for the volumes of the *Seven Gables* that he circulated among his friends.[20]

Hawthorne's jokes about decapitation condense his complex reactions to his recent ordeal and, in simplifying his commingled sense of shame, punishment, and revenge, make those reactions into something he could accept. Exposed as a man of practical affairs actively serving mammon instead of the man who lives in the conviction that happiness comes from his artistic commitment to living by one's "highest sensibilities," Hawthorne could arrange his various irritations and find relief in the form of a joke.[21] Thus he could subdue his fear of betraying himself by observing wryly that his "greatest apprehension" was that he would settle to become a "tolerably good Surveyor." Even here, given the potential metaphor of writer-as-surveyor, Hawthorne keeps his anxieties under guard through a play on words. The psychological processes of such jokes temporarily lessen the weight of guilt and suffering that Hawthorne associates with the public display of the private mind. In the novel, however, he communicates his sense of the agony involved in public display when he describes the peculiar torment that Puritan criminals suffer at the pillory: This "portion of a penal machine" had been considered "as effectual an agent in the promotion of good citizenship, as ever was the guillotine among the terrorists of France." This "instrument of discipline" could "confine the human head in its tight grasp, and thus hold it up to the public gaze." Although Hester is spared "undergoing that gripe about the neck and confinement of the head," she still has to withstand the "very ideal of ignominy . . . made manifest in this contrivance." Perhaps Hawthorne knows all too well the "essence of this punishment" when he writes, "There can be no outrage, methinks, against our common nature,—whatever be the delinquencies of the individual,—no outrage more flagrant than to forbid the culprit to hide his face for shame" (SL, 55).

Oddly appropriate as Hawthorne may have found images of decapitation, they do not suddenly appear in his consciousness as a result of the political controversy. The fact is, a complication of visions of dismemberment—the root anxiety for decapitation, according to Freud—occurs to Hawthorne in an even more curious reflection recorded in his notebooks. This complex of images would be startling in any context; here it is especially arresting because it follows Hawthorne's musings upon the scarlet letter as the subject for a novel, perhaps as much as five years before he was fired and began to write his romance:

> The life of a woman, who, by the old colony law was condemned always to wear the letter A, sewed on her garment, in token of her having committed adultery.
> To make literal pictures of figurative expressions;—a man suddenly turned into a shower of briny drops. An explosion of laughter—a man blowing up, and his fragments flying about on all sides. He cast his eyes upon the ground, staring up at him in wonderment &c &c &c.[22]

It just cannot be determined whether Hawthorne made these entries at one sitting or whether hours or days intervened. But on whatever occasion, their psychological association is strong. Although these reflections may show that adultery coincidentally provides Hawthorne with an opportunity to engage the "question of metaphor and the problem of literal versus figurative language that claimed the attention of his Puritan forefathers," we may also see that in the second passage, the question of metaphor is subordinated to literalizing dismemberment, whereas in the first passage, the effect is to make the literal (letter) into a metaphor (fiction).[23] Why Hawthorne would link images of castration with adultery is the subject of an orthodox psychoanalytic inquiry, but we can at least conclude that the coupling of adultery and dismemberment, if not consecutive or concurrent in Hawthorne's mind, is duplicated when he comes to write the preface to his romance about the consequences of infidelity.

In the novel, Hawthorne makes metaphoric the literal charges against him by enlarging the allegation of political misconduct, which so mortified him, into an indictment significant enough to include the social extent of private transgressions. Adultery must have seemed appropriate, first, because its punishment in Puritan New England required such public confessions as Hawthorne pretends to make in "The Custom-House," but which often really were as exacting as Hester's ordeal. Moreover, as Tony Tanner argues, adultery comes to occupy the attention of nineteenth-century novelists because of its fundamentally subversive nature. It threatens the very structure of a middle-class society that values domesticity as an expression of personal and social worth.[24] Hawthorne's Boston surely would have understood adultery as a substantive danger, though not as severe as the Puritans held it to be against theirs. Adultery would readily suggest the sense of private sin that public exposure makes into a torment. To a culture priding itself on its edifying gentility, the image of the sexually directed or possessed transgressor would still bring down the weight of communal disapproval. Indeed, the Romantic enshrinement of adulterous lovers as promoting a value for the self beyond community could not have competed with Puritan social imperatives still in effect by 1850, as the novel seconds by refusing to ratify the lovers' claim that their union has "a consecration of its own." The choice of adultery, so recognizably a subject of mid-century fiction, must have seemed to Hawthorne as compelling an alternative as it was a popular one for representing secret crime to be publicized and punished. Perhaps as a guilty consequence of blinking at Custom House graft, Hawthorne believed his transgression betrayed an image of himself, thus violating Sophia's redemptive love in being untrue to the spirit of bourgeois respectability that he believed had graced their marriage. If so, this secret would be in keeping with the apologia he makes in the preface: his real crimes were against his own spirit.

Hawthorne's professional misconduct may have been so negligible that it really warrants the aloofness and wit with which he treats it. Out of his humiliation, however, Hawthorne wrought a story of sin and response that could broaden the scope of his recent experience in the life of public politics. In reshaping the circumstances of guilt and exposure into a novel about the effects of adultery, he enlarges allegations brought against him and gives them a more profound cultural resonance than his indiscretions, such as they were, literally merit. So intensified is the sense of guilt, the horror of self-recognition, the demand for revenge, the conviction of failure, that Hawthorne's characters become repositories for this deepening of a secret. Yet just as the characters can be understood as the splintering of so many fragments of Hawthorne's temperament, they also summarize the diverse social meanings a writer will project for a secret. Demonstrably as the characters resemble aspects of Hawthorne's psyche, they also configure various responses, in Hawthorne's New England, to values of privacy violated, needs of public life manipulated.

Even as Hawthorne may have meant the characters to correspond to historical personages, they also remark of mid-century values for voicing personal or modulating public positions.[25] Hester's characterization as the rebellious victim looks forward to the growing uneasiness over the subjugation of women, just as it alternately celebrates and criticizes the Romantic commitment to individual sovereignty. In harbingering the conflicted moral leader seeking compromises, even disastrously, Dimmesdale suggests the enfeebling ambivalence of moral authority in an antebellum society evading confrontation with its own sins. Chillingworth operates as the driven scientist of Romantic fiction to be sure, but he also exemplifies the new cultural figure of aggrandizement who abrogates all socializing influences in the pursuit of one's limited, selfish interests. Pearl, who is given as the very embodiment of the future, is dually predicated on contradictions that beset mid-century moral, social, and political life—American innocence and unruliness—perhaps expressing the feared illegitimacy or inauthenticity of a culture which, like Pearl, is "made afresh, out of new elements . . . a law unto herself" (135).

Marking each character's cultural expression of a secret is the *A*, and its fluidity of significance suggests the novel's preoccupation with the concealed. Even at the close, secrets remain: What will happen to Pearl? What finally did the parson confess? Just as "The Minister's Black Veil" closes with an image of a secret's intransigent indeterminacy, so too does *The Scarlet Letter* end with the letter *A* gleaming in all its meaning and mystification. Throughout, Hawthorne imparts to it suprarational and supersensible meanings, making secret and pregnant its exact senses. As he remarks at a famous moment in the preface, "but how it was to be worn, or what rank, honor, or dignity, in by-past times, were signified by it, was a riddle . . . I saw little hope solving. . . . Certainly, there was some deep meaning in it, most worthy of interpretation, and which . . . streamed forth from the mystical symbol, subtly communicating itself to my sensibilities, but evading the analysis of my mind" (31). The riddle of the letter's meaning invites the reader's probing, continuing inquiry into the secrets it betokens. In a sense, the reader joins Hawthorne in the search for its meaning, becomes part of a community of interpreters, as in Hester's case, that wants to scourge the "moral badness" (that secrecy signifies) from its presence.[26] Not satisfied with branding Hester an adulteress, this community insists that she name her paramour, divulge her secret. Until she does, Hester stands outside even while she seems regenerate. As long as she withholds her secret, however, the letter's "mystical" powers continue to stimulate the action and the rhetoric of the romance.

Through the various senses ascribed, the scarlet letter instructs Hester's community and Hawthorne's readers in how its secret may be learned. Either through a complex process of inference or after long single-minded pursuit, some knowledge can be ascertained. Because a secret resists articulation and takes its form of disclosure out of the "dark necessity" of its unfolding, it can be understood through the sympathy that a secret's approximated statement inspires. That sympathy may be the quasi-medical doctrine Chillingworth practices, but more normally it comes out of the "great and warm heart" of the general populace. As Hawthorne draws this distinction, an "uninstructed multitude" is likely to be deceived when it "attempts to see with its eyes." "When, however, it forms its judgment, as it usually does, on the intuitions of its great and warm heart, the conclusions thus attained are often so profound and so unerring, as to possess the character of truths supernaturally revealed" (127). Here Hawthorne's trust in Democratic political principles is a qualified affirmation of sympathy as "transcendent good faith."[27] The crowd will "usually" respond generously, but it cannot be counted upon to intuit sympathetically. Its literal vision is neither profound nor even accurate but can be shallow and mistaken. That audience, Hawthorne's potential readers included, needs to be taught how to see, and that vision should come out of the heart rather than the eye.[28]

Under this light, the novel's fixed relation between secrets and sympathy becomes clear. Literal-mindedness, familiarity, intimacy, even love do not obtain. Only through "sympathy" can others confirm a knowledge of the "worst," no matter how untellable. "Best discerning friends," such as Dimmesdale's, who find it providential that the parson and the physician enjoy a close proximity are likely to miss the hints of Chillingworth's already-rumored evil purposes. Their love for the parson and the urgency of their desire to see him healed blind them to both the true nature of his torment and the true character of his tormentor. Like the closest friends that Hawthorne declines to address in the preface—those in "perfect sympathy"—such observers cannot perceive the secret in the sinner's soul. "Another portion of the community," however, comes to doubt the wisdom of Dimmesdale's relation to the doctor and to guess the terror in the patient-victim's nearness to his hunter. This kind of observer is like the "friend" Hawthorne does address—"kind and apprehensive," chronically, if mildly, suspicious, though also charitable.

The sympathy of the scientist, on the other hand, descends from the primitive medicine Chillingworth has studied, the "many new secrets" he has learned in the wilderness and the curative recipes he already knows "as old as Paracelsus" (72). His medical knowledge is based upon a theory that "proceeded from the assumption of a universal connection between all things, basing its alchemical remedies upon supposed correspondences between the injured member and the cure."[29] Chillingworth's passion to know, like Ethan Brand's, transforms this healing power of sympathy into a destructive and self-distorting faculty. Like Brand, Chillingworth's mastery of formulae makes him lose his hold of "the magnetic chain of humanity," having ceased to partake of the "universal throb." Like Brand, in the story from the abortive romance Hawthorne meant to publish with *The Scarlet Letter*, Chillingworth is no longer a "brother-man, opening the chambers or the dungeons of our common nature by the key of holy sympathy, which gave him the right to share in all its secrets" (99).

According to the traditional categories, Chillingworth sacrifices the heart for the power of the mind, yet even so he possesses a special awareness:

> Never know him! Believe me, Hester, there are few things,— whether in the outward world, or, to a certain depth, in the invisible sphere of thought,—few things hidden from the man, who devotes himself earnestly and unreservedly to the solution of a mystery. Thou mayest cover up thy secret from the prying multitude. Thou mayest conceal it, too, from the ministers and magistrates. . . . But, as for me, I come to the inquest with other senses than they possess. . . . There is a sympathy that will make me conscious of him. I shall see him tremble. I shall feel myself shudder, suddenly and unawares. Sooner or later, he must needs be mine! (75)

And upon hearing this speech, Hester "clasped her hand over her heart, dreading lest he should read the secret there at once." Here Hawthorne may be giving voice to his sense of his presumed antagonist's demonic relentlessness, but just as surely he is articulating his conviction that the "worst" can be sympathetically ascertained, if only through the most dogged, single-minded pursuit.

And that effort is, inevitably, conceived as reading, a sympathetic act of interpretative appropriation, here understood as violation.

Chillingworth enjoins Hester to preserve their "secret bond," to "breathe not the secret" of her husband's true identity. The physician needs to conceal his purposes; anonymity is integral to perpetrating his design successfully, in Hawthorne's prescient sense of how an investigator, like the early psychoanalysts in treating their patients, ought to reveal nothing of himself to his victim.

> Few secrets can escape an investigator, who has opportunity and license to undertake such a quest, and skill to follow it up. A man burdened with a secret should especially avoid the intimacy of his physician. If the latter possesses native sagacity, and a nameless something more,—let us call it intuition; if he shows no intrusive egotism, nor disagreeably prominent characteristics of his own; if he have the power, which must be born with him, to bring his mind into such affinity with his patient's, that this last shall unawares have spoken what he imagines himself only to have thought; if such revelations be received without tumult, and acknowledged not so often by an uttered sympathy, as by silence, an inarticulable breath, and here and there a word, to indicate that all is understood; if, to these qualifications of a confidant be joined the advantages afforded by his recognized character as a physician;—then, at some inevitable moment, will the soul of the sufferer be dissolved, and flow forth in a dark, but transparent stream, bringing all its mysteries into the daylight. (124)

Unlike the nineteenth-century psychiatrist Krafft-Ebing, who would treat his patients through a "sympathetic nature, penetrating eyes, and a persuasive voice" and find exactly the salutary words to placate their turmoil, Chillingworth haunts his patient with the eventuality of exposure and taunts him in language calculated to prey on the guilt-laden minister's despair.[30] As the doctor observes of some medicinal herbs he finds growing on a grave: "They grew out of [the dead man's] heart, and typify . . . some hideous secret that was buried with him, and which he had done better to confess in his lifetime" (131). The case exemplifies Chillingworth's conviction that even if men "bury their secrets," ultimately they will be discovered. As if to ward off the desire to confess that the physician's scenario arouses, Dimmesdale argues the case for the helpless man in impossible circumstances, for even if one "earnestly desired" confession, there can be "no power, short of Divine mercy, to disclose, without uttered words, or by type or emblem, the secret that may be buried with a human heart. The heart, making itself guilty of such secrets, must perforce hold them, until the day when all hidden things shall be revealed." Although Dimmesdale couches his defense in biblical locutions, Chillingworth is not fooled, arguing that such men "deceive themselves," even if they succeed in deceiving the community. The physician easily disparages the Puritan minister's self-deceiving, faith-denying rationalization that confessing his own "hideous secret" would subvert his good works. The argument that the minister advances, in this thinly disguised effort to excuse his own impenitence, stands directly antithetical to his Puritan creed. By way of veiling his secret, Dimmesdale creates a hypothetical case, a fiction that reproduces his hypocrisy, but it is an example that his merciless sympathizer handily rends. So when Chillingworth chides those who deceive themselves for hiding these "miserable secrets," its chastening force is not lost on Hawthorne, who seizes on the scarlet letter as a "type or emblem" by which he may disclose his own secret without uttering the words.

For other than through cold-hearted investigation, secrets can be perceived through the "great and warm heart." In creating a fit audience out of the "uninstructed multitude," Hawthorne complicates the terms by which secrets may be understood and searches for an indirect method of disclosure, one that tries to ensure the most appropriate response. Abjuring the reader of "perfect sympathy," Hawthorne prefers a less intimate friend—"kind and apprehensive"—who apprehends in the sense of *discern* as well as of cautious anticipation in sharing a writer's nervousness over self-exposure. In still another sense, this reader must apprehend, as in arrest, an author for disclosures in which he incriminates himself personally and for those revelations by which he attacks the complacencies of a public that dwells too much in the sunshine, with too little sympathy for the dark or shadowy in American history or culture. A reader so wary is likely to catch the clue that even as Hawthorne professes to be freely expressive, his "native reserve" inhibits open admission and makes him seek another, disguised way of revealing the truth.

■ Tied to biographical assumptions as my study has been, it remains that even if Hawthorne had no such secret as I have indicated as very likely being much in his mind when he began writing *The Scarlet Letter*, a rhetoric of secrecy lies at the very center of his romance, in ways that previous criticism has only partially suggested.[31] How secrets operate in the shaping of narrative is, as we shall see, a more appropriate question for *Seven Gables* where they explicitly figure in developing the novel's plot and design. In *The Scarlet Letter*, however, secrets signify the ambiguous, perhaps indeterminate, nature of experience; they do not so much stimulate the plot as contribute to a psychology of representation, one that works through Freudian categories of displacement and condensation. Secrets do not operate here as they might in a detective story or a realistic novel, the missing clue in the action, the ultimate cause of the literal results to follow, the motor of desire that generates and predicts closure.[32] Instead, they provide and protect that element of mystification Hawthorne deemed necessary for both engaging and frustrating his readers' apprehensive attention, as is so markedly the case at the novel's close. The activity, the pressure, of keeping secrets, prevents the world from seeming knowable or readily explicable, even as it arouses readers' desire to know. In this, it establishes a screen through which imitations of the truth can be advanced as being as reliable as the naked truth, where metaphor exists on equal footing with the literal, thus preserving the ground where the Actual and the Imaginary might meet while requiring readers to find their footing there.

Furthermore, the perpetrating of the secret, or untold, lends the romance much of its psychological density. The literal facts of the case are never really in doubt, though every student of the novel can wonder that whatever confirmation readers get that Dimmesdale really is Hester's lover comes only after one has lost interest in that question. Less definable, however, is the underlying reality by which a character lives and to which readers react: Dimmesdale's guilt, Hester's impenitence, Chillingworth's obsession, Pearl's outlaw nature, the bases for all of which, like the *A*'s meaning, resist superficial clarity. These "motive secrets," as Hawthorne elsewhere calls the galvanizing features of personality, give the romance its nexus of things that cannot be quite expressed, its primary, affective sense of marvel, like the sexton's astonishment at finding Dimmesdale's glove on the scaffold. There, the sexton responds with a homely interpretation, based on Puritan allegorizing, that this perhaps is God's admonishment for Dimmesdale to fight Satan's workings ungloved. Curiously, this moment presents what may be the one moment of conscious or deliberate humor in the narrative, as if Hawthorne were warning readers that easy, formulaic interpretative responses will prove insufficient, no matter how piously they observed existing social and spiritual criteria. At the same time, the sexton's unwitting joke should also alert readers to seize upon evidence left by mistake, to pursue the logic of traces.[33]

The romance, for Hawthorne, depends on imparting this power of wonder, the obfuscating of literal explanations for psychological texture and complexity. The author's refusal to verify that for which the reader has every reason to expect objective confirmation will always cause frustration and annoyance, as Lionel Trilling observes.[34] Hawthorne's concealings, equivocations, appositions, alternative choices suspend the very expectations the reader wants fulfilled, coiling the reader within the unresolvable terms of the text. The purposes of this method are as paradoxical as the conundrums it creates. On the one hand, Hawthorne's refusal to grant literal verification incites the reader to greater expenditures of imagination, a more continuous involvement with a text's urgent marshaling of ambiguity. On the other, Hawthorne's veilings prevent the reader from fully appropriating the text, which remains the author's, never to be fully relinquished. Although Hawthorne's precluding of representation—as in the *A* on Dimmesdale's breast or the text of the Election Sermon—might lead a reader to suppose that a work can be what one chooses or that the plurality of interpretations invites us "to construct our own conclusions," the text, we shall see, remains the writer's.[35]

The primary means of enacting this mechanism of exacting mutually exclusive claims derives from the author's insistent desire to show that secrets either cannot or ought not to be known. Sometimes, this insistence is cannily directed; just as often, it will seem gratuitously habitual, even random. In either case, whether to protect himself from too personal an exposure or to defend his text from misprision, Hawthorne issues a warrant of secrecy. For once secrets are told, as Hawthorne dramatizes in "The Intelligence Office" and "Earth's Holocaust," they lose their fiction-making province. In these sketches, Hawthorne's rhetorical method of cataloging human desires in the one, sources of pain in the other, is undone, made self-consuming, by the revelation of a supreme case, the "secret" that has occasioned the fantasy and that shows how futile is the enterprise of learning all. Once named, a secret loses its promise of possible meanings; the writer is forced into assigning a fixed value or static explanation. Moreover, a secret told also risks making the author's tactics of mystification obvious in retrospect, as Hawthorne dramatizes in "Egotism; or, The Bosom-Serpent" and explicitly addresses in *The Marble Faun*.

When the secret can be withheld, as in "Rappaccini's Daughter" or "Roger Malvin's Burial," the play of ambiguity is seemingly endless, as if to undercut a story's most apparent purposes, so that possession of the text redounds to the writer, though it will seem to belong to readers by catering to their penchant for making sense. The author gives only those terms through which a secret might be guessed, some approximation of its meaning or configuration of its identifying status. To literalize, then, is to deny secrets their fundamentally suggestive power, as Holgrave comes to see upon reading "Alice Pyncheon," when revealing the source of Maule's Curse would not only undo the story's effect on the listener but would also silence the tale's resonances for the teller.

For Hawthorne, the terms that imitate disclosure are often metafictional—"chimney-corner legend," "moonlight" visions, interpolated stories—all offering versions of the truth without laying it bare. In *The Scarlet Letter*, however, these techniques are not given any real place. Occasionally pointed out are examples in nature that seem to correlate meanings, like the comet or the wolf that eats out of Pearl's hand, but these allegorizings are too overt, even when modulated, and for many readers constitute the novel's weakest moments. Instead, the instructing terms are found in "The Custom-House" that Hawthorne believed so necessary to add. Essentially, those terms are humorous, as if to treat in jest what is cast so earnestly in the romance.

The dialectic between "jest and earnest" that Hawthorne repeatedly refers to in his notebooks and fiction so preoccupies him that this dual principle for casting the life of meanings proves characteristic of his art. In both the short stories and sketches, where narrative strategies often share a functional analogy with the telling of jokes, Hawthorne again and again exploits the presence of a secret by bringing tragic themes to bear on trivial experience, sometimes discovering serious characters in potentially ludicrous situations or revealing how the most profoundly felt desires often end in ridiculous results. Or he hints, through the crazed power of laughter, as in "My Kinsman, Major Molineux" or "Ethan Brand," at the close connection between the somber and the humorous. In "The Custom-House" this combined rhetorical voice is sustained through Hawthorne's mocking caricatures of other officials and through his jokes about losing his head. Yet this humor is also subordinated to Hawthorne's serious explanations of his involvement in the seamy business of local politics and the predictable end of trying to serve two gods at once—art and mammon. He wryly notes that it is "sadly curious" how so "slight a taste of office" infects a person with the "singular disease of graft": "Whoever touches the Devil's wages should look well to himself," Hawthorne cautions, for even if one's name is safe, one's "better attributes," "all that gives emphasis to a manly character," are risked: the soul's "sturdy force," "courage and constancy," "truth," and "self-reliance" (39). Troubled by assaults upon these "better attributes," Hawthorne tells us, he "endeavored to calculate how much longer I could stay at the Custom-House and yet go forth a man." Although he confesses to having bartered his imagination for a "pittance of public gold," his deepest fear and the real cost to his dignity, ironically, is that he would cease literary labors and be satisfied to become as lethargic as any "tolerably good" surveyor.

In this convoluted effort to admit his shame, Hawthorne chooses a romantically darker crime than any that his adversaries alleged— a crime not only against his manhood but also his high standards of moral conduct. Furthermore, he confesses to an artist's crime of indolence, equated with the lethargy of which he has just made so much fun, echoing the voice he has earlier imitated in evoking his Puritan forebears' disdain for him as a trifling writer of story-books. This indolence will surely trouble "a man who felt it to be the best definition of happiness to live throughout the whole range of his faculties and sensibilities!" (40). Surely the misdemeanor charges must have seemed to violate his best sense of his "better attributes." In this sense, Hawthorne's confession is strikingly sincere, but under the circumstances of his firing and his scheming to keep the post, this Olympian detachment does not do justice to the humiliating liability to which his conduct exposed him, the crime—as Nissenbaum has said—of being no better than everybody else.[36]

Hawthorne's posture corresponds to Freud's description of the "exaltation of the ego" that humorous defense achieves. "I am too big [artig] to be distressed by these things." Following Freud, we call such a reaction a defense mechanism, wherein an assumed aloofness can ward off the threats that pedestrian actuality presents, a "peculiar technique" comparable to displacement. According to Freud, "humorous pleasure is derived when a threatening truth, already in preparation," is "disappointed" by being "diverted on to something of secondary importance." That is, an unacknowledged source of distress is interrupted from coming into conscious recognition, when a humorous remark can target an easier, more acceptable charge, one closely enough linked to the deeper threat. That connection needs to be at least metaphoric, so that the form of the preferable response can absorb the more serious one, reflecting its truth, and can thus dispel the anxiety being created. Freud parallels "humorous displacement" with defensive processes, insofar as they are both "correlative of the flight reflex" and prohibit "internal sources" from generating "unpleasure" (as the standard translation puts it). For Freud, humor is the "highest" of these defenses because it scorns the mere repression of anxiety from "conscious attention" and insists on facing some version of the "ideational content" of a secret threat in order to surmount its "distressing affect," a common ploy of irony, for example. Humor does this by converting the energy in the "release of unpleasure" through a more manageable "discharge" into pleasure, something to be smiled over or laughed about. This displacement of troubling pressure into a pleasurable form is a "transformation" that spurns the "automatism of defense" and tries to recommend to the consciousness a converted, discernible alternative form for disclosing unconscious promptings.[37]

In this context, Hawthorne's own "peculiar technique" can also be seen. By confessing his secret under the guise of aloofness, of being above such pettiness, he avoids what may be the bitterer truth: not only did he seek "Uncle Sam's gold" at the expense of his imagination, but he also, according to his partisan enemies, let that gold be diverted into pockets where it did not belong. The "ideational content" remains the same, but it is pleasurably distorted in the satirical treatment he affords himself and his cohorts. His satire seeks to prove the defense that he really is much better than these superannuated sloths, while he also pleads that he is merely a man among other men, subject to the same temptations, susceptible of the same "singular disease" of getting money for doing nothing on the public payroll or winking at an everyday practice of graft. This is not to say that Hawthorne did not really accept his version of the story or that he was undismayed by his unproductive years. The defensive strategy of confession, however, qualifies the genial sunshine the sketch was intended to radiate, concealing through humor what might have been a still darker secret—the dark necessity of sin—even from himself. That this edited account itself suggests a pained awareness of human limitation further demonstrates Hawthorne's desire to reveal the secret indirectly. Discharging the pain in a preferable form, his admission that he is a man subject to the same seductions as any other works by "withdrawing energy from the release of unpleasure." Hawthorne heightens his pleasure by caricaturing the other officials and admitting that, in the end, he was glad to lose the job he tried so hard to keep. His defensive posture preserves entirely his insistence on his relative superiority while ignoring the publicized reasons for his dismissal, even as he moved to retain his position. In this way, Hawthorne continues to exalt the ego and exult in the triumph over his enemies, now changed from political adversaries to versions of what he might have become. He may thus emerge as finding the whole business all too distasteful.

Freud sees this triumph as humor's underlying purpose. Its "ultimate grandeur" lies in the "victorious assertion of the ego's invulnerability":

> The ego refuses to be distressed by the provocations of reality, to let itself be compelled to suffer. It insists that it cannot be affected by the traumas of the external world; it shows, in fact, that such traumas are no more than occasions for it to gain pleasure. . . . Humour is not resigned; it is rebellious. It signifies not only the triumph of the ego but also of the pleasure principle, which is able to assert itself against the unkindness of real circumstances.[38]

Whereas jokes, in Freud's scheme of things, are primarily fabricated to create pleasure by aggressively dismantling inhibition through condensation and displacement, humor tries to transform "unpleasure" into pleasure, to countervail the feelings that threaten the ego's invulnerability. The defensive process of humor is not so socially motivated as a joke's eliciting another person's laughter to corroborate the successful allaying of a restive inhibition. Instead, humorous defense denies, for personal satisfaction and for public perception, that the pressures of reality are too intense to tolerate and must find an alternative way of easing the disquietude they can cause. Even one who declines Freud's distinctions can still concede that humor's primary purpose is to lessen the impact of disturbing feelings. Freud teaches that humor works to the degree that it efficaciously diverts the threat in the "provocations of reality" onto something of "secondary importance"—a lesser characteristic from which the deeper threat can be learned.

Humorous defense remains true to the self by freely showing a somewhat better trait whereby the worst may be inferred.

Often the pleasure in humor's transformation can only be enjoyed by the humorist alone. As a "vague confession" of the truth, humor's disburdening offers only "momentary relief" from the distress of real circumstances. To some degree, humorous evasion or detachment makes this "vague confession" inadequate to its task; if the secret truth is pressing enough, it ultimately defies humorous treatment and seeks a more effectively pleasurable disclosure. Hawthorne understood this compulsive need, following the failure of initial formulations, to find ever more precise versions of the truth: "The minister well knew—subtle, but remorseful hypocrite that he was—the light in which his vague confession would be viewed. He had striven to put a cheat upon himself by making the avowal of a guilty conscience, but had gained only one other sin, and a self-acknowledged shame, without the momentary relief of being self-deceived. He had spoken the very truth, and transformed it into the veriest falsehood" (144). Here Hawthorne describes how approximate confessions work by substituting a specious version of a secret to deflect the pressure of imminent confession.

Hawthorne recognizes here that insofar as an approximate confession is dishonestly incomplete, too deeply private, or overly general, it fosters self-loathing by compounding the original source of guilt with hypocrisy and paralysis. In Dimmesdale's "secret closet," this self-loathing leads to a peculiar punishment: "Oftentimes, this Protestant and Puritan divine had plied the scourge on his shoulder; laughing bitterly at himself the while, and smiting so much more pitilessly because of that bitter laugh" (144). The pastor's pleasure lies in the releasing of an inhibition, a pleasure that induces him to lash all the harder as a partial fulfillment of the punishment he feels he so richly deserves. His whipping himself imitates that punishment feebly, while Dimmesdale avails himself of a pleasure so private that only in secret can it be enjoyed. So too does Hawthorne keep his secret in "The Custom-House," approximating a punishment for his misdemeanors by joking about decapitation. Thus he humorously defends himself against the mortification that his enemies' allegations occasion and, more important, his own guilt.

Hiding his "inmost Me behind its veil," Hawthorne obscures his confession and engages in an elaborate self-defense of keeping yet hinting at a guilty secret. Typically, the characters uphold this dual process of disclosure by avowing one secret to conceal another or by distorting the substance of one so that it will seem like something else. Hester's secret is surely the name of her lover, but the interest of her refusal to divulge his identity is, for the community, her still worse defiance against authority.[39] Her dream that she and Dimmesdale may yet be happily united is both an unacknowledged desire and a yearning for an identity beyond the one proscribed for her.

Dimmesdale's secret is his sin, and this leads to the crippling guilt of paradoxically fearing to perform a pastor's duties while enjoying a gruesome delight in the adoration he wins out of his avowals of pollution. The self-hatred and self-punishment that his dilemma imposes find expression in his simultaneous effort to publicize his sin, however apprehensively, and mask it, as in the "lurid playfulness" that aims to subvert the morals of the young and faith of the elderly. Until his sin is made naked, it "burns in secret" (192), inciting him to further attempts of approximately expressing his guilt. Until he finds this means, the secret propagates even more self-disdain.

Fundamental to Chillingworth's keeping his identity secret is his outraged sense of violation, the compromised vision of purity that his vengeance on Dimmesdale will never repair. Although he believes it is Hester's betrayal that transforms him into a fiend, the doctor's radically distorted desire for retribution bespeaks a secret that Chillingworth, poignantly, seems really to know: his own sense of physical, even sexual inferiority. For Chillingworth has been injured where perhaps he was most vulnerable, his "folly" in hoping that he actually could encourage and enjoy his young wife's lush sensuality. His torture of the man who cuckolds him is to appease, by projection, the gnawings of his inner emptiness.

Pearl's secret is understood as a question of whether she can ultimately be brought into human sympathy, for beyond the element of strangeness in her characterization lies a deeper sense of inscrutability. The question, is she human? is subordinated to the way she embodies the mysterious past, bewildering present, and uncertain future. She is at once the "living hieroglyphic, in which was revealed the secret they so darkly sought to hide" (207), the key to the present—is she an outlaw spirit of misrule or a supernatural innocent?—and the legacy to the future, posing the question of what will happen to America once its child of illicit passion and enduring sympathy departs.

These secrets of guilt and its consequences express Hawthorne's diversified sense of the roots of transgression. More important, they indicate the overarching rhetoric of secrecy spread across the narrative. Hawthorne's relentlessly hinting indirection, his multivalent shifting sense of what these secrets are, will remind us of the stream that Pearl disparages for its "sighing" and "murmuring." Like the "profound and continual undertone" of Dimmesdale's sermon, the stream's "murmuring babble" echoes of the known but untold life. The brook "would not be comforted, and still kept telling its unintelligible secret of some very mournful mystery that happened—or making a prophetic lamentation about something that was yet to happen. . ." (213, 186, 187). The stream "had gone through so solemn an experience that it seemed to have nothing else" but this "unintelligible tale" to "say." Although the aggrieved stream is intended to qualify the scene of nature's sympathy with the lovers, the murmuring brook also remarks of another "unintelligible secret," the answer to Hawthorne's rhetorical (in both senses of the word) question, which takes the form of Hester's response to Pearl: "What has the letter to do with any heart, save mine?" (179).

■ *The Scarlet Letter* opens onto a nightmare made real. Emerging from the prison, Hester trudges to the scaffold where she is scrutinized for her sins, "under the weight of a thousand unrelenting eyes, all fastened upon her and concentered upon her bosom. It was almost intolerable to be borne" (57). The attention that Hawthorne gives to the crowd's punishing gaze documents a primal moment when secrets are exposed to public examination. While Freud teaches that the dream imagery of a staring crowd expresses the fear of publicly revealed guilt, the power of this scene also suggests Hawthorne's sense of the humiliation brought by fixed and steady attention to shame.[40] That he initiates the romance with this very incident of combined sin, punishment, and display will also attest to the connections among wrongdoing, publicity, and writing that the events of the previous few months very probably aroused.

Just as certain is the lack of any easily awarded mercy. In all her courage, mistakenly founded on the belief that "whatever sympathy she might expect lay in the larger and warmer heart of the multitude" rather than the elders, Hester braves the "stings and venomous stabs of public contumely, wreaking itself in every variety of insult" (64). In fact, at least one among them—the "ugliest and most pitiless"—wants the adulteress put to death, since "marks and brands" are too lenient punishment for Hester's shame. Hawthorne concludes, "Meagre, indeed, and cold, was the sympathy that a transgressor might look for from such bystanders at the scaffold" (50). Only one, the youngest, and perhaps kindest and most apprehensive, observes how painfully and truly telling is Hester's badge: "Not a stitch in that embroidered letter, but she has felt it in her heart" (54), as if to testify, at the outset, that the private story of sorrow and lawlessness can be sympathetically apprehended from its public "mark" of punishment and display.

Hester's unkind observers at the scaffold demand that her secret—the name of her bastard's father—be told, made unqualifiedly explicit. Yet the Reverend Mr. Wilson himself reminds all that "it were wronging the very nature of woman to force her to lay open her heart's secrets in such broad daylight, and in the presence of so great a multitude" (65). Without the shadowy guard of moonlight, the very atmosphere of romance, the revealing of a secret, it seems, violates the sanctity of the heart, especially if the general audience is wanting in sympathy and needs to be instructed in the shared human community of guilt. That lesson first comes from Dimmesdale whose "tremulously sweet, rich, deep, and broken" appeal not only bids Hester to reveal the unconfessed sinner in their midst, but also reminds all others that they cannot resist its enchantment: "The feeling that it so evidently manifested, rather than the direct purport of the words, caused it to vibrate within all hearts, and brought the listeners into one accord of sympathy" (67). Hawthorne's sense here ought not to be obscured: like the "essential plaintiveness" underlying the Election Sermon, the tone of Dimmesdale's call registers how the "feeling that it so evidently manifested" presides over the "direct purport of the words." That emphasis on tone as overriding literal meanings lies at the center of Hawthorne's rhetoric, for in the heightened moral response evoked is the necessary eliciting of sympathy. When an audience— townsfolk and readers alike—can be brought into "one accord" of kindness and apprehension, the revelation of secret guilt is readied. That unveiling works through transferring the burden of confession from Hester to Dimmesdale, from exposed criminal to hidden one, as Hawthorne describes how the "inward and inevitable necessity" to confess can be met, if only indirectly.

The pastor's address speaks to the townspeople's individual needs to confess. Dimmesdale's appeal wraps itself in language that charms the listeners into corroborating Hester's sin with their own secrets: "So powerful seemed the minister's appeal, that the people would not believe but that Hester would speak out the guilty name, or else the guilty one himself, in whatever high or lowly place he stood, would be drawn forth by an inward and inevitable necessity." What the community understands as the compulsion to confess is only their ordinary sense of a sinner's burden. Under the sway of Dimmesdale's moving prosecution of his duty, the multitude supposes that any criminal, so gently but powerfully beseeched, would necessarily reveal himself.

Dimmesdale's rhetoric bespeaks a collective desire and value for confession; what it suppresses is his own. The pastor shares the "inward and inevitable" compulsion, yet by generalizing the necessity, he works a private defense of indirection. Although he sincerely exhorts Hester to disclose "that mystery of a woman's soul," his speech is at least ironic, even self-consciously so. Dimmesdale implores his lover to expose him because punishment would be better than "to hide a guilty heart for life. . . . Heaven hath granted thee an open ignominy, that thereby thou mayest work out an open triumph over the evil within thee, and the sorrow without. Take

heed how thou deniest to him—who perchance, hath not the courage to grasp it for himself" (67). Paralyzed by his fear of exposure
and his conflicting desire for punishment, Dimmesdale pleads
urgently and sincerely, but conditionally. He introduces his appeal
by qualifying that Hester should confess "If thou feelest it to be for
thy soul's peace," not his. When we learn Dimmesdale's secret, the
self-reference of the speech becomes evident. Here the parson de-
fers and thus diverts the necessity to confess. Publicly addressed,
his speech is also a private disclosure.

In fact, at this early moment, Dimmesdale does reveal himself. His
need to expose himself is as strong as his need to obscure the truth.
When Hester refuses to say his name, his relief is the very breath of
life. But the minister confesses only indirectly, by uncovering the
mere necessity for disclosure, rather than by baring his heart. As a
defensive ploy, his lament disarms the listeners into thinking that
any sinner would now indict himself, so sincerely does Dimmesdale
search for a way to make his grief public. But the minister's private
joke, if one may call it so, is also the author's. In describing these
listeners' response, Hawthorne notes unobtrusively that the sinner
may be of high or low social status, even as Dimmesdale tells Hester
that she should name the father "though he were to step down from a
high place, and stand beside thee, on thy pedestal of shame" (67). The
reader readily assents to Hawthorne's aside, the leveling passion implicit in Dimmesdale's appeal, and may further conjecture that her
lover must be of a higher social station; position in the community
ought not to save the sinner from the punishment he deserves. At the
same time the sinner must be lower, at least in the sense that an
unconfessed adulterer (like an unconfessedly corrupt customs official) has no open avenue to penitence. The reader knows that
Dimmesdale is, in a very literal sense, higher than Hester. Even as he
speaks, he is "leaning over the balcony, and looking stedfastly [sic]
into her eyes": "Thou hearest what this good man says, and seest the
accountability under which I labor" (67). For Dimmesdale, on the
scaffold, both stations of being higher and lower equally apply. Indeed, Hawthorne recurs to this construction, as a virtual compulsion, when Dimmesdale mounts the scaffold the final time to make

his guilt explicit. There Chillingworth berates the parson for his decision to make his sin known and thereby deprive his tormentor of a *raison d'être:* "There was no one place so secret,—no high or lowly place,—where thou couldst have escaped me, save on this very scaffold!" (253). The scaffold, as the scene of guilt, confession, punishment, and display, marks the place where both alternatives exist and where the reader can detect, from the outset, Dimmesdale's guilt, the "accountability" under which he makes his address. Therein does Hawthorne also offer his account of a secret-keeper's "accountability," even if that secret can be known only by the feeling a voice "so evidently manifested, rather than the direct purport of the words." Through writing, the novelist gives voice to the "inward and inevitable necessity" of confession, even as he withdraws from giving an explicit account. Instead, the writer presents his disclosure through a series of inferences or directed choices that a reader can pursue.

The setting of a choice, as between high and low, is a function of narrative method that Yvor Winters described as Hawthorne's "formula of alternative possibilities."[41] Hawthorne's inveterate technique of ascribing one explanation only to qualify it with its opposite or his promoting one motive only to withdraw it, his suggesting one rationale but refusing to confirm it, all participate in what is essentially a defensive procedure. The writer frustrates the reader's desire to know something definitively. The confounding multiple possibilities tease the reader, while the writer willfully refuses to say which answer, if any, applies. Thus the writer need not be responsible for any one version and can still protect the text from the antipathetic interpretation of the meanings he imagines to be most private. In this way, a reader can be led away from misconstruing a text's secrets and toward a sympathetic apprehension, while the writer's own sense is kept under the guard of dubious distinctions. Out of his reluctance to specify, Hawthorne can submit the reader's efforts to appropriate a text to the test of ambiguities, ensuring a more careful response, yet preserve the essential element of mystification. This willful obscurity, however, is more than a "minor cause of irritation" but rather a major defense against a readership that the author perceives as hostile or ignorant. The formula of alternative possibilities leaves the text's secrets safe from misprision or easy violation and allows the author to exploit the intractable ambiguities those secrets create, indeterminacies that yield implications of "secondary importance" out of which a secret—like the relation between Dimmesdale's guilty appeal and the writer's voice—may be coaxed.

Or the writer can deliberately give an interpretation to make the reader dismiss its veracity. But in doing this, the reader must also apprehend the feeling "evidently manifested," even if he rejects the "direct purport of the words." When Hawthorne offers several explanations—the authority for each of which is suspect—he diverts the reader from the ones he has called attention to as merely secondary, although they may really edge toward primary disclosure. By allowing the reader to choose among several possibilities, Hawthorne invites the reader into what seems otherwise to be an autonomous text, for once the choices that the reader makes engage him in the general problem of discerning secrets, that attention more nearly matches both the characters' and the author's. One critic concludes that such narrative choice "leaves us alone to complete the novel by determining its imaginative procedure as we do so" and that by so engaging the reader's curiosity, Hawthorne can regain "access to the mysteries of the psychic life," the secrets that elude both formal and psychological definition.[42] Yet insofar as this mystification promotes the rhetoric of secrecy, it does not do so by "absconding" with the work's meanings and surrendering those meanings to pluralistic reception. It presents those mysteries in ways that can specify the reader's understanding.

One such mystery is described in "The Custom-House" when Hawthorne records his reaction to the very material of the scarlet letter: "I happened to place it on my breast. It seemed to me,—the reader may smile, but must not doubt my word,—it seemed to me, then, that I experienced a sensation not altogether physical, yet almost so, as of burning heat; and as if the letter were not of red cloth, but red-hot iron. I shuddered, and involuntarily let it fall upon the floor" (31–32). In this oft-remarked passage, Hawthorne anticipates the reader's hesitancy to accept so supernatural an explanation and emphasizes his own tentativeness in offering this strange incident by repeating that the letter only "seemed" to have this effect. The reader, Hawthorne apprehends, may smile indulgently at this eccentric anecdote but should still take seriously the author's perception of the fabric as fiery hot, as being susceptible of metaphoric functions. Once the cloth covers his breast, the letter produces a visceral reaction that Hawthorne cannot dismiss. Hawthorne's experience corresponds to the complex statement of sin that the letter symbolizes; once he attaches the letter to his person, it loses its merely literal properties; once he associates it with himself, it gains metaphorical functions. Paradoxically, the letter both displays and covers a burning secret. As the rhetoric of this passage establishes, the value of the symbol accrues to the degree that readers suspend their conventional interpretations of an experience that cannot be explained. In describing this moment as arousing a smile and only tentatively suggesting that the writer's experience be taken literally, Hawthorne defends himself from the complaint that this moment is neither true nor subject to verification and informs the reader that such doubts are inappropriate.

To see this defense at work in the romance, let us consider a parallel moment in Hawthorne's account of the reaction that the letter provokes. At the close of "Hester at her Needle," Hawthorne again presents a choice between literal and metaphorical understandings where neither alone suffices. The setting of this choice defends one answer against another and elicits more precise, apprehensive acts of the reader's imagination in determining the worst that may be inferred, as long as the reader does not succumb to a certain vulgarity.

> The vulgar, who, in those dreary old times, were always contributing a grotesque horror to what interested their imaginations, had a story about the scarlet letter which we might readily work up into a terrific legend. They averred, that the symbol was not merely scarlet cloth, tinged in an earthy dyepot, but was red-hot with infernal fire, and could be seen glowing all alight, whenever Hester Prynne walked abroad in night-

time. And we must needs say, it seared Hester's bosom so deeply, that perhaps there was more truth in the rumor than our modern incredulity may be inclined to admit. (87–88)

The passage demonstrates, for a second time, Hawthorne's sense that a merely literal response is inadequate, that, as his notebook entry indicates, figurative expressions can be submitted to literal pictures.

Vulgar or naive interpretation of the symbol's meaning instructs modern readers better than they might think. Whereas the reader of the preface is supposed to smile, Hawthorne expects the reader of the novel to be justifiably dubious that the letter should gleam so brightly on Hester's breast. A consciousness too refined has much to learn from a "grotesque" one, though the former need not subscribe faithfully to the latter. Still, the vulgar imagination of the "uninstructed multitude" proceeds out of the "great and warm heart" and settles on the fantastic in the face of what it cannot understand. To the unrefined consciousness, the pain that the letter would cause can only be communicated superstitiously. So strenuously do the vulgar observers allegorize the letter that, by interpreting Hester's grief in this way, they give the letter's secret meanings generalizable powers. In their effort to find a correspondence between these meanings and the physical pain that they attribute to Hester's stigma, they conflate these two realms of experience, thus imitating Hawthorne's own practice of working up a "terrific legend," one that appeals to their unlettered imaginations. Fanciful meanings replace literal ones through the supernaturally conditioned apprehension of the original grief that the letter was intended to instill. By the heat of that sympathy, they forge a representation of a painful secret into their own fears that Hester's humiliation arouses. This fanciful apprehension illuminates their own secrets; the townspeople's guilty passions are collocated with the adulteress's crime, "whenever Hester Prynne walked abroad in the night-time," which for Hawthorne is when one is most likely to recall dark realities. And the coarse-minded vaguely confess to these private sins by defensively displacing their anxieties onto the already known, already visible one that Hester's badge signifies.

Hawthorne warns that "our modern incredulity" will dismiss the vulgar interpretation, but he cautions that our doubts alone will not dispel the symbol's curious capacity to organize a collective sense of sin, its irruptive manner of bringing secrets closer to articulation. Nor does the modern response explain the terror that the legend of the letter imparts. The letter leads the townspeople to crude attempts at metamorphosing Hester's pain into their own, and though the readers are meant to dismiss these efforts, they must not do so peremptorily. While the letter certainly does not bear the physiological effect the vulgar ascribe to it or that Hawthorne suggests in the preface, finally the smiling or doubting reader must apprehend the sensuousness of the letter's display. To dispel the rumor too readily is to deprive the viscerally felt symbol of its collectivizing, parable-making functions. For the rumor's very vividness and popularity legitimate Hester's "new sense," "the sympathetic understanding of hidden sin in other hearts" (86). Plagued by "intimations, so obscure, yet so distinct," Hester fears a loss of faith, one that the rumor's imagery of hell would confirm. The "sympathetic throb" by which Hester recognizes the secrets of others affirms that this loss of faith may indeed be merited but, as Hawthorne ambivalently suggests, must be resisted.

Although the story the people tell is not believable, its lessons should be remarked. By fixing the proof of Hester's speculations on so suspect an understanding as the "grotesque horror" that the vulgar express, Hawthorne deliberately obscures the lessons, though he gently insists on the allegorical value of the evidence. As Angus Fletcher has remarked, herein lies the defense within any allegory, for "allegorizing always demonstrates a degree of inner conflict we call ambivalence."[43] Hawthorne's ambivalence imbues the letter with an affective intensity and widens the symbol's range. He refuses to state finally that Hester's loss of faith is warranted; instead, he offers a rumor as to the symbol's general applicability, which challenges the reader to interpret the letter further than modern incredulity allows. The letter then must be seen as fulfilling the criteria of both Actual and Imaginary laws and as resting in the "neutral territory" where the real and imagined meet to make romance possible, where secrets may be told indirectly without being exposed. This ambivalence relieves Hawthorne of expressing his accord with Hester's "so awful and so loathsome speculations," his own urge "to believe that no fellow-mortal was guilty like [him- or] herself" (87).

The lurid fantasies of the townspeople allegorize Hester's secret (and their own ambivalence), yet their indecorous search for a suit- able metaphor frees Hawthorne to discover one that can corre- spond to his requirements of romance. Placing the burden of parable-making on the vulgar, Hawthorne reserves for his narrator the more refined tone, a voice that can "express the highest truths in the humblest medium of familiar words and images," the "power of addressing the whole human brotherhood in the heart's native language" (142). Thus does Hawthorne describe the "sad, persua- sive eloquence" in Dimmesdale's "Tongue of Flame," a "voice that angels might . . . have listened to and answered!" This voice re- sounds of the burdensome "black secret of his soul," one that makes the parson capable, like Hester, of "sympathies so intimate with the sinful brotherhood of mankind." Later, Hawthorne de- fines this rhetoric as the "complaint of a human heart . . . telling its secret . . . to the great heart of mankind, beseeching its sympa- thy or forgiveness . . . in each accent," the "profound and continual undertone that gave the clergyman his most appropriate power" (243–44). Here, however, the "Tongue of Flame" speaks also of Hawthorne's own guilty secret, metaphorically represented in Hester's and then crudely allegorized by the community. By this democratizing process, readers can be led to apprehend their own secrets and to see how they share in the novel's community of guilt.

Rumor, like equivocation, apposition, qualification, thus oper- ates to protect the text from vulgar misappropriation, insofar as it gives the reader a model of how not to interpret the A. The vul- garity of allegory is the risk it takes in developing a schema and assigning values. Not only, then, does allegory incite crude misap- propriations, but also does it encourage antipathetic interpreta- tion, for readers have been insufficiently led through the range of moral choices.[44] Their capacity for sympathy is too weakly exer- cised; their apprehensiveness, too impatiently surrendered. So crucial to Hawthorne's narrative method is this exploiting of ambiguities to enlarge and refine a reader's response that it is the feature most popularly associated with his twentieth-century reputation, the nodal point amidst our own changes in critical assumptions. To the extent that Hawthorne's mystifications—self-conscious or otherwise—inspire his modern readers' efforts to clarify his purposes and strategies of representation, the pervasive riddling is among the primary sources of his work's appeal. The setting of alternative choices creates the very impasses that they are supposed to solve, perpetrates the riddles that, paradoxically, the choices are meant to answer.

Surely the riddle that continues to fascinate readers the most is whether Dimmesdale wears an *A* on his breast, the problematic closure of plot that enrages some readers and challenges all to penetrate the mystery Hawthorne insists on preserving. Throughout the book, the reader is taunted with the possibility, though at the ultimate moment of disclosure, Hawthorne demurs from making Dimmesdale's secret sin literal. An innocent reader may estimate that, just as the witches' sabbat in "Young Goodman Brown" may have been either a dream or a reality, the appearance of the *A* does not really alter the novel. Yet Hawthorne's refusal to show the *A* incites the apprehensive reader to wonder why Hawthorne would call attention to the "ghastly miracle" only to foreclose representation. The gap he thereby creates between the text and reader encourages a recursive interpretation to appreciate why it would be "irreverent" to disclose the letter openly. By offering multiple possibilities of interpretation, Hawthorne defensively reveals the necessary, though deceptive, clues.

For F. O. Matthiessen, the value of Hawthorne's multiple choices "consisted in the variety of explanations" to which this technique gave rise. Hawthorne used this variety to make emblematic the "continual correspondences between external events and internal experience."[45] A more recent critic suggests that multiple choice leaves the conclusion of the novel as much up to the reader as up to Hawthorne. Richard Brodhead observes, "By absconding with the book's climax and providing alternate visions of it instead, he allows us to construct our own conclusions, to see something or nothing on Dimmesdale's breast, but either on the condition that we be aware of the nature of the vision that will make what we see meaningful to us."[46] So reader-centered a principle of interpretation is actually at odds with the value Hawthorne places on the apprehensive reader's response, for the narrative method of disclosure by defense seems to posit but one solution to the problem. The variety of explanations reveals a number of possible readings, none of which apply; the ploy tantalizes because the reader's desire to know can never be consummated, while the secret stays enshrined. For in the end, there is just one secret, which is implied but which in remaining unspoken creates a host of others.

Perhaps the chief reason that Hawthorne resists making explicit the physical proof of Dimmesdale's guilt is that showing the letter would not accord with Hawthorne's tactic of making the reader apprehend meanings from evidence of secondary importance. For all the allegorical interest of all that has preceded, meanings are always presented tentatively or speculatively. The effect of making Dimmesdale's guilt explicit would then be to undermine Hawthorne's rhetorical purpose of inspiring the reader to believe that other than actual experience is just as accurate as historical truth.[47] For the cautious, anxious, charitable reader, this other than actual world of meanings is verified by the "great and warm heart" that renders truth as if supernaturally revealed, putting that meaning on par with the truths of history. Like Hawthorne on the "second story" of the Custom House, the reader of the romance comes to see the present as shaped by history's invariable multiple choice of secrets that can be guessed, coaxed out of the evidence. Just as the novel begins with the townspeople's trying to uncover what has happened before—who was Hester's lover?—so must the reader look to the past to recover the answer to riddles that continue to affect the present.

Riddles remind us—in their essential arbitrariness—that we cannot always know either by intuition or by reason the proper reply to difficult, vexing questions. A given question, riddles tell us, has but one answer, and the frustration this provokes is that their solution depends on both the suppleness of consciousness and the vagaries of the unconscious, or both. Consciousness will most often fail to yield a satisfying response, and it must combine with intuition to narrow the numerous possibilities. Like multiple choice, a riddle inevitably resists the first attempts at resolution. An easy solution makes for a bad riddle, for the purpose of riddles is always to conceal.[48] How many people guess them right? How pleasing to do so; how cheated the teller feels. All the time the teller intended to mystify the listeners with what was imagined to be a virtually unintelligible secret, the listeners could discover it and thus confound the teller. The pleasure that a successful riddler feels will come from revealing an answer only after the listeners have exhausted all guesses and admit that they do not, even cannot know; then they are ready to share the teller's delight in the secret's worthiness and the effectiveness of the riddler's typology of concealment. Multiple choice performs the dual process of preventing the riddle from being solved even as it, simultaneously and paradoxically, places the clues before the reader, if only the reader will see the clues. Then, like a riddler exulting in triumph, Hawthorne can proclaim of Dimmesdale's confession: "It was revealed!" (255).

By not showing the sign of Dimmesdale's guilt, Hawthorne frustrates the reader's now heightened interest in seeing the A at the very moment that the reader wants incontrovertible confirmation. At this moment, Dimmesdale falters, "as if the minister must leave the remainder of the secret undisclosed" (255). In preserving that secret, Hawthorne deceives the reader into the conjecture that the interpretations the onlookers venture are more important than the appearance of the A, the inscription of guilt. Most of the spectators testify to the presence of the letter, but the apprehensive reader understands that their witness is doubtful, because "when an uninstructed multitude attempts to see with its eyes, it is exceedingly apt to be deceived." These observers believe that Dimmesdale either conjured the stigma or branded himself during his seven years' trial. Other viewers speculate that the letter was gnawed by the "ever active tooth of remorse," but that interpretation is also suspect, for these observers may consider themselves the ones "best able to appreciate the minister's peculiar sensibility" and who earlier would have supposed that the relation between the doctor and his patient was a salutary arrangement. Throughout, they are unaware of Dimmesdale's need for self-punishment, his secret whippings and midnight vigils. In their admiration for Dimmesdale they point to the "wonderful operation of his spirit upon the body" but cannot comprehend its source of self-loathing, blind as they are to their own hypocrisy. At this juncture, Hawthorne avers that the reader "may choose among these theories," as if to close the matter by leaving it open. But before he can "erase [the letter's] imprint out of [his] own brain," as he "would gladly" like to do since "long meditation has fixed it in undesirable distinctness," he practices a further deception that deprives the reader of that right. Consider that the "undesirable distinctness" that Hawthorne would happily blur is a phrase both literal and ironic. Even though he does not want the reader of the preface ever to mistake the deep sorrow of the romance for any despondency in the writer's life, the "long meditation" on his own secret guilt makes so sharp an imprint on his consciousness that he not only longs to erase its effect, but he also wants to inscribe the story that his secret suggests, for throughout the narrative Hawthorne is speaking, in a veiled way, as much about himself as about his fictional characters.

A few spectators willfully disbelieve the direct purport of Dimmesdale's words and attend instead to the feeling evidently manifested. They "professed never to have once removed their eyes from" the parson and claim that there was no mark on his breast. These spectators kindly and apprehensively take Dimmesdale's revelation to mean that "he has made the manner of his death a parable in order to impress on his admirers the mighty and mournful lesson, that we are sinners all alike" (259). Yet their testimony cannot be credited too highly. There is a little too much kindness and not enough apprehension here, even if this interpretation considers, as the others do not, the pastor's masked final words. Their denial of Dimmesdale's guilt is too forgiving a sympathy, but the error it makes is more on the side of accuracy than understanding; like the "infernal fire" the vulgar imagine has seared Hester's bosom, the "parable" that these observers wish to create is a "terrific legend," one that subordinates literal statement to figurative expression, though here the reading is too fine rather than crudely allegorical. Because they desire to see Dimmesdale's death as a parable, as perhaps the pastor means it to be, these spectators sacrifice verisimilitude of representation but not of apprehension. Like the "grotesque horror" the vulgar invoke to satisfy their imaginations, these interpreters transform the pastor's consciousness of universal blameworthiness into an angelic consciousness of blamelessness. Thus the proposition that the manner of the parson's death is a parable still stands but not for the reasons that the witnesses give. These spectators find Dimmesdale's consciousness of sin to be a comfort because it disburdens them of confronting immediately and finally their own participation in that vision—their own secret guilt—just as the townsfolk displace their fears of such guilt onto Hester's badge, an able and comfortable symbol that we are sinners all alike. A kind and apprehensive reader sees that these too forgiving, somewhat perceptive observers too easily ignore Dimmesdale's confession in their eagerness to ease the burden that the pastor's parable would leave them. But the kind and apprehensive reader will see that such an appreciation of parable, however misappropriated, however much it resists "our modern incredulity," is of a piece with the kind Hawthorne asks for in the preface, when his "vague confession" makes a parable out of his controversial dismissal.

Not yet is Hawthorne finished with instructing his reader in the character of sympathetic response, for he follows this deceptive clue with another one to disclose further the autobiographical relevance of this "truth so momentous." Hawthorne offers the speculations of these well-meaning observers, but he does not dispute their interpretation so that readers can "consider this version of Mr. Dimmesdale's story as only one instance of the stubborn fidelity with which a man's friends—especially a clergyman's— will sometimes uphold his character; when proofs, clear as the mid-day sunshine on the scarlet letter, establish him a false and sin-stained creature of the dust," a man whose secrets have been revealed. This further qualification might deceive a modern, incredulous reader to dismiss this talk of parable and believe himself free to choose among these theories. Hawthorne was not so free: he carefully, and characteristically, qualifies that a clergyman's friends are so likely to want to protect a good name, by way of suggesting the same thing about a writer's friends. Although he wants the reader of the preface to believe that, so dim was the memory of the preceding eventful summer, he cannot even recall the names of his charges at the Custom House, his "long meditation" on the difficulties of a few months before could not have easily erased "the undesirable distinctness" of another memory: the active letter campaign that Hawthorne prevailed upon his friends to wage, in private and in the newspapers, on his political behalf. One may even wish to suppose that the embarrassment he caused his friends when his name was besmirched worsened his guilt and still weighed heavily on his mind, that he had betrayed both an image of himself and his friends' esteem. Thus the final interpretation of Dimmesdale's guilt is still another clue of secondary importance by which Hawthorne tries to satisfy his need for confessing. In offering this mistaken rationale, that the parson makes a parable of blamelessness out of his guilt, Hawthorne diverts the reader from seeing a less vague confession, while he also offers a sop to those other readers who too readily assent to a vision of universal guilt without acknowledging and confronting the turmoil that underlies this sense.

Quite as if the "inward and inevitable necessity" to confess now too dangerously verges toward the page, Hawthorne assumes for the first time his pose of being the mere editor of these proceedings, the posture he sustains in the preface, and its double sense will seem almost a joke: "The authority which we have followed . . . fully confirms the view taken in the foregoing pages." Facing exposure, Hawthorne withdraws behind his veil, but not without explaining the defensive technique of giving indirect hints which express secrets: "Be true! Be true! Be true! Show freely to the world, if not your worst, yet some trait whereby the worst may be inferred!" Rather than a plea for total honesty, this exhortation tough-mindedly denies the possibility that the secrets in human life can all be known, much less told plainly. (The confusion on this point comes, in part, from the way the expression "if not" is commonly misused to mean that which is ultimately included instead of excluded.) Here Hawthorne urges not a case for dissembling but for recognizing that only through the efficaciously expressive masking of a secret—the replacing of primary traits with secondary ones—can a community, including the one between writer and reader, be served, for only then does a secret lose its individualizing, here tragically isolating effects. Then the truths that one should not or cannot bear to disclose may be known, since the "worst" can be guessed out of sympathy.

Finally, it is unnecessary to rely on Hawthorne's own sense of parable-making to see how *The Scarlet Letter* dramatically shapes a rhetoric of secrecy. To preserve a sense of Hawthorne's making the novel into a confession is thus to see it, like Dimmesdale's "vague confession," as a "vain show of expiation." We need not suppose that "Hawthorne had been acting the part of each of these characters concealing something of the shame of one and guilt of the other, urgently feigning both a composure and an innocence he knew he had lost"—as Nissenbaum has shown so well.[49] For quite apart from Hawthorne's personal relation to the novel is the text's own means of communicating and intensifying what cannot be said. Not only do the characters connect with each other across these lacunae, but out of the gaps between what the reader apprehends and what cannot be verified emerges the novel's eerily intransigent uncertainty of meanings. The strange, muted violence that bears the novel along—the ravages of the mind, the compromising of the passions, the involutions of the spirit, the dehumanizing power of desire—emerges from the denial of sympathy that underlies nearly every exchange and that animates virtually every conversation. Emerson's famous response to the novel is perhaps more appropriate than at first it might seem: "Ghastly, ghastly," he is reputed to have remarked. That ghastliness is the profound uneasiness into which a reader can fall, the effect of the novel's commitment to balking explicit senses and keeping a secret. As Georg Simmel writes, "the hiding of realities by negative or positive means" is "one of man's greatest achievements. . . . the secret produces an immense enlargement of life: numerous contents of life cannot even emerge in the presence of full publicity. The secret offers . . . the possibility of a second world alongside the manifest world; and the latter is decisively influenced by the former."[50]

An important scene in which this "second world" conditions the "manifest" one occurs when Dimmesdale keeps his vigil while waiting for the Reverend Mr. Wilson's lantern to "reveal his long-hidden secret," so the parson's sin can finally be fully publicized. His "secret" produces an "enlargement of life," or so he allegorically interprets the comet. But in the end, his effort to authenticate this "second world" fails, paralyzed as he is by the "impulse" of "that Remorse which dogged him everywhere" and which drives him "to the verge of disclosure" only to be frustratingly and invariably drawn back into the "tremulous gripe" of "Cowardice." Dimmesdale could neither "endure" nor "fling" his guilt "at once." Instead, "this feeble and most sensitive of spirits could do neither, yet continually did one thing or another, which intertwined, in the same inextricable knot, the agony of heaven-defying guilt and vain repentance" (148). Described here is the duality of keeping a secret, simultaneously wavering between concealment and revelation. For not only does a secret contain "a tension that is dissolved in the moment of its revelation," but also does this moment constitute the "acme in the development of the secret; all of its charms are once more gathered in it and brought to a climax," as seen both in this pivotal episode in the novel (the second of the three scaffold scenes) and in the final revelation. In the earlier scene, the release of a secret's charms is stalled, but in being so, a secret's dual energies redouble, while the pulls acting upon Dimmesdale—Cowardice and Remorse—postpone the climax. The secret is thus "full of the consciousness that it can be betrayed; that one holds the power of surprises, turns of fate, joys, destruction—if only perhaps of self-destruction." The "external danger of being discovered" with which Dimmesdale flirts is "interwoven with the internal danger, which is like the fascination of the abyss, of giving oneself away"—the ever-present potential for a secret's evacuating itself of meaning. For Simmel, "The secret puts a barrier between men, but at the same time, it creates the tempting challenge to break through it, by gossip or confession—and this challenge accompanies its psychology like a constant overtone."[51]

When the anxiety over his imminent betrayal is disappointed, the minister consoles himself with a "grisly sense of the humorous," an overtone to which Hawthorne decidedly gives way in the preface. In Dimmesdale's belief that he need not confess because the coming dawn will reveal his mortification publicly, his "crisis of terrible anxiety" makes an "involuntary effort to disclose itself by a kind of lurid playfulness." Just as he now substitutes himself on the scaffold for Hester and as he will later replace his impenitent self that was lured by his beloved's call for human happiness, Dimmesdale pretends, by fabricating a vision, that he can replace his confession with mediating versions of mortification and debasement. Whether he imagines that the town virgins will expose their breasts to him—inverting his desire—or that he might teach dirty words to children, subvert the spiritual confidence of the old, or trade lewd jokes with sailors, the parson playfully reproduces, as secondarily important, versions of his original sin.[52] These proxies duplicate his sense of his earlier fall to sexual temptation and, as imitations, provide a distorted clue whereby the worst may be inferred. The pleasure that this indirect method affords him is the vicarious one of an originating secret's multiple replications. The "grisly sense of the humorous" can only propel him so far, however; his secret untold, the necessary sympathy not forthcoming, he searches compulsively for more and more precise ways of uncovering his heart to the multitude. Only near the close when confession is imminent does Dimmesdale give the secret voice, in the Election Sermon's resonating "cry of pain," which the reader does not hear. Then can he bare his breast, the final denudation, which the reader is forbidden to see.

Why does the reader not see and hear these most precise versions? Of Hawthorne's belief that he could not, and should not, make a full disclosure but only hint at the worst, thus beseeching the reader's sympathy, Lionel Trilling suggests that the difference between Hawthorne then and now is implied by our impatience with this procedure of masking, hinting, withdrawing. Why not the very worst? Trilling asks. Why keep the secret?[53] For Hawthorne, making the revelation into a riddle is an act of disclosure that elicits the reader's most complete involvement. Rather than divulge the secret of his own experiences or the minister's, Hawthorne attaches this lesson in how to be true "among the many morals which press upon us from the poor minister's experience" (260). It would be "irreverent" to show the worst because it would violate the "sanctity" of the human heart, the sanctity that readers would violate by rending the veil, behind which the author's inmost Me purportedly remains. By the same logic, to show the A would be to unmask the worst rather than represent it, however defensively. Exposure would make this moment too much of a lurid sideshow for the multitude Hawthorne was trying to instruct as an audience, especially for the lessons in sympathy he meant to inculcate. Not only would the narrative method of dually promising and postponing a secret's revelation be effectively disrupted, but both the psychological rationale of defense and the moral basis regulating response would also be subverted and undone. Sympathy would no longer be required to apprehend the "black secret in [the] soul" (143).

In *The Scarlet Letter*, Hawthorne devises a system for romance narrative that actively brings the reader into the text. The tactics of representation would seem to suggest that once readers become "kind and apprehensive" they can learn the identity of the novel's "black secret." As the novel develops, however, the very notion of the determinate value of a secret recedes. Instead, the novel's fundamental secret—the meaning of the A as one that can be ascribed to Hawthorne—really exists to concentrate the psychological, social, and rhetorical range of several secrets. This concentration of meanings perpetrates a fiction of determinacy through which the reader's sympathy is intensified.

The reader's assurance, then, that one secret needs to be named is a false one. If readers are troubled by Hawthorne's seeming to renege on showing an A on Dimmesdale's breast, it is because they are returned to the bewilderment that both preface and romance have promised to relieve. Yet the numerous secrets—of emblem, character, history, and text—would not be accommodated by identifying one secret, for these have been concatenated throughout, from chapter to chapter, scene to scene.

Orchestrating these elements of secrecy, the novel's text, like the *A* itself, offers answers less definitive than organic to the questions it poses. The reader is less a Daniel reading the handwriting on the wall than a member of a community. The text means to shape this society by presenting and reproducing the anxiety of reading, first in the actions of the characters and the interests ascribed, then in the fiction of Hawthorne's reading Surveyor Pue's documents. This anxiety, in Hawthorne's view, will be appeased to the degree that readers are schooled in sympathetic response. When readers are so instructed, they are brought to a knowledge of their own secrets through the leveling process this novel invokes, and a community of readers, like the community of citizens Dimmesdale foresees, can be achieved. This lone note of optimism in Hawthorne's tragic romance must be observed, not merely to be true to the author's characteristic sentimental exertions of hope in the face of evidence he so readily mounts against a society blind to its own lack of sympathy, a society to which the readers of Hawthorne's texts belong. Doomed to live out the logic their secrets demand, the characters collide with or evade each other, embattled as each one is with a "motive secret," caught as they are in conflict with other characters also embroiled in their own secrets. Moreover, this psychological drama is conducted in a community abounding with secrets. Preoccupied with questions of private life and public behavior, this private history of the New England colony suggested, for Hawthorne, still another dimension of secrecy: how the secrets of the past make their presence felt, how the historical present presages the future. In *The House of the Seven Gables*, the secrets of the past and their effect in the present—how the "wrong-doing of one generation lives into the successive ones"—underlie problematic issues of genre and form. The resolutions that Hawthorne finds are to be understood in the ways that the relation between secrets and sympathy illuminates the novel's dynamics of disclosure.[54]

CHAPTER TWO

The House of the Seven Gables and the

Secret of Romance

In turning from the Puritan past and its implied effect on the present to the explicit treatment of that history in *The House of the Seven Gables*, Hawthorne meant to explore the limits of genre even as he tried to fashion a work that would sell. So the story of Holgrave's progress, his redemption and reconciliation through marriage to Phoebe, is set against the story of corrupt claims to empire. This coupling of plots has long been understood as so forced that it cannot seal the narrative's fracturing into several different plots and styles. These plots seem to conflict with one another; one set of conventions belies the dominion of another. Indeed, much of the novel's criticism has centered on the question of the plot's coherence, perhaps because its narrative procedure and rhetorical assumptions are the issues that seem most to engage Hawthorne.[1]

Contemporaneous commentators sounded a similar note. An anonymous reviewer in 1855 saw the novel as the "most pleasing and complete" of Hawthorne's three recent romances but conceded that it would not serve well "as a model to apprentice fiction-mongers," while granting that "Hawthorne may be allowed to let his genius find its own vent, and diverge as often as it pleases from any path it may ostensibly follow." The novel, by this estimate, would lose the "best part of its attractions, had the author rigidly repressed the promptings of his luxuriant fancy, and clearly pursued the even tenor of his narrative."[2] The reviewer's sense that Hawthorne must have his freedom to create is more than an indulgence; it sanctions Hawthorne's experimenting with various representational modes in the novel. For at times, *Seven Gables* relies as much on gothic devices or sentimental conventions as it does on the verisimilitude for which Hawthorne was often praised: "scenery, tone, and personages of the story are imbued with a local authenticity which is not . . . impaired by the imaginative claim of romance." Through "intense sympathy," says one critic, Hawthorne's "elaborate and harmonious realization" of the Puritan past—a whole "New England character"—is achieved, even more fully in *Seven Gables* than in *The Scarlet Letter.*[3]

Split between its aspirations to cultural prophecy and commercial appeal, the novel is divided in its purposes. This break propagates disunities of plot, structure, and theme that the treatment of secrets, and the disjunctive forms of their disclosure, typifies. Sympathy is held out as the means by which narrative and social order can be validated, but even when bolstered by this moral and political faculty of response, *The House of the Seven Gables* collapses under the weight of its unresolved contradictions. For *Seven Gables* tries to do what *The Scarlet Letter* eschews. At the close, it names its secrets fully. These ostensible disclosures, however, seem more to participate in the techniques of gothic fiction than in the inferential processes that *The Scarlet Letter* encourages. At its conclusion, *Seven Gables* seems like one of those novels that tie up all matters of plot by telling the reader one or two key details. Heretofore left out, these details usually concern some coincidence or unknown circumstances of birth, knowledge which now enables a hero or heroine to establish right relations to other characters or correct misdeeds. This information is often characterized as bringing the secret of happiness, the secret of true love, the secret of true wisdom, or the secret of wealth. Not surprisingly, once told, such secrets often allow a marriage to proceed and signal a new harmony.

This naming of secrets lies at the root of the problem of organizing the several styles, plots, and themes of *Seven Gables*. After devising a complex system of representation, Hawthorne cannot create an adequate means of easing the tensions within it, tensions that naming secrets should disperse. For *Seven Gables* portrays two kinds of secrets—determinate and not—to be associated with the other oppositions that undergird the novel's structure. These two kinds of secrets warrant two forms of disclosure—"ostensible" and "more subtile"—that reflect the romance's two temporal frames, past and present. Moreover, these two kinds of secrets often correspond to the two lines of education plots and can be understood as gender coded. Thus there are at least two stories to *The House of the Seven Gables:* the tale of American virtue that takes place on the floor of moral wisdom and domestic stability over which Phoebe reigns and the story of economic rise and decline, the level where Holgrave's education is conducted. The two stories of enterprise and virtue are meant to be made one, just as ostensible representation and mystery are meant to be fused through the intercession of "comprehensive sympathy." Then the narrative framework will be seen as aligned, "chimney-corner legend" or fantasy from the past, the equal to ordinary, everyday stories in the present.

■ Oppressed by the unyielding gloom of *The Scarlet Letter,* Hawthorne sought to relieve the somberness of his next romance with doses of geniality and a happy ending. He called *Seven Gables* a more "characteristic" work, by which he meant that it represented his whole nature rather than relied exclusively on the grim aspect that vivified its predecessor. Hawthorne hoped that in being truer to his temperament, he was also being more attractive to his readers. But eager as he was to gratify popular and sentimental tastes, along with his own brighter side, the novel darkens "damnably toward the close," as he admitted while composing it.[4] While the happy ending that he wrought out of Maule's Curse and the Pyncheon heritage of evil pleased his favorite reader, Sophia, it has generally been regarded as problematic ever since. Its exuberance may come from the relief of telling an obsessive secret, but the closure inadvertently creates more secrets.

The dissatisfaction with the ending is usually based on requiring of it more than Hawthorne may have intended. It can readily be seen as a romantic explanation of the preceding or a realistic promise of the future or an ironic view of their conjunction.[5] In a novel where history is storied and the plot emerges out of the conflicts between competing ideological claims for social predominance, the ending raises expectations that one or the other of these factions will succeed or that some easy truce can be achieved between elitist and egalitarian views of political and economic order. The argument over who owns America, however, will never be finished, and Hawthorne seems to withdraw from the very debate that the ending is supposed to resolve. The spectacle of Holgrave's ascendancy and marriage can be understood as an allegory of democracy's vanquishing of elitist power, even as this victory of the populace is suggested to have its own elements of corruption. Establishing a new house will ultimately destroy democracy's claim to power, which may well prophesy the rise and ultimate decline of middle-class culture. Yet Hawthorne is also willing to invoke democratic principles as transhistorical. Despite the local specificity with which Hawthorne treats Holgrave's progress, he awards the young man's tale with the timeless quality of a story about coming into adulthood.[6]

The ending purports to hold nothing back, but the secrets finally disclosed do not counteract the effect of the novel's tragic premise that "No great mistake . . . is ever set right." Or so E. P. Whipple, the critic whom Hawthorne credited as having "helped me to see my book," suggested when he first observed that the conclusion "departs from the integrity of the original conception, and interferes with the strict unity of the work."[7] For all of its enthusiasm, the ending inevitably disappoints many readers for its contrivance and conventionality. Although readers might guess that Holgrave is really a Maule and that what seems to be the historical necessity of evil is really subject to human control, it cannot be said that the success showered upon the characters is commensurate with anything they have endured. After setting loose the forces of ineluctable evil, Hawthorne seems to call them back, as if to observe how much damage might have been done. Rather than pursue the consequences of his premise that evil lives from one generation into successive ones, Hawthorne tries to put aright the effects of a great mistake and confers on his characters a fairy-tale bliss that is only somewhat more qualified than the happy endings of conventional romances. Phoebe integrates her personality, Holgrave learns moderation, and their marriage becomes a foregone conclusion. Yet Clifford's guilty air is never explained away; Hepzibah does nothing to transcend her alternately comic and pathetic proportions. When Uncle Venner is included in the family felicity for being a good companion to Clifford, Hawthorne seems to have tumbled over the precipice of absurdity that he claims a romancer must always avoid.[8] Even when viewed in the duskiest of the author's characteristic light—that this happiness may be only temporary—Hawthorne's explanation of how the burden of the past may be lifted is too easily reduced to the revealing of a few technical details, such secrets as the spring behind the Colonel's portrait, the family history of apoplexy, Holgrave's true heredity. Nor do these secrets provide a solid enough foundation for the cultural criticism that the novel mounts.

Once these secrets are told, they lose their suggestive power and become unsatisfyingly literal. They prove insufficient for the legacy of material acquisitiveness and spiritual manipulation that they initiate. Readers who feel betrayed at the close may hold that such family traits as apoplexy or a predilection for the occult do not justify the facsimiles of gothic representation which Hawthorne suggests can be found in contemporary life. Not only do the answers given seem inadequate to the questions of history and the possibilities of social rejuvenation, but if the secrets Hawthorne finally tells did accommodate the novel's political, economic, and social meanings, the romance would instruct readers to dismiss legends or supernatural tales and look for literal explanations in the face of the concealed or fraudulent.

Perhaps Hawthorne believed that naming these secrets would appease or entertain readers used to elucidated mysteries as a convention of closure. Still, the mechanical explanation of the impact of the past on the present does not correspond to the feeling that the resolution is intended to allay. When they are ultimately disclosed, the previously hidden secrets inspire neither responsibility in the present nor awe of the past. The horror that has proceeded from these secrets, however, still needs to be communicated if Hawthorne would "convince mankind (or, indeed, any one man)" of the "high truth" that the "wrongdoing of one generation lives into successive ones" to become "a pure and uncontrollable mischief."⁹

Such secrets as Holgrave's genealogy or the Pyncheons' congenital susceptibilities do not warrant the effects their concealment produces. Such secrets say more than the simple notion that behind any great controversy lies the mundane or even the trivial. These secrets suggest that at the source of any great question is an obvious reality that we have foolishly ignored or have obscured as a result of our money-minded dull-wittedness. However mysterious or magical the answers we seek, the root causes of questions concerning social turmoil, political hegemony, and economic power are plain or should be, once the mystifying veil is lifted. Then secrets seem to matter little. To reach this exaltedly demystified state, secrets must be stripped of at least two kinds of their power: first, the power to individuate or to isolate the secret-keeper; second, the faculty to suppress or to obliterate. The first power means that one of the secret's basic premises—of making special, or granting identity—is controverted. In place of the prestige of having a secret is the somewhat debased position of having forfeited the mastery that privileged knowledge confers. One is left among all the others who lack the status that having a secret means. Furthermore, relinquishing a secret also means surrendering the faculty of filtering everything through the mentality that a secret erects or props. A secret imposes this controlling premise of reception and thus can either allow some information or dismiss evidence that does not support its necessity, as if the secret can guarantee its own existence and negate all that would interfere with its sovereignty.

Such a transaction simply overturns the point of Holgrave's story of reconciliation. If the once-secret realities fomenting upheaval are as ordinary as we are asked to conclude, then Holgrave's adjustment is not really taxing and edifying. If he already knows that he has no power to make Pyncheons choke on their own blood and that his retribution is the working of sexual and class humiliations, then his struggle seems less a personal sacrifice than a vehicle that bears the plot along while commenting upon it. In this sense, perhaps, such simplification appeals to a strain of impish wit observable throughout Hawthorne's short fiction and sketches; great complexity is finally reduced to everyday rationales or simple explanations that human beings in their never-ending folly, self-importance, or blindness, learn only after they have exhausted themselves in futile travails.

While readers are given a sense that a central mystery, like the truth behind Holgrave's conversion, is being elaborated, *Seven Gables* does not elucidate this issue by basing its narrative logic on sequence. The romance's secrets do not become increasingly apparent as the pages turn; their disclosure is not subordinated to a direct or linear process of accumulating evidence, giving up false leads, and following clues. The detection of these secrets, moreover, is not derived from the gothic ploys with which Hawthorne experiments in "Alice Doane's Appeal." Nor do these secrets substantiate the human need to seize clues in an age no longer committed to theocentric explanations of mystery. There is no key to a central mystery as in Balzac, or one to be found through ratiocination as in Poe. The novel will suggest at various points that knowledge of a secret will make all clear, but no single secret really predominates. In fact, several appear crucial. There is no single determinate mystery to be solved by the clever deduction of coincidences, no tissue of connection to be guessed, as in Dickens. There is little pressure to go beyond what the logic of a situation warrants, as in Conrad; no Jamesian "grasping imagination" is heralded. In *Blithedale*, Hawthorne initiates a complex procedure of narrative induction that James later extends and elaborates; but in *Seven Gables*, there is no such indeterminate cause, toward which the reader steadily advances though never learns, to account for the bewilderments the narrative produces. Conventional as the happy spectacle is at the close, it clarifies nothing the reader was ever incited to conjecture. As Todorov remarks of the structure of a Henry James story, in a formula applicable to Hawthorne's plotting of this novel: "The appearance of the cause halts the narrative; once the mystery is disclosed, there is no longer anything to tell. The presence of the truth is possible, but it is incompatible with narrative."[10] Moreover, no matter how multivalent the symbols such as the house or Alice's posies, the narrative is not guided by some rigorous search for meaning to dramatize the relation between secrecy and reality, as in *Moby-Dick*. Nor does the narrative specifically lay obstacles amid that search, as in *The Marble Faun*. Although all of Hawthorne's romances treat the compromised quest for a secret, its identity remains unclear, while the means for unearthing it usually create further opacities.

Instead of sequentially, the novel moves by a process of accretion, its tableaux embellishing upon or undercutting one another. The narrative can be understood to take detours or to vacillate, so that its middle may seem "inert" or its conclusion "impotent."[11] A secret is invoked, its search sustained, from chapter to chapter, yet no clear, unilateral logic of disclosure is asserted or can be inferred. For instance, when the possibility is raised that Clifford may have murdered the Judge, Hawthorne suspends the operations of the plot, not to elaborate on Clifford's possible culpability or even to heighten and exploit the reader's uncertainty, but to chortle over the Judge's round of missed appointments. Although he wishes to leave open the question of Clifford's guilt, in "Governor Pyncheon" Hawthorne invites the reader to join him in what is virtually a communal act of desecration. Such detours often follow the twists of a gothic plot, a narrative structure which Hawthorne's conventional readers could immediately identify and to which they would easily respond. For such readers, the Judge might yet emerge alive from his death chair. The explanations educed from these abrupt changes, however, also fail to satisfy.

Rather than merely reflect given rhetorical and social orders, the lines of plot are the entanglements of two visions of order, associated with Holgrave and with Phoebe. On the one hand, there is the story of the novel's bildungsroman, in which the thoroughly marginalized young drifter is brought into accommodation. His claims to power and society's power of victimage are finally balanced, by dint of his cleverness and Pyncheon feebleness, once he is given entry into the body social. That story, however, is both the tale of Holgrave's coming into centrality, retrieved from the margins, and the cost of that reconciliation when his antagonism is domesticated. This plotline works on the grounds that Holgrave's identity prohibits him from achieving his apotheosis. Who he is must be kept secret, although traces may still appear. Holgrave's story—the American male's moral progress—follows the fiction that some true self must be hidden even as it is being reshaped, a mask or two donned while a new self can be fashioned and tested. Although unacknowledged, this reshaped self is very much like the old, since it is usually a provisional response to newly felt urgencies. At last, he is ready to be redeemed by a princess who will reconnect him to the life of primal pleasures, personal responsibilities, and social standing.

The princess in Hawthorne's novel is the American democratic version of the morally simple girl, like Phoebe, who preserves ethical and emotional priorities while making the outcast respectable. Phoebe's role as this princess is still another story in the narrative, another example of how a past wrong lives on into successive generations. Yet that plot is played down to suit the purposes of a legend, like Holgrave's, which serves the patriarchy. Phoebe's story of love and marriage is subordinated to her place in the narrative. Her development is incorporated as a stage in Holgrave's education. Ironically, the crucial effect of minimizing Phoebe comes during the telling of "Alice Pyncheon," for that is the climax of Holgrave's triumph over the antagonisms, the very point at which Phoebe's truncation is signaled in her predecessor's victimage. In Phoebe's case, the past wrong is the humiliation of the female, the princess who is never allowed to accede to power but is instead bartered in the males' negotiation of the right to govern. The molesting of Alice exemplifies the physical abuse that corresponds to the psychological stunting that males would visit upon females. The violation recorded, the violence portrayed and threatened, shocks Holgrave into a new awareness, as we shall see. That new vision, however, is not so startling that Holgrave's change of heart should seem illogical. The image of Alice's misery, the abuse she suffers, represents basic childhood fears of being beaten. Freud tells us that males and females alike dream that a male authority will strike and injure them but that males conveniently repress a middle stage of this dream, the image of themselves as female victims of their fathers' wrath and brutality.[12] Holgrave's narrative of violence suffered and enacted may lead to his own reconciling of opposites, but it also perpetuates the diminishment of females and their own quest for power. For the story of Alice's degradation is woven together with Phoebe's bildungsroman to create a submerged plot that complements and competes with Holgrave's.

The Phoebe-Alice plot combines mythic and historic explanations, while it also emerges as a conjugate plot that integrates the novel's issues of temporal and spatial order, individuality and collectivity, norm and excess.[13] These two lines of plot, then, provide the romance with two modes of representation, one corresponding with commonsense understandings of secrets, the other ensuring mystification. These two modes, in turn, define the novel's dualisms of structure, temporality, and cultural understanding. For the novel's disunions also can be understood as the faulty compromises between male and female that the marriage plot dramatizes. In response to the novel's questions of class structure and domestic ideology, the wedding between economic power and morality proceeds on the hope and promise of establishing a collaborative sympathy, a social vision dear to nineteenth-century American values.

█ The structure of *The House of the Seven Gables* is neither a parody nor a Yankee variation of the constitutive features of a gothic novel.[14] Instead, the process of representation reveals secrets in ways conventionally direct and characteristically, for Hawthorne, indirect. It is a dual procedure, which also helps to define Hawthorne's sense of a romance's "definite moral purpose" (2). Although Hawthorne does give answers to particular secrets, the ostensible disclosures explain only marginally the conduct of the characters. When, for example, Hepzibah is reluctant to open the door to her cent-shop, Hawthorne ascribes her anxiety to the memory of a former Pyncheon, a "petty huckster," who first defiled the house with commerce. But even while Hawthorne proposes that "the reader must needs be let into the secret" (28), Hepzibah's degradation is really imitative of the shame that the Colonel first brought upon the house and, more important, is secondary to the indignity she now feels for descending a rung on the aristocratic ladder. When Hawthorne explains Clifford's nervousness, we learn: "The secret was, that an individual of his temper can always be pricked more acutely through his sense of the heavenly and harmonious, than through his heart" (112). But surely this revelation does not explain his suicidal urge or his apparently guilty conversation once he and his sister take flight. While the reader may have supposed that Clifford's detention robbed him of his sanity, Clifford's behavior is so startling that the reader, along with the people who meet the "pair of owls," may suspect that the childish lover of beauty is, after all, a murderer: "What a treasure trove to these venerable quidnuncs, could they have guessed the secret which Hepzibah and Clifford were carrying along with them!" (255). What could this secret be? That Clifford has killed the Judge? That the Judge has died of natural causes? If the first, the reader of melodramatic novels would expect some detailed account about this madman, which Hawthorne expressly does not give. If the second, why would a quidnunc care that Clifford now feels free?

Rather than through sequence or gothic apparatus, secrets in *The House of the Seven Gables* are disclosed through a dual process of narration, a process that becomes the very vehicle of the romance's "definite moral purpose." For Hawthorne, this relation between representational technique and moral issues is central: "When romances do really teach anything, or produce any effective operation, it is usually through a far more subtle process than the ostensible one" (2). A romance can "really teach," even as it eschews verisimilitude, as long as it relies on its subtler method. The "ostensible" procedure is Hawthorne's equivalent to telling a straightforward tale, one that is bound by conventions of representation through which the world of the novel is rendered directly and literally. The ostensible procedure is rooted in the desire for determinacy. The subtler method, by contrast, produces its "effective operation" through a suggestive power, what Hawthorne calls the "legendary mist" that settles over the narrative. This process of entangling the lines of plot and of offering two modes of representation is defined in Hawthorne's preceding paragraph where he describes his narrative structure as "woven of so humble a texture" as to require that legend be used to connect a past era with the present. Legend lends a mist of possibility that literal representation of the gothic cannot supply. Pared of its excess, legend conveys and intensifies the horror of the past and makes it accessible for the present.[15] Hawthorne realizes that this reliance makes his narrative "more difficult of attainment." To solve this problem, he searches for modern sources of wonder—photography, mesmerism, technology—that can approximate the dread or bewilderment that gothic rendering of the sublime and fantastic traditionally evoked.

Freighted with mystifying elements that demand finer interpretation than the merely literal affords, "chimney-corner legends," such as "Alice Pyncheon," make their impact by being provocative and elusive. Their unverified explanations, as Holgrave's tale exemplifies, swell the novel's atmosphere with an enlarged sense of the possible and perhaps also the shocking. Legends work to the extent that they make the past and its secrets more vividly discernible, more cogently explicable than the present case may allow, locked as the present may be in the demand for plausibility. Legends preserve the strangeness of the past, preserving it as the time of original causes, which weigh so heavily on the present. Countervailing the urgency for verification, legends keep the strangeness of the past oppressively vital and hence are more authoritative in their suggestiveness than any authorized version in the present. The authority of legends comes from their self-containment as explanations, however inexplicit, yet they produce their "effective operation" by producing an even allegorical correlative wherein the present may find its own resemblance. In *Seven Gables*, legend brings into contact with the "ostensible" a heightened value of possibility, a range of suggestion seemingly grounded in history but one that is also psychologically accurate. This "more subtile" procedure guards the past against subversive or trivializing demystification, keeps the past actively shaping the present.

Hawthorne's announced purpose in developing this dual procedure is to "really teach," an obvious pun in this context where Hawthorne means to distinguish between the realistic demands of novels and the wider latitude of romance. The reader of the preface must be doubly alert to Hawthorne's crafty diction; "ostensible" conceals another ambiguity, for the word can mean both "open to view" and "apparently though not necessarily true." Furthermore, "subtile" refers to a sense of fine discrimination yet may also mean "deceptive" or "deceitful." The defense that this double meaning provides is then fortified when Hawthorne, declining "to impale the story with its moral," professes that he considered it "hardly worth his while" to make the moral explicit. The various disquisitions on the past and the present in the novel suggest, however, that Hawthorne adopts this characteristically defensive posture in the preface because he may have suspected that readers would respond only to the sensational or sentimental elements in the narrative and disregard the social and historical implications of the speeches that the characters make. Thus his subtle method could supplement even as it legitimated his ostensible one. For example, the house that gives the book its title is both literally a house and also the novel's central symbol. Its metaphoric properties are evoked from the outset through the "subtile" procedure of transforming the house from an ancestral home, replete with the accoutrements of romantic traditions, to a mind (as we will later see in the description of Jaffrey's psychology), to a myth concerning pre- and postlapsarian American history, to an apocalyptic image of a regenerated, newly entitled society. Like the figures at the bottom of Maule's Well, the house becomes one of Hawthorne's "castles in the air" through the "effective operation" of a romance that changes with the beholder's eye. For the instruction Hawthorne finds in the "effective operation" of romance is how the representation of secrets is also the structuring of response. Insofar as readers become the repositories of the moral values and cultural history that Hawthorne invests in the narrative, the response to be achieved in the method of subtly representing secrets is inevitably the broadening and refinement of sympathy.

The relation between this process of representation and the disclosure of secrets may first be suggested in an incident that occurred after Hawthorne published *The Scarlet Letter* but before he began his next book. In May of 1850, he sat for a painting by Cephas G. Thompson; at that time, he recorded in his notebooks his reservations about portraits: none of his earlier ones pleased him or proved "satisfactory to those familiar with my phiz. In fact, there is no such thing as a true portrait; they are all delusions; and I never saw any two alike, nor, hardly, any two that I could recognize merely by the portraits themselves as being of the same man." Hawthorne's initial dissatisfaction was apparently quieted during these sittings, especially as he came to recognize the mutuality between Thompson's endeavor and his own. Observing the artist's increasing "eagerness," the writer could "recognize the feeling that was in him, as akin to what I have experienced in the glow of composition."[16] Portraiture, Hawthorne came to understand, shared affinities with romance. Whereas the fiction writer doubted the efficacy or even possibility of literal rendering, the portrait artist could make vivid the special senses beyond the literal that Hawthorne valued as the domain of romance's "subtile" schemas of representation. One critic has observed that Thompson's enthusiasm must have been communicated to the author, who immediately began to document in his journal the pictorial interest of the faces that he saw. This interest, according to Taylor Stoehr, is also extended to the novel where the representation of faces is an active, organizing motif.[17] Not only does the picture of Colonel Pyncheon stare down upon the characters, but the house itself is described as having a "human countenance." Virtually every character's face is described, and some characters are identified by their facial gestures, a "smile" or a "scowl." Hawthorne even examines the face of so innocuous a character as Uncle Venner to find what "secret meanings, if any, might be lurking there" (64).

Well known as Hawthorne's interest in faces is in the novel, it becomes especially noteworthy if we also consider how sitting for Thompson excited Hawthorne's complex, psychological response to the anxiety of self-representation that the novelist had meant to case in "The Custom-House." Even if writing that sketch had quelled Hawthorne's misgivings about his publicized troubles of the preceding summer and allowed him to keep securely behind its veil his "inmost Me," the nervousness of exposure was irritated again when he viewed Thompson's completed work. The portrait, he wrote, was "afflicted with a bedevilled melancholy" and showed "the very head that had been cut off" when Hawthorne was dismissed from the Custom House.[18]

While this incident reveals a secret that is, as we have seen, susceptible of psychological explanation, the interest of Thompson's
uncanny portrait also lies in the emphasis that Hawthorne discovers in the process of representation for romance narrative. The
truly striking aspect of the episode, for Hawthorne, is that representation itself can realize the secrets belonging to a subject. Not
the subject but the process exposes and exhibits a subject's true
character. Mimesis is less fixed, more plastic than the author had
heretofore understood. Usurping so much from its subject, this
process makes itself accessible to the sympathetic understanding
of both writer and reader. Similarly, the activity of representation
more and more stimulates the reader's apprehension, to complete
what the artist leaves unsaid or even unrealized. To some degree,
Hawthorne's new understanding is really the adumbration of the
lessons learned from *The Scarlet Letter*, but here they are applied
to mimetic rather than metaleptic properties. In addition, the recognition that he could treat a contemporary milieu with the same
"romance" as he could a historical one permits Hawthorne then to
develop his dual sense of the novel's temporal logic and its corresponding "ostensible" and "more subtile" procedures. The "ostensible" method represented could be extended and enriched by the
"more subtile" one, thus avoiding the distortion that, Hawthorne
feared, literalization encouraged. Through his experience at
Thompson's studio, Hawthorne came to see how representation
both configures and transforms, is both ostensible and subtle, and
thus conveys a subject's hidden life. In *Seven Gables*, Hawthorne
means to bring together two kinds of representational strategies—
one appealing to the literal or "ostensible," the other appealing to
the suggestive or "subtile"—for rendering secrets, or at least point-
ing to their viability. As Hawthorne demonstrates at the close, the
literal or determinate value of a secret always can be ascribed to
some meaning or other, but secrets also give rise to the "legendary
mist" spreading across the novel's tableaux, the indeterminate
character of which remains provocative.

This dual sense of representation is first seen in the "magical"
mirror in the Pyncheon home. Rather than the typically Augustan
use of mirrors as imitative that we find in some of his early stories,

here transformative properties are invoked. As in "Monsieur du Miroir," the mirror reflects the "secret footsteps" in the process of representation.[19] In *The House of the Seven Gables*, the mirror reflects the images of the whole Pyncheon family, but not as they prefer to present themselves or as they appear in their prosperity. Instead, this magical mirror reveals them in their secret family spirit—"as doing over again some deed of sin, or in the crisis of life's bitterest sorrow" (21). Its reflective capacities transform rather than imitate, a process fundamentally, even ideally, fictive. As Hawthorne laments, "Had we the secret of that mirror, we would gladly sit down before it, and transfer its revelation to our page" (20). Rather than a perfect imitation, the mirror projects the family heritage of wrongdoing and regret that its members have always sought to conceal. The mirror abstracts the unacknowledged guilty passion animating their appearance while remaining hidden beneath the image each would present.

Real mirrors have no such properties. This suggestive power of Hawthorne's version of transformative reflection finds a more modern example of portraiture: the daguerreotype. Because a daguerreotypist can "make pictures" out of daylight, he can find the "wonderful insight in heaven's broad and simple sunshine" that "actually brings out the secret character with a truth that no painter would ever venture upon, even if he could detect it" (91).[20] Both the daguerreotype and the mirror transform the literal, make it suggestive; they portray what cannot otherwise be illustrated and imply what is not immediately perceptible in the subject itself. Both kinds of image express the "secret character" of their subjects, whether this representation is based on the legends of the past or the thin air that illumines the here and now. Thus the transformative process of representation, in its capacity to transfigure what it portrays, also defines the novel's two temporal frames: the past that resists explanation and the present that is generally more secretive than the bright sunshine of American life would admit. As we will see, the fantastic quality of this transformation will also align the past and present with the future.

When Hawthorne discloses the literal truth at the end of the novel, the "more subtile process" expends its power of intimation, and the secrets lose their effect. No longer concealed, the facts about the Pyncheon and Maule families are no longer equal to the passions that they have aroused and deployed. As a matter of course, secrets lose their spell once they are told. A secret's charm consists in its remaining still to be guessed and, hence, still capable of being transformed. So much of the action and effect of *The House of the Seven Gables* follows from the withholding and culminates in the disclosure of these secrets that merely enumerating them indicates their importance to the plot. The fundamental secret is the way in which the corruption of the past lives into the present, a "prehistoric deed," as Leslie Fiedler calls an event that antedates a narrative and is the armature around which the lines of the plot are wound.[21] Also secret is the cause of death for both Colonel Pyncheon and Clifford's uncle. Although various explanations are given, none is confirmed. For much of the novel, Clifford's thirty-year absence is unexplained, Jaffrey's guilt left undetermined. Clifford's very identity is briefly withheld; Holgrave's real name told only in the last chapter.

The secret that centers the ostensible plot is the "connecting link" which "had slipt out of the evidence, and which could not anywhere be found" (18), the missing deed that certifies the Pyncheon land claims. The Judge describes it as "the secret of incalculable wealth" and comes to the house to "wrench a secret" from Clifford, arguing with Hepzibah in an exchange punctuated by the word *secret*. At the conclusion, Clifford finally remembers that as "a child, or a youth, that portrait [of Colonel Pyncheon] had spoken, and told me a rich secret." Holgrave then prods him to recall a "secret spring" and observes that "there are a hundred chances to one, that no person unacquainted with the secret, would ever touch the spring." This comment leads Phoebe to ask "How came you to know the secret?" which, in turn, compels Holgrave to confess the secret of his true identity. Indeed, the word appears constantly in the novel, for however simply chosen, it carries the special value of that "formal assumption" which *is*, yet is not articulated. In the case of the missing deed, the "secret" both is and is not present in the imaginative recreation of history, but it is absent from the literal reality. Its very absence provides its interest for the characters and the plot. In effect, the story hinges on this absent cause, perhaps creating in Jaffrey an anxiety of the void, the fear that an essential nullity underlies his life of appetites, his dream of empire. The chance of gaining the crucial link—the written proof—drives Jaffrey to initiate the climactic set of developments in the ostensible plot. At the same time, the fundamental fact of the deed's absence leads to and participates in the novel's general procedures of mystification, the stuff of legendary mists.[22]

Hawthorne's characteristic sense that, as a matter of process, fiction discloses a secret to a sympathetic respondent is demonstrated and qualified when Hepzibah tries to comfort Clifford by reading aloud. She desires to provide Clifford with some clue, which she herself cannot find, for a way out of his helpless misery. This faith in fiction's arranging of a secret responds to one of narrative's most socialized functions, that of offering some balm or refuge to the dispirited or distraught. Her library of eighteenth-century works—"with tarnished gilding on their covers and thoughts of tarnished brilliancy inside"—offers nothing to relieve Clifford's anxiety: "Hepzibah then took up Rasselas, and began to read of the happy valley, with some vague idea that some secret of a contented life had there been elaborated" (134). But her halting voice and the "tedium of the lecture" fail to make Johnson's wisdom accessible. The "life-long croak" in her voice conveys her "whole history of misfortune," even if she could get the rhythms of Johnson's prose right. Sounding as if she is in "mourning for dead hopes," she unwittingly belies any optimism that the narrative authorizes.

Hepzibah's ridiculous reading of Johnson illuminates Hawthorne's version of how a work of fiction performs some consoling or moral service for the reader. Ironically, this is the situation for Clifford and Hepzibah, since Johnson's *Rasselas* is a particularly inappropriate text either for Hepzibah to choose or for Clifford to enjoy. The irony verges on a cruelty made comic; Clifford's reaction is only a deepening of despair, while Hepzibah virtually exacerbates the very malaise she meant to gladden. Thus Hawthorne suggests that the authorizing of a moral vision that fiction enacts is legitimate only to the extent that the writer (here, the public reader) and reader (or listener) can achieve some accord, a sympathy of interests and purposes that fiction read aloud can correlate. What is particularly at issue about this scene of reading is that Hawthorne dramatizes how integrally sympathy functions in communicating a secret.[23] In Hepzibah's grimly silly failure, Hawthorne posits the conviction that a text's secret meanings do not arise unless the narrative is appropriately apprehended by the right audience. Otherwise, the secrets that a text is supposed to impart recede from view, get garbled in the reading. On the one hand, this valorizing of the communiqué asserts the primacy of a secret's particular moral purpose; on the other, Hawthorne designates how peculiarly difficult it is for the writer to make known a certifiable meaning that a secret concentrates. Instead, we observe the dispersion of Rasselas's lessons: they lose their educative thrust, seem irrelevant, or remain inexplicit.

This narrative condition is chronic, however satirical the treatment is here. Readers may like to imagine that a novel has some secret to be determined, one crucial for the "receipt of a message," and that the author possesses an "authentic and normative sense of what he has said." This limited sympathy, however, actually suppresses a text's latency of possible secrets, since "it is not uncommon for large parts of a novel to go virtually unread: the less manifest portions of its text (its secrets) remain secret."[24] And many of these secrets can be recovered, as rereading a text proves so often. For Hawthorne, the central secret that his own romance communicates is detonated when Holgrave reads his tale to Phoebe. While its moral will seem to affect Phoebe as little as Johnson's does Clifford, the secret that Holgrave discloses to himself is conveyed through his act of reading. Yet that reading is really a rereading of his story and his biography that leads him to reconceive the very meaning of his secret and the very basis of sympathy. The circumstances of reading his story aloud help Holgrave to see that secrecy may be a question of information, determinate answers to particular questions, but it is also an issue of mystery, uncertainty, and indeterminacy. When Holgrave reads "Alice Pyncheon" aloud, the interpolated tale demonstrates how secrets and their forms for disclosure are clarified and enlarged through the process of narration. Holgrave ostensibly knows the secret that his work is supposed to communicate, yet only through the circumstances of retelling do the less manifest, more undecidable, and more urgent secrets become clear.

■ Piqued by Holgrave's aspersions against the house and its former inhabitants, Phoebe asks the daguerreotypist why he continues to live there. Holgrave first responds that only by living there can he know "better how to hate it," then adds immediately: "By-the-by, did you ever hear the story of Maule, the wizard, and what happened between him and your immeasurably great-grandfather?" (184). Although Phoebe already has heard the family legend, Holgrave wants to give his version of the story. Far from a merely mechanical excuse for Hawthorne to render Holgrave's thriller, the question is scarcely as incidental as the daguerreotypist wishes it to sound. Just a few moments before, when Holgrave wryly remarks of the essential mystery of every human being, he reveals his reason for abruptly changing the subject: "Men and women, and children, too, are such strange creatures, that one never can be certain that he really knows them; nor even guess what they have been, from what he sees them to be, now. Judge Pyncheon! Clifford! What a complex riddle—a complexity of complexities—do they present! It requires intuitive sympathy, like a young girl's to solve it. A mere observer, like myself, (who never have any intuitions, and am, at best, only subtile and acute,) is pretty certain to go astray" (178–79). Perhaps nervous that Phoebe's "intuitive sympathy" will discover his secret or perhaps because he anxiously wishes to confess his lineage by means of a defensive, mediating fiction, Holgrave is stirred to reveal his identity but only under the disguised form presented in "Alice Pyncheon." When he admits that he wants to learn better how to hate the Pyncheons, his secret activates the logic of defense and disclosure, not some non sequitur in the conversation. Through covert suggestion, Holgrave can represent, in this family romance of abused sexual and economic power, the love that he does not yet dare to admit openly.

Holgrave mesmerizes Phoebe through his narration and thereby assumes and enacts what Laurence Holland describes as Hawthorne's "authority": this "mediating action both defines and creates the authority of the actual author who inscribes it. . . . If one were to claim that Holgrave in some measure 'betrays' Hawthorne's authority by exceeding limits that Hawthorne himself would respect, or by falling short of Hawthorne's more persuasive power and tact, one would have to recognize that to betray is also to reveal, as with secrets, the design of the author." For Holland, Holgrave's tale creates an "interactive transferral of power and its sanctions," a translation of authorial intention into narrative enactment. This translation of the narrator's "exercise of powers into sanctions" constitutes the "governing authority of Hawthorne's art."[25] The "interactive transferral of power" suggests how Hawthorne supplants the "ostensible" procedures with the "more subtile" method insofar as Holgrave's force is qualified, even as it is asserted. For the powerful effect of his tale is on the teller more than the listener. Hawthorne may use the interpolated story to shoulder a rhetorical burden he would prefer not to carry, but in Phoebe's insufficient response, and Holgrave's heightened one, Hawthorne begins to construct how secrets are disclosed, a story of gender-coded reception that keeps the fiction of cultural harmony in balance.

The tale is an argument intended to convince Phoebe of the storyteller's powers, which he demonstrates to be erotic and aesthetic. He mesmerizes her, although Phoebe is not pitted against the daguerreotypist, as Alice is against Maule insofar as some "sinister or evil potency was now striving to pass her barrier." The story's effect, however, is just as seductive as Maule's incantations are for Alice. Like the auditors of "Alice Doane's Appeal," Phoebe is subject to narrative manipulations directed at her heart that are calculated to bring her into sexual submission or, at the very least, into an awareness of Holgrave's potencies. To the extent that Holgrave's purpose is to conquer the threat of a young girl's power of sympathy, he must prove, even shamanistically, that his power of being "acute" and "subtile" is equal to a girl's defenses. Not only does Holgrave arrogate to himself the shaman's divining power that is associated with some exotic, inspired performance, but he also proposes to cure Phoebe through telling a story, his way of purifying her to become his wife. The coded message to Phoebe is clear: this is your legacy as a Pyncheon female; you too will be betrayed by your father and made a victim by his enemies. Furthermore, in telling Phoebe a story about the humiliation of her ancestor, Holgrave also implies his power as a Maule to save or damn her.

If Holgrave's point is chilling, Phoebe's response is also to be understood as a warning, albeit an inadvertent one. Rather than rise to Holgrave's challenge, Phoebe is rendered passive, even compliant. Hers appears the appropriate reaction, especially to this story about opposing males who collaborate to abuse the virgin both regard as precious yet whom both would destroy. Phoebe's response is to pretend not to hear or understand the significance of what she has been told, and understandably so. She discovers in the story that a woman's calls for help will be ignored. Phoebe, we learn, is as "unconscious of the crisis through which she had passed as an infant of the precipice to the verge of which it has rolled" (212). It is not merely enough to infantilize Phoebe at this point; Hawthorne must also make her unconscious in spite of herself, insofar as she thinks she is being "very attentive" though she does not recall the incidents "quite distinctly." She has only an "impression of a vast deal of trouble and calamity," which seems to her justification that the "story will prove exceedingly popular" and will fulfill the expectations of a reading public hungry for excitements. Yet that unconsciousness also suggests Phoebe's keener sensitivity to mystery. She is better than Holgrave at translating a knowledge of secrecy into forgiving sympathy. Sympathy, we see, becomes the female's cultivated position, her one sanctioned exercise of power. As Alice's legacy suggests, she has little recourse.

Holgrave's story is a latter-day reenactment of the violence between the two families, an inscribing of hatred that ultimately turns inward on the participants. At the request of the greedy Gervayse, the wizard Maule conjures the "departed personages, in whose custody the so much valued secret [the missing deed] had been carried beyond the precincts of the earth" (206). Through the medium of Alice's "pure and virgin intelligence," Maule conjures the ghosts of Colonel Pyncheon and his own antecedents, but the Maules prevent the Colonel from imparting this knowledge: "Fi-

nally, when he showed the purpose of shouting forth the secret . . .
his companions . . . pressed their hands over his mouth; and forthwith—whether that he were choked by it, or that the secret itself
was of a crimson hue—there was a fresh flow of blood upon his
band" (207). At this vision, Maule realizes that the secret cannot be
told and tells Gervayse: "The custody of this secret, that would so
enrich his heirs, makes part of your grandfather's retribution. He
must choke with it, until it is no longer of any value" (207).

The secret is that the Pyncheons will inevitably spill their own
blood as a result of their avarice. When Gervayse sacrifices his
daughter, he repeats the family shame. When he submits Alice to
the mesmerist and ignores her "dismal shriek" for help, he violates
her as cruelly as Maule will himself. By turning from her muffled
cry of pain, he turns to his grandfather's policy of abuse. The father's betrayal is further to sentence his daughter to silence, since
that is the language of his response when she calls for him to help.
Like the Colonel, Gervayse does not understand what is really precious; "his head full of imaginary magnificence," he condemns her
to the wizard's power.

Gervayse's treatment of his daughter is even more disturbing for
the insight it reveals about the pursuit of secrets. So rooted is the
desire to keep and extend empire that fathers, this story suggests,
routinely and typically betray their daughters, sell them into an
even sexual bondage with the fathers' sworn enemies. This description only barely overstates the case in "Alice Pyncheon." The
female becomes the token of exchange between father and suitor as
they adjust the relation of power. The daughter is negotiated into a
wife or concubine, takes on the identity of a gift (to be entrusted to
one's care). The extremity of Hawthorne's representation of this exchange should not distort the ordinary character of fathers' abusing
the autonomy of their daughters, fathers making their daughters
the medium of their own purposes, which are the attaining and
advancing of power. Alice thus becomes the literal and figurative
medium through which the secret can be communicated. Her
story reveals both the secret of a "crimson hue" and the original sin
of violation, replicated from generation to generation. Once
Holgrave learns the secret—the respect for the fundamental mys-

tery of another person and the subsequent necessity for the "rare and high quality of reverence for another's individuality" (212)—he is restrained from visiting Maule's Curse upon the present, with Phoebe as his victim.

Thus the ostensible meaning of the tale is communicated to readers fixed on Holgrave, but Hawthorne also elucidates the secret of romance and its subtler method to readers who likewise learn from Phoebe. Here Hawthorne may be said to reclaim his power from Holgrave, when the storyteller is instructed in the ways fiction should excite sympathy. Although the aesthetic power of "Alice Pyncheon" is trivialized as soporific, the story's sexual power of suggestion remains strong; it promises to reveal secrets, and so it does. Holgrave refuses to become the "arbiter of a young girl's destiny" and forbids "himself to twine that one link more, which might have rendered his spell over Phoebe indissoluble" (212). By opening his heart to sympathy and by renouncing the kind of sexual dominion that predicates Alice's humiliation and death or Phoebe's violation, Holgrave resists the compulsion to relive and repeat the crimes of the past. Sitting in the moonlight that enlivens his sympathy, Holgrave sees that the garden's "common characteristics were now transfigured by the charm of romance," the grounds of Hawthornean "neutral territory." Animated by the success of his story, brought to sympathy by the circumstances of the setting, alerted by the example of Matthew Maule, Holgrave achieves his great realization. He learns the lesson that his story has taught him, and perhaps Hawthorne as well: "I have told you a secret which I hardly began to know, before I found myself giving it utterance" (215).[26]

The secret that Holgrave finds himself uttering is respect rather than hatred for the mysterious, the other, the female. Instead of discovery per se, the circumstances of telling his story and the transformative light of sympathy lead him to apprehend what was secret even to himself, for this great secret bids him to live with and love the mysteries of the other—in the person of Phoebe. He can thus be liberated from the legacy of resentment that has supported but also burdened him.

Prompted by Phoebe's lament over the lost gaiety of youth,

Holgrave explains that first "bemoaning" of mortality and the memory of the "heart's joy at being in love" "are essential to the soul's development." When the "two states come simultaneously," as they do now for Holgrave though not for Phoebe, they "mingle the sadness and the rapture in one mysterious emotion" (215). Although Phoebe is moved by the story, Holgrave is really the more shaken. Knowing his true relation to Matthew Maule, as Phoebe does not, and the meaning of his choice of Phoebe as the object of desire, Holgrave grasps his own secret connection to the sins of the past and learns a psychological and historical rationale for not ravishing Phoebe, one that becomes knowable "by a charm of romance," again both fictive and sexual, a charm that also portends death and grief.[27] Insofar as he is awakened into sympathy, he sees that as doomed as the Pyncheons are by their greed, the Maules too are cursed by their vindictiveness. Maule has supposed that he had merely "taken a woman's delicate soul into his rude gripe, to play with," but Alice's death makes him the "darkest and wofullest man that ever walked behind a corpse" (210). To avoid this fate, Holgrave resists the family compulsion of "acquiring empire over the human spirit," as Hawthorne describes the temptation most seductive "to a disposition like Holgrave's." For "empire over the human spirit" is the reprisal the Maules have always sought, once their real property was taken from them. The Pyncheons' wealth and social status (which both Matthew Maule and Holgrave wish to see in order to know better how to hate it) lead the Maules to curse their enemy or gain sexual empire, as in "Alice Pyncheon."

Here Hawthorne makes sympathy the requisite condition of reception for romances, as it was for Holgrave, and sets them apart from novels. In novels, sympathy is not essential to perception; readers may sympathize with a character or situation, but they face an "ostensible" world. The logic of its report is one of inclusion and imitation rather than intuition and suggestion. Romances, on the other hand, need to be sympathizing and to inspire sympathetic apprehension, moral qualities that set the romancer apart from mere fictionists. When Hawthorne condemned the "damned mob of scribbling women" and their value for Christian salvation, for example, he feared that he should ever be as formulaic in his vision. Hawthorne's lonely pleasure is that he would fail his own ideals of excellence and of moral complexity if he were ever as popularly successful as Susan Warner. Instead, it becomes his consolation that one day an audience will understand his strategies and purposes, that readers will intuit what he has left unsaid, will know what he is thinking, will have sympathy for his secrets. Such a frame of mind can be understood as the writer's chronic conviction of himself as one who governs a world, atop one's hermitage as in *Blithedale* or the roof over Saint Peter's Cathedral in *The Marble Faun*, and one who surveys history from one's "castle in the air," according to the omnipotence of thought.[28] Under this light, the romance becomes the fictive domain of wish-dream, but with a difference: the writer of romance can be likened (as Hawthorne says of romance's guiding spirit, the moon) to an "ambitious demagogue, who hides his aspiring purpose by assuming the prevalent hue of popular sentiment" (213). Occupying as it does a "neutral territory," the romance is colored by the feelings that all are presumed to share, but really the romance's "aspiring purpose" is much more sharply reckoned. As a matter of a will to power, the purveyor of romance seeks to make his vision assume the form of "popular sentiment," even as "demagogue" he would subvert the popular grounds of power.

The circumstances under which Phoebe also learns the "one mysterious emotion" of love and mortality further suggest how Hawthorne's "more subtile," even demagogic process of representation reveals the secret. The commingled consciousness of love and death as a momentous perception is not particular to Hawthorne in American romance of the mid-nineteenth century; Cooper's *The Pilot* proves as much. The motif is archetypal, but the effect of this scene lies in its parallel, even compulsive repetition of the earlier one, not necessarily in its thematic statement. Just as Holgrave has learned the secret as a result of a representation, Phoebe's awareness of love and mortality also comes through mediation. Even as he tells Phoebe of Jaffrey's death, Holgrave wishes to spare her the direct sight of the corpse, the "fearful secret hidden within the house." So he shows Phoebe the daguerreotype of death that he has taken that morning. Whereas once the Judge's picture revealed the "secret character" of his resemblance to the Colonel, now the portrait transforms that face into the very image of death. Although "it still seemed almost wicked to bring the awful secret of yesterday to her knowledge," Holgrave explains the natural causes of Jaffrey's demise after she recognizes the Judge. Not only does Holgrave's explanation exonerate Clifford, but it also lifts the gloom that has settled on the house and predicts a world where sympathy rules. Like the Lord and Lady of May in "The May-pole of Merry Mount," Holgrave and Phoebe share an understanding which separates them "from the world" and binds them to each other: "The secret, so long as it should continue such, kept them within the circle of a spell, a solitude in the midst of men, a remoteness as entire as that of an island in mid-ocean;—once divulged, the ocean would flow betwixt them, standing on its widely sundered shores" (305).

"This secret takes [Phoebe's] breath away," and she can barely be restrained from publicizing the news. Holgrave prolongs the secrecy in the hope that the subliminal affections that the Judge's death arouses in him may also be shared with her. Holding this secret encourages an intimacy in which they may also share the secret of sexual romance, when they declare their love for each other. Then "they were conscious of nothing sad or old. They transfigured the earth, and made it Eden again" (307). While some critics have observed Hawthorne's visions of cultural prosperity in this statement, the scene also dramatizes the value that Hawthorne places on the transformative process of romance: to reveal secrets by a process of representation enacted through the sympathetic understanding of love. For Hawthorne, love frees because it transfigures. The charm of fictive and sexual romance can suggest the secrets of mortality through forms both ostensible and subtle, as it has for Holgrave earlier and as it does for Phoebe now. Merely naming the secret, as Holgrave does upon finishing his story, does not assure that it will be apprehended. When Holgrave first tells Phoebe the secret of mortality and love, she cannot yet comprehend; she must be brought into sympathy more subtly than Holgrave's ostensible method permits. Indeed, "Alice Pyncheon" may very well ensure that Phoebe turns a deaf ear. Perhaps appreciating the secret requires eliminating the oppressive surrogate father of the Judge, as Crews and Porte argue, but the dismantling of patriarchal power may also require a conversion to female ways of understanding.[29] In "The May-pole of Merry Mount," Hawthorne treats the telling of this secret as sobering; now, in his middle age, having been saved by his own Phoebe—as he sometimes called Sophia—he finds that bringing the secret to light is a joyous occasion.

That joy of romance is akin to the pleasure that daydreaming and creative writing are reputed to share. For Freud, this pleasure is found in the way a story or playful experience brings together not two but three time frames—past, present, and future. Indeed, how an author does this is his "innermost secret": a "strong experience in the present," says Freud, "awakens in the creative writer a memory of an earlier experience . . . from which there now proceeds a wish which finds its fulfillment in the creative work. The work itself exhibits elements of the recent provoking occasion as well as of the old memory."[30] Freud even apologetically offers such a "formula" in explaining how these two types of activities share in expressing a wish and fears that "it will prove to be too exiguous a pattern." Yet while the psychoanalyst stresses the "childhood memories" of a writer's life, the student of culture is also careful to recognize, as part of the formula, that the "re-fashioning of ready-made and familiar material" contributes to the transacting of a secret. Such works derive "from the popular treasure-house of myths, legends and fairy tales," the "distorted vestiges of the wishful phantasies of whole nations, the *secular dreams* of youthful humanity." In this context, a writer like Hawthorne may keep "a certain amount of independence, which can express itself in the choice of material and in changes in it which are often quite extensive."[31] So when Holgrave reads Phoebe his tale, he performs still another function of the storyteller: the binding together of past, present, and future. For the secret Holgrave dramatizes is the necessity of intercessive sympathy. He inscribes the memory of sympathy, as the lesson of the past, for present and future generations. Through his story, his "chimney-corner legend" that has the effect of a daydream, he keeps the experience of collective past alive in the present, imparting to his listeners and presumed readers a moral responsibility now and in the future.[32]

■ The ending of *Seven Gables* represents a "secular dream" of mid-century, capitalist America's "youthful humanity," a dream that concludes when a dominant culture's antagonist is defeated and appetitive excesses are reformed. Holgrave's story of moral progress becomes the medium for this youthful dream, and his ambivalence is expressive of his culture's antinomies. Too often, Holgrave is understood as a lonely radical whom Hawthorne is at pains to bring into society, when primarily the daguerreotypist is one of the dispossessed. His career has been tenuous, and his new trade offers little emolument. Holgrave wants to be led back into the world from which his family has been cast out. His protestations to the contrary, his commitment first is to wresting back, as a member of the once-subsistent but now dependent class, the power of economic self-determination. His hatred of the past marks his resentment of this disenfranchisement and the isolating distortions it occasions. In fact, Holgrave sees himself as having been driven a "little mad" by the subject of Pyncheon greed. The whole history of the families is fixed with the "strangest tenacity" in his mind, so much so that he finds "one method of throwing it off" in putting an "incident" from that past "into the form of a legend" and to "publish it in a magazine" (186). Not only does he see "writing stories" as a means of restoring his health, but he also hopes for his share of "literary fame" as a measure of regaining prestige.

In Hawthorne's prophecy of the marriage between American virtue and enterprise, Holgrave integrates the conflicting drives in his character by recognizing his bond of sympathy to others, the learning of a "great secret" that also allows for the resolving of his ideological contraries. This bond is the conviction of reverence for another's individuality that the combined vision of love and mortality affords. The deliberate telling of this secret, unlike the deliberate concealment of the scarlet letter, disrupts the accretion of meaning by which the narrative proceeds. Once the secret is both told and understood, the process of representation is unalterably changed. No longer to be perpetually repeated, the wrongdoing of the past can be explained away. And nothing is left to be represented, it seems, except the relief of being rid of the past. The happy ending finds its source in the joy of no longer being bound to that "awful secret of yesterday," no longer to "laugh at Dead Men's jokes" or "cry at Dead Men's pathos" (183). As compelling as Hawthorne intends this vision to be, it also unhinges the question of the narrative function of disclosing secrets.

Holgrave's recognition of the relation between mortality and love—the secret he hardly knew before he found himself giving it utterance—constitutes his reliving a social, psychological, and historical trauma. We do not need to reserve the word's literal application to understand that a plot—the story Holgrave tells and its part in the story Hawthorne tells—operates as a "working-through" of its own secrets.[33] Reliving a trauma may lead one out of its perpetuating and paralyzing effects, as is Holgrave's experience when he resists the temptation to violate Phoebe in a manner akin to Matthew Maule's invasion of Alice. Later, when the consequences of the Pyncheons' obsessions are repeated and relived in the apoplectic death of the Judge, the secret of Maule's Curse can be known and communicated. And once a secret is thus disclosed through a narrative, it loses its symbol-making and inhibiting power, as it also may during psychoanalysis, where the formal representations of secrets from the past are "remembered, repeated, and worked-through."[34] In recognizing and, in turn, resisting his familial urge toward the vindictive desire to gain human empire, Holgrave removes himself from the family trauma of dispossession. This removal is effected when he sits in the transfiguring moonlight and is brought into sympathy, the "rare and high quality of reverence for another's individuality." For Hawthorne, this "moonlight, and the sentiment in man's heart, responsive to it" are "the greatest of renovators and reformers" (214). Moonlight renovates because it changes the appearance of things from the way they are to the way they could also be, the distinction that Hawthorne makes in the preface as definitive of romance.

Once this scene is repeated with Phoebe, Holgrave can begin
wholeheartedly to reform the social structure, and Hawthorne can
reform, ambivalently, the course of his romance. The revelation of
secret springs and secret identities seems to offer a complete
closure, a promise to the reader that all has been told. Under this
condition, the author is left with little else than to give a sentimental resolution, one that seems to replace the gothic narrative discourse that has taken over much of the final movement of the
novel. Hawthorne thus creates a closure that will make congruous
the emotional effect that *The House of the Seven Gables* has accu-
mulated. For the triumph that he records lies in the intensity of
wish rather than the fulfillment of intent. That victory lauds the
transformative power of romance, but the sheer force of the recommendation may make the reader suspicious that this closure, even
if it satisfied the logic of the plot, is little more than an enforced
fiction that reveals how fictive the happy ending really is. Perhaps
under the illusion that the book's deepest secret has been told,
Hawthorne does "hold something back," as Phoebe charges Holgrave with keeping "any secret the disclosure of which would benefit [her] friends." Holgrave replies, "Nothing—no secrets but my
own" (217). So may readers suspect of the conclusion to this narrative. There, the sentimentality celebrates the secret of romance,
concealing Hawthorne's characteristic procedure of masking the
secret he professes to reveal. As in "The Threefold Destiny" or
"The Great Stone Face," the sentimental vision of prosperity glit-
ters so luminously because such happiness has seemed unattain-
able. Insofar as the conclusion embraces this sentimentality, it attests to the strong desire to find romance redemptive as well as
transfigurative. Thus the ending means to renovate the plot, reforming it as no longer subject to vacillation, no longer ambivalent.

The way that ambivalence conditions the narrative and qualifies
the process of representing and revealing secrets finds its fullest
expression in the house itself. By presenting a "human countenance" that is "expressive also, of the long lapse of mortal life; and
accompanying vicissitudes, that have passed within" (5), the house
gives shape to the human and historical drama that has ensued

within its confines. This symbol has been frequently discussed, even as a fundamental metaphor in Hawthorne's aesthetic.[35] In its role in the telling and keeping of secrets, the house also suggests the reciprocal relation between the ostensible and the subtler forms of representation. Just as the house configures a legacy of evil, so can the soul from which this evil emerges be represented as a house. Out of the house's description, in carefully limned detail, comes a portrait that captures this evil secret in the likeness of Judge Pyncheon. It is one of Hawthorne's most extended images of representation as the process that evokes a hidden secret:

> With what fairer and nobler emblem could any man desire to shadow forth his character? Ah; but in some low and obscure nook—some narrow closet on the ground floor, shut, locked, and bolted, and the key flung away—or beneath the marble pavement, in a stagnant water-puddle, with the richest pattern of mosaic-work above—may lie a corpse, half-decayed and still-decaying, and diffusing its death-scent all through the palace, and the incense which they bring, and delight to burn before him! Now and then, perchance, comes a seer, before whose sadly gifted eye the whole structure melts into thin air, leaving only the hidden nook, the bolted closet, with the cobwebs festooned over its forgotten door, or the deadly hole under the pavement, and the decaying corpse within. Here, then, we are to seek the true emblem of the man's character, and of the deed that gives whatever reality it possesses, to his life. And, beneath the show of a marble palace, that pool of stagnant water, foul with many impurities, and perhaps tinged with blood—that secret abomination, above which possibly he may say his prayers, without remembering it—is this man's miserable soul! (229–30)

This passage would surely delight a reader used to the excesses of gothic prose, but Hawthorne also wants the reader who would be a "seer" to perceive the "secret abomination" beneath the show of splendor. The reader with "tender and acute" vision whom Hawthorne anticipates can perceive the secret and will behold "in the man some shadow of what he was meant to be" (139). For such a sympathetic observer, appearances never tell the entire story; for such a reader, there are always secrets.

The reader who is also a "seer" recognizes that the gothic form transfigures "this man's miserable soul" into a house, the various details of which suggest the wickedness it tries to conceal, an outward sign like the scarlet letter, that is meant to be read. Handily demystifying the obvious fiction that appearances construct, this "tender and acute" vision seizes on the secret recesses, like the "hidden nook," "bolted closet," and "deadly hole." In these forbidden and dangerous places lies the "true emblem" to be interpreted. Here Hawthorne suggests that there is some secret deeper even than sympathy can reach. The various images of aporia beckon the reader to dismantle this schema of signification, but Hawthorne cuts short that exercise when he confesses to leaving indeterminate the very secret that the passage directs readers to hunt. The confession, then, intends to ward off the truth that the soul can be detailed, that the emblem can be read. The passage exalts sympathy only to stress its limits. For sympathy to succeed in making readers easier with intractable mysteries, the response must be "comprehensive," the sympathy, we shall see, that comes from the "sadly gifted eye," the vision that responds to life's double aspect.

This passage also suggests what it was in Hawthorne's own "sadly gifted eye" that made him less popular than he would have liked. The canniness of his psychological portraits may excite some readers, then and now, but it is precisely such powers to lay bare the habits of the mind that make so many of his readers uneasy. Some contemporaneous readers openly expressed their displeasure in Hawthorne's writings and found them distasteful, unhealthy, even repulsive. As one reader puts it, there is a "want of living tenderness" in Hawthorne. For all of his own high sense of his fine capacities for sympathy, the writer is estranged, as Hawthorne himself feared, from the common lot of humanity: "It is a pity that he displays nature to us so shrouded and secluded, and that he should be afflicted with such a melancholy craving for human curiosities." Rather than a bond of sympathy, Hawthorne creates a "poetry of desolation" in which "the doings of the characters awaken only a faint, dream-like interest in our hearts." If some critics praised Hawthorne's "genius for realities," this doubting reviewer can complain that Hawthorne's fictions are but "strange drama replete with second-hand life. An air of unreality enshrouds all his creations. They are either dead, or have never lived, and when they pass away they leave behind them an oppressive and unwholesome chill."[36]

Such a response is typical of many readers who discover mainly antipathy, rather than sympathy, in reading Hawthorne. The complaint is against the writer's coldness and his morose fascination with unpleasant, unhealthy fantasies, on the grounds that these are plays of mind rather than real ills. Like other antipathetic readers, the anonymous critic that I've cited must also impugn the author as being unwholesome, even spiritually diseased. While such readers echo Hawthorne's worst anxieties about himself and his choice of writing as a profession, they condemn Hawthorne's mind as contaminated, the life of secrets polluted. Indeed, the very sense of seeking secrets is associated with something dirty. This unseemliness is criticized as a lapse of taste that is also a moral, temperamental, or hereditary defect. As Freud was also charged, the writer is accused of taking some perverted pleasure in exposing what no one wants to think about.[37] If the writer could be brought to a sunnier disposition, the complaint runs, then the so-called secret would disappear and the need for sympathy would be abated, just as several of Hawthorne's scenarios turn on the undercutting of a mystery through correcting a sick brain or troubled eye.

As if to balance the author's tendency unduly to credit claims of middle-class triumph and moral certainty, in *Seven Gables* Hawthorne's unwholesome quality is given at least equal expression. The sources of potential disgust in this novel are many: Hepzibah's quasi-incestuous feeling for Clifford, Clifford's enfeebled lust for Phoebe, Jaffrey's lecherous advances toward Phoebe and sexual exhaustion of his wife, Gervayse's betrayal of his daughter, Maule's humiliation of Alice, even the monkey's barely concealed genitalia. In characterizing any and all of these elements, Hawthorne solicits the reader's awareness of what many would consider unsavory concerns. Even against their wills, readers find themselves concerned with topics that may repulse them, secrets they would rather not know. The result complicates sympathy, to the extent that readers either praise Hawthorne's grasp in a prepsychoanalytic age or denigrate his interest in obsessional neurosis, compulsion, incest, and erotic vagaries. Forced to broaden and refine their sympathy, either for characters or their secrets, readers may even feel betrayed into discovering that they must recognize and forgive what they would otherwise ignore or dismiss. In this respect, as we shall see, Hilda figures as a model of response in *The Marble Faun*, unable as she is to reconcile the existence of corruption and virtue within a single phenomenon or event or person. So too are the terms of sympathy stretched here; *Seven Gables* requires that readers sympathize with the degenerating Pyncheons, the aggressive principle of progress in Holgrave, and the stable values of domestic power in Phoebe. To do so is also to make shift with aristocratic arrogation, hostile subversion, rural complacency, all amid a social life growing ravenously more commercial and property minded. If readers fail to respond with sympathetic approbation at the close, it is perhaps because Hawthorne so adeptly conveys the divisions to be unified that we doubt any resolution is possible. Any claim to victory that the "show of a marble palace" makes over a "secret abomination" will seem false.

A "secret abomination" is but one aspect of the house's mystery. As Hawthorne's metaphor suggests, any text, like the world itself, can be seen as double sided. For along with the secret behind the "true emblem" here, there is another one that an apprehensive observer can learn. According to Hawthorne, one must have faith in a "comprehensive sympathy," which provides "poetic insight," the "gift of discerning, in this sphere of strangely mixed elements, the beauty and majesty which are compelled to assume a garb so sordid" (41). This dual vision, which ambivalence underlies, responds to the necessity of seeing "This contrast, or intermingling of tragedy with mirth, that happens daily, hourly," a gift that becomes especially precious "to us, who know the inner heart of the seven gables, as well as its exterior face" (294, 295). The reader who doubly discerns can perceive that the "second story" of the Pyncheon house projects "such a meditative look that you could not pass it without the idea that it had secrets to keep, and an eventful history to moralize upon" (27). A passerby, Hawthorne tells us, who presented the easily plucked "mystic branch" of the Pyncheon elm would then have the "right to enter, and be made acquainted with the secrets of the house" (285).

An imaginative observer, one used to seeing secrets beneath appearances, would need no such talisman. In any house, "Doubtless, the whole story of human existence may be latent," but the Seven Gables has the "picturesqueness, externally, that can attract the imagination or sympathy to see [the whole story of human existence] there" (27). This observer could learn from his perusal of its "picturesqueness"—the form of its representation—that the Pyncheon house has "something deeper" and more "inviting" than its gloomy appearance promises. The Seven Gables was not exclusively the haunted scene of the wicked acquisition of wealth or the cruel manipulation of the soul. The mansion is founded on another secret that the Pyncheon elm suggests in its "mystic expression that something within the house had been consummated" (286). The foundation of the house is really laid on two secrets: Maule's Curse and the "blessing" of the "stubborn, old Puritan, Integrity." For Hawthorne, the efficacy of this benison "was to be seen in the religion, honesty, moderate competence, or upright poverty, and solid happiness, of his descendants to this day" (285).

The conflict between these two secrets expresses the novel's ambivalence toward the past and the present, an attitude that also shapes representation. Vacillating between two extremes as Freud has described it, ambivalence speaks in two seemingly irreconcilable voices, as Hawthorne does when he is alternately virulent and reverent about his Puritan heritage, a habit of mind long associated with his work.[38] Clearly, it is the psychological characteristic underlying the framework of dualism in the novel: the split characterization of the house's foundational secrets, the vision of the world as being both mud and marble, the tension between past and present, the opposition between male and female, faces as either scowls or smiles, narrative as ostensible and "more subtle." At the close, the force with which Hawthorne portrays the transfigurative

capacity of love indicates the strength of the desire to believe it so
and thus to be reformed, no longer ambivalent. The hallmark of
ambivalence is its method of denouncing one of its components,
its refusal to countenance one of two conflicting desires. Ambivalence vanquishes itself by proclaiming victory and suppressing
the "secret abomination" that would undermine the fiction of reconciliation that the fact of ambivalence insists upon.

In *Seven Gables,* the fiction of reconciliation is that American
virtue and economic power can be united in one "marble palace,"
where the nurturing, domestic power of Phoebe can rehabilitate
Holgrave and help him to return to a community that both needs his
politics of amelioration and sanctions his spirit of enterprise. When
moral and economic powers are wed, the future of America seems
very bright, its house in order, its potential for destructive violence
muted. In this house, male and female live together without the
oppressive weight of class and gender prejudices. Phoebe converts
Holgrave to this wisdom, and he will build a house where her virtue
can be safely and beneficently exercised. This is Hawthorne's vision,
a "secular dream" of "youthful humanity," as well as the cultural
fantasy of union toward a harmonious end that a nation entertains.
Plaguing American society's reality, however, is the series of un-
satisfying compromises that would only postpone the actual and
destructive disunion to come. Acutely characteristic as it is,
Hawthorne's fiction of reconciling ambivalence also betokens his
country's. As Lincoln warned, a house divided against itself would
fall.

Whatever else the ending achieves, it represents the sense of release that comes from believing that ambivalence is finally overcome and that we are truly rid of the past, the conflict it causes
undone. The wrongdoing of earlier generations is finally set right,
the past seems "worked-through," silenced at last. Having told all
its secrets, the novel may hold back another one. This secret is not
just a "formal assumption," insofar as it is a "lost object, grail,
primal scene, spectral and identifying name, seductive charm." Instead, this secret "has the status of anticipation, something known
yet not as a direct object, something known as if always already
forgotten."[39] The secret that the novel demonstrates but cannot

say is the disharmony underlying its sentimental vision of union and progress. Prodded by a secret subversion within this fiction, Hawthorne bestows a daydream of how past, present, and future are unified by coloring the castle-in-the-air aspect of his romance with the "hue of popular sentiment." Yet this fantasy only disguises and cannot undo romance's "more subtile" and demagogic extension. In the hope that his characteristic doubt could be allayed in this "characteristic" work, Hawthorne may have masked this secret even from himself and, in so doing, created fissures in his house of fiction that sympathy cannot repair.

The attributed power of sympathy as a formal principle of genre, one that brings together issues of theme, method, and reception, really creates a blind for Hawthorne. Caught as the novelist is between the process of reading that his dual method is designed to encourage and the pressure of revelation that consists with the gothic ploys he invokes only to withdraw, sympathy becomes the means of evading rather than of meeting the novel's implications of form, like the illusion that violence underlying ambivalence can be so readily defused. Only provisionally does sympathy complete the connections among narrative procedures, psychological analogies of form, and historical themes or cultural concerns. For *The Blithedale Romance*, these forced connections create conflicts which, in large part, become the novel's disintegrated subject. There, sympathy as solution becomes so distorted that its fictive quality is exposed, its failure to resolve any of the issues it addresses cemented. That failure will also suggest how secrets bear the weight of social meanings and how a text responds to the cultural urgencies that bring it into being.

CHAPTER THREE

The Blithedale Romance: Secrets, Society, and Reform

Hawthorne's most overtly social novel is also his only one written in the first person. The subject matter and the narrative perspective of *The Blithedale Romance* have been the novel's two most distinguishing features and its two dominant critical concerns, yet the dynamic relation between the novel's uncharacteristic point of view and utopian issues remains insufficiently explained. Why does Hawthorne conceive of a retired poet's pronouncing his unrequited love to be an appropriate conclusion for a narrative about reformist communities, philanthropy, and transcendentalist politics? I argue that, rather than an aberration, the first-person perspective of *Blithedale* responds to and emerges from Hawthorne's vision of a mid-century American crisis of individuality. Coverdale's problematic report duplicates pressures on the individual, a tension that erupts out of the split between the demands of the psyche and the failure of a social matrix to define an integrated self. This public sphere is represented in *Blithedale* as not only the efforts of political reform but also the necessary enterprise of reshaping intimate relations. Indeed, the politics of reform are so closely associated with the state of intimate life, and its effects on the individual, that the story of Coverdale's reaction to his milieu reveals a normative concern for the ways in which private anxieties register public tensions. Coverdale's "adventurous conjectures" signal how the private self is projected onto public experience, even as that self absorbs the social forces that define the novel's historical moment. His beleaguered first-person narrative replicates the very disintegration of self which reformist movements mean to correct but which ultimately, for Hawthorne, exhibits their failure, a paradox that also generates Coverdale's story. Reform projects fail, as we shall see, because they enact a secret bid for power rather than the courting of redemptive sympathy, blind as their proponents are to the rift between ideals and motives. Coverdale's response, we may say, particularizes these conditions.

So closely linked has Hawthorne been to his narrator that the romance has invited two kinds of biographical criticism: as a roman à clef based on the author's experiences at Brook Farm and as a psychological self-portrait of the author had he not escaped his lonely bachelorhood.[1] However much Hawthorne discouraged the former—to the disappointment of his original audience—and however arresting subsequent readers have found the latter, the tendency to hear writer and narrator as univocal ought to be resisted, and not merely out of respect for a New Critical tenet or for the Jamesian legacy that Hawthorne's Coverdale first endows. The poet's anxious responses to violated privacy and bewildering public conduct may have been Hawthorne's, but this reaction is also more generally and variously shared in the age. In a still larger sense, Coverdale's exaggerations of Hawthorne's personality render the novelist's critical version of an American scholar. Emerson had called upon his scholar to be a poet who "learns that in going down into the secrets of his own mind he has descended into the secrets of all minds."[2] By contrast, Hawthorne confirms this point in making his poet too preoccupied with others' secrets to take a metaphysical interest in his own. Instead, Emersonian energies of introspection are turned outward, wildly. Rather than follow the new logic of self-reliance or the principles of self-culture, Coverdale searches everywhere for the secrets of others, as if to provide a clue to his own unobserved, untold motives.

Hawthorne's poet achieves little of the stature that Emerson believed possible for his scholar; Coverdale, as virtually every reader comes to understand, is nothing more than a voyeur. In fact, *Blithedale* is centered on Coverdale's self-conceived mission to guess his friends' secrets. Much of the novel consists of the narrator's struggle to find the hidden motives and meanings in the social arrangements that so fascinate him. The record of his search provides the plot developments with their structure, though his pursuit itself makes nothing happen. Coverdale's inquiries cover nearly every dimension of the characters' relations: Who is Priscilla? What is her relation to Zenobia? to Westervelt? What is Zenobia's relation to Westervelt? to Hollingsworth? Hollingsworth's to Priscilla? What, finally, have these relations to do with Coverdale? "For was mine a mere vulgar curiosity? Zenobia should have been able to appreciate that quality of intellect and the heart which impelled me (often against my own will, to the detriment of my own comfort) to live in other lives, and to endeavor—by generous sympathies, by delicate intuitions, and by taking note of things too slight for record, and by bringing my human spirit into manifold accordance with the companions whom God assigned me—to learn the secret that was hidden even from themselves."[3] Time and again, Coverdale invokes his powers of "generous sympathies" as his highest recommendation as observer-narrator, but his fashioning of himself as a "priest" of sympathy ultimately discredits him. His inflating of his faculty of compassionate understanding and implicit perception actually distorts sympathy so violently that its moral quality is negated.

Readers of Henry James are used to the way that Coverdale's defense rationalizes his predilection for learning secrets and tries to convert it into a moral fineness. Richard Poirier is surely right in observing that in this work Hawthorne anticipates James's later sensibility rather than that of *The Bostonians,* the social novel with which *Blithedale* so obviously bears comparison.[4] While strong similarities exist between Hawthorne's romance and James's early realistic foray into the "very American" subject of the public meanings of intimate life, James's later narrative procedures for secret-guessing are much more elaborate and respond to social conditions that Hawthorne, fifty years earlier, was encountering in a much less complex way. Were Coverdale really a Jamesian sentient consciousness, along the lines of the narrator of *The Sacred Fount* or Strether, he would not need to visit the boarding-house across from his hotel room when he sees his friends behind a curtain. He would think that he knows just by looking through the window—the spectacle would seem so rich—the precise nature of the relation between Zenobia and Westervelt. Instead of *The Bostonians*, the novel from James's middle period that *Blithedale* may have influenced most, however indirectly, is *The Princess Casamassima*, where James situates his sentient artist manqué in a confusing milieu of politics and sexual intimacy, while charging Hyacinth Robinson with the responsibility of deducing meanings from both the life of personal relations he witnesses and the hidden, obscure world of the London streets: "The value I wished most to render and the effect I wished most to produce were precisely those of our not knowing, of society's not knowing, but only guessing and suspecting and trying to ignore what 'goes on' irreconcilably, subversively, beneath the vast smug surface."[5] In *The Princess*, one may say, James extends and broadens Hawthorne's sense of voyeurism as a response to a newly complex social life, one which is rife with the interests of reform, by investing this act of specialized vision with the politically felt urgency of spying.[6] Yet in their emphasis on this specular aspect, both *The Princess* and *Blithedale* also testify to the failure of sympathy. Coverdale's failure to find a reciprocating love indicts him, though it also suggests the selfishness of his fellow utopians, just as Hyacinth's failure to do so condemns the political reformers for their own moral bankruptcy.

Coverdale's rationalization of his prying—his "duty"—suggests Hawthorne's focus on private relations as reflecting public concerns, though here the emphasis is on the individual's response to a world that more and more threatens the possibility of privacy. In the poet's reaction against the publicity of daily life at Blithedale, Hawthorne has been understood to score his revenge against the Brook Farmers who distracted him from his purpose in joining the commune, which was to live frugally while writing productively enough so that he could soon afford to marry Sophia. The pressures of living among others too often interfered with his plans, as he complained in his letters. Yet in Coverdale's need for privacy Hawthorne suppresses the true cost of life in such confined quarters. "Fond of society," as the poet says he is, he also needs "occasional retirements." "Unless renewed by a yet farther withdrawal towards the inner circle of self-communion, I lost the better part of my individuality" (89). Coverdale's response to the enforced intimacy of Blithedale, then, suggests two opposing anxieties. On the one hand, public life demands "retirements" into even farther reaches of "remoteness from the world," such as he had first sought in moving from the city. On the other, Coverdale's reaction to his predicament is also, paradoxically, directed outward. Instead of simply shunning other people and their encroachments against the "individual soul," Coverdale reacts by encroaching in the most intense way into their private lives.

The poet's spying is an aggressive policy of surveillance, one that is self-protective and self-communing. In this respect, Coverdale's voyeuristic concern for self-guessing is a function of the novel's general political interest in the status of and challenges facing the individual. For Coverdale, close personal relations intrude upon the best parts of one's individuality. The poet fears that once his vigorously reserved privacy is surrendered, his individuality will be lost, and he will be seen under the unsettlingly democratic light of being certainly no better and perhaps a good deal worse than others. Even as the adventure at Blithedale commences, Coverdale discusses with Hollingsworth the relative merits of Fourierism, a doctrine that the philanthropist scorns for its reliance on individualist motives for amelioration. Coverdale withdraws from the argument, but not from the conviction that the self as the primary agent for social change needs to be preserved. Coverdale's "vulgar curiosity" insists on the principle of self-promotion, which, instead of bringing his "human spirit into manifold accordance" with others', really subsumes his faculty for sympathy and thereby widens his distance from the very people he avows that he means to help. As Zenobia describes his voyeur's motives, "Bigotry; self-conceit; an insolent curiosity; a meddlesome temper; a cold-blooded criticism, founded on a shallow interpretation of half-perceptions; a monstrous scepticism in regard to any conscience or any wisdom, except one's own; a most universal propensity to thrust Providence aside, and substitute one's self in its awful place" (170). Zenobia decries Coverdale's confusing his "fancied acuteness" of vision with his "idea of duty," his self-authorizing of his interest in others' lives, and warns him that he steps "blindfold into these affairs!" So thoroughly mediated by his voyeurism is Coverdale's conception of the self that he cannot even see "these affairs," but only his own distortions, which obversely become reliable. His prying is for his enlightenment and protection, since he spies on others only to shore up his own conceptions, to make the world fit his interpretations. In living vicariously through others in this way, he derives his own satisfactions, his spurious cultivation of the self.

In "these affairs," as Zenobia knows, the self is risked; individuality is wagered. Coverdale's effort to secure his individuality against the assault that intimate life makes is to conceive that others have secret relations to be fathomed, desires to be substantiated, conduct to be detailed. When he first arrives at Blithedale, he is frantic with irritated curiosity—about Zenobia especially—and can scarcely control his aroused desire to know. Subject as she has been to a great deal of "eye-shot," Zenobia asks Coverdale "What are you seeking to discover in me?" to which the poet, "surprised into the truth by the unexpectedness of her attack," responds: "The mystery of your life. . . . And you will never tell me" (47). Immediately does the pressure of intimate life beset him with the fear of losing control of his fantasies, of being "defrauded" by Zenobia's sexual history, a sense of himself as inviting betrayal, even a loss of self-command. His reaction to this denial is to deny to himself his own passion and transform it into a mission or "duty" of coaxing out the "mystery" by using his most reliable instrument, his vision. The eye then protects the self from its passions, and it does so by creating the fiction that other people, not he, are enmeshed in desire—guilty pasts, base motives, selfish obsessions.

Coverdale's conjecture is right, since these others do have secrets, even as his methods guarantee his failure. Like Parson Hooper or Goodman Brown, Coverdale cannot overcome the unnerving realization that other people's motives are disguised and indiscernible. Their secrets, in fact, define them as other, and it is as other than himself that others draw the voyeur's strictest attention. A voyeur is, after all, someone who must believe that there may be something to see which he is not supposed to know. If others have secrets to be learned, he gains some measure of his will to power over them; they can be controlled, directed as actors on the voyeur's "mental stage." The voyeur looks out upon an eminently theatrical world of social experience where dramas are played for his private delectation. Furthermore, this unlicensed learning of secrets, through a perverted sympathy, is pursued in the hope of shoring up one's own uncertainty of self. If the world is a stage, the theater is the unstable self made restless in the quest for consolation or peace. Even "in the midst of cheerful society," Coverdale reflects, "I had often a feeling of loneliness," especially in the recognition that "these three characters figured so largely in my private theatre," while "I . . . was at best but a secondary or tertiary personage with either of them" (70). As if to ward off such feelings of marginality, the voyeur trains his inquiring gaze onto others and observes them in the process of involuntarily disclosing themselves so that he may find the secret to his compromised position, that is, the life of personal and direct intimacy from which he has been excluded.

In this invasion of other people's privacy, the voyeur becomes an audience of one whose right to observe is granted to him by "Destiny," "the most skilful of stage-managers." Thus he appoints himself to his position, under the aegis of an aesthetics of fate: social life "seldom chooses to arrange its scenes, and carry forward its drama, without securing the presence of at least one calm observer. It is his office to give applause when due, and sometimes an inevitable tear, to detect the final fitness of incident to character, and distil in his long-brooding thought the whole morality of the performance" (97). Here Coverdale rationalizes his penchant to seek concrete evidence in life for his fantasies by invoking his right as critic to judge a work of art. The poet-voyeur turns social experience into an artistic production, one that he both sits through and directs. He submits the world in all its complexity and mundaneness to his individual capacity to shape and interpret it, for the scope of this world as a grand performance is nothing less or more than what the voyeur can encompass and subsume.

The voyeur reacts to the dangers posed by the "tyranny of intimacy" to his individuality by making himself, through his powers of detection, responsible for the very being of others.[7] By "custom," Coverdale makes "prey of people's individualities," the distinguishing characteristics he wants to blur or obliterate in order to preserve his teetering sense of self (84). His response to the fear of having his individuality subjugated is to dehumanize others by forcing them into roles and projecting the voyeur's private psychodrama onto them. Beyond this, the voyeur seeks to "insulate" a "friend" from "many of his true relations, magnify his peculiarities, inevitably tear him into parts, and patch him very clumsily together again." Out of this torturous inspection comes the voyeur's hideous production: "What wonder, then, should we be frightened by the aspect of a monster, which, after all—though we can point to every feature of his deformity in the real personage—may be said to have been created by ourselves!" (69). Here Hawthorne makes explicit the anxious stimulus behind *Frankenstein*. Just as Victor Frankenstein creates a monster out of his nervous fears of sexual relations, so does Coverdale make a monstrosity to reflect his own trepidations about intimacy. His dehumanizing of others mirrors the monster in himself, his own social and sexual inadequacies. By taking himself out of the world of "these affairs" and living more intensely in the world of his own imaginings, he guards himself from having his own monstrosity detected, from having his own secret prized. That secret is the fear of having the self exposed, of having one's individuality shattered.

Merely being privy to others' secrets does not grant passage into intimate relations. Coverdale's voyeurism fixes him in a double bind of insisting on his individuality and of vicariously participating in the intimacy that voyeurism seeks to approximate. Coverdale's search for secrets really works to restrict him, even as he sometimes seems to edge closer to ultimate knowledge. Intimacy would provide the basis for sympathetic understanding, but it is exactly Coverdale's debased sense of sympathy—the voyeurism shaped by an overvalued individuality—that excludes him from ever establishing the necessary ground. For Hawthorne, intimate relations enhance the close bond of sympathy in which secrets can be communicated by one, intuited by the other, with the bare fact of secrecy preserved. Coverdale's power of sympathy, like Chillingworth's, is aggrandizing, protecting his individuality and subverting the individuality of others by examining their passions and coming into contact with their very spirit without reciprocating.

Hawthorne was particularly alive to this corrupt kind of sympathy, for it distorts intimacy and risks degradation. When Sophia expressed her wish to visit a medium to assuage her headaches, her fiancé desperately warned her against the decision. His hatred for this voguish treatment was vehement, a suspicion we now recognize as distinctly sexual in its origin; Hawthorne speaks of these practitioners as invading their subjects' souls, touching their most personal passions. But as sexual as Hawthorne's fear may have been, it more tellingly expresses an anxious lover's worry over the loss of his privileged intimacy with his betrothed, a bond of sympathy that would be ruined for being shared: "There would be an intrusion into thy holy of holies—and the intruder would not be thy husband!" Hawthorne's phrase may seem to be just a genteel, spiritualizing euphemism for genitalia, but he means more than that. His literal suspicion is that the "sacredness" of Sophia's being "an individual" could be debased. His worry over the "sacredness of an individual," he explains, "is caused by no want of faith in mysteries, but from a deep reverence of the soul, and of the mysteries which it knows within itself, but never transmits to an earthly eye or ear."[8] Hawthorne may mean to recall this sense when Coverdale fearfully observed Priscilla's performance as a medium, as I shall discuss; here, at least, he reveals the strict regard for privacy and reserve, always associated with his temperament. Yet even as that privacy is insisted upon, the effect of that insistence is to uphold the "mysteries which [the soul] knows within itself"—secrets—in the name of protecting the self as individual. In this context, Hawthorne suggests that the individual retains the "sacredness" of that status when the divisions it suffers are kept to oneself, if the soul's secrets are what risks its division, its profanation. For it is the "transfusion of one spirit into another" that violates individuality, exposes secrets to someone other than one's properly sympathetic intimate, if these secrets must be communicated at all. This kind of exposure is potentially ruinous in Hawthorne's scheme of things. The author of "The Devil in Manuscript" and "The Haunted Mind" continues his plea to Sophia, though really he seems to be exhorting himself: "Keep thy imagination sane—that is one of the truest conditions of communication with Heaven."[9] The sane imagination—the redemption sought for in so many of Hawthorne's short stories— emerges out of an individuality that comes only with the urgent concealment of the soul's "mysteries."

Precisely here one may consider Coverdale's immediate and irrational contempt for the mesmerist, Westervelt, who turns out to be the voyeur's double. Westervelt's first offense is not simply that he presumptuously calls the voyeur "friend" (the term the voyeur uses for *his* victims); Coverdale's anger is virtually preconscious, emerging out of a "latent hostility which is sure to animate particular sects, and those who . . . have sequestered themselves from the crowd" (90). Coverdale instinctively sees Westervelt as an intruder who violates the poet's privacy and who threatens his belief in the divine core of individuality. Coverdale has retreated to the "innermost sanctuary" of his wood, and through the same "side-aisle" that Coverdale compares to a "casual opening" that "all of a sudden" gives access to the "long-sought intimacy of a mysterious heart," Westervelt disturbs Coverdale's reverie. That the mesmerist disturbs Coverdale's "spiritual state" is hateful enough, but that he intrudes "almost without impressing the sound or sight upon my consciousness," arousing a "feeling . . . which may be hidden in some dog-kennel of the heart," further suggests a considerably deeper source for Coverdale's "ludicrously irate" humor. Coverdale's immediate perception of the intruder as an "enemy" is heightened by an awareness that this adversary is almost unreal, that the "stranger" "had almost the effect of an apparition."

Although Westervelt may ultimately deserve Coverdale's contempt, not yet does he really merit it. His calling the poet "friend" in a tone that betrays his insincerity is only the excuse Coverdale finds to take offense. Yet Coverdale cannot ignore that he and the stranger have a good deal vaguely in common. The mesmerist is about the same age; like the poet, he is extremely handsome, but, unlike the former urbanite, Westervelt is dressed in fine rather than "homely garb," as Coverdale takes note. Their likeness, moreover, is not merely physical. Once Westervelt leaves, Coverdale intuits that he may have been mistaken to dismiss this man who takes so keen an interest in the friends whom the poet himself is investigating, for Westervelt's "evident knowledge of matters, affecting my three friends, might have led to disclosures or inferences, that would have perhaps been serviceable" (96). What the mesmerist and Coverdale share is more than an interest in the three others, but a secret. Through the "side-aisle" of the uncanny and into the secluded wood of "self-communion," Westervelt confronts Coverdale with an image of the poet's darker self.[10] Suggesting the counterfeit friend, meddlesome and secretive, the mesmerist disturbs Coverdale in both senses of the word. He makes the poet nervous by intruding into the private self, in the refuge where the self's other aspect is also at home, where the soul communes with its own "mysteries," where the individual meets its divisive, darker aspect, embodying one's secrets. Just as Westervelt violates Coverdale's privacy, so he also projects, through his questions about the other three, Coverdale's own sense of treading uninvited into others' intimacies and makes that sense loathsome to the poet. Thus Coverdale glimpses the relation between the voyeur and the mesmerist; both have the power of subverting—as we will consider in due course—one's "holy of holies," the private self held to be at the core of individuality.

Coverdale's revulsion bespeaks his fragility of self. He has retreated to his "sanctuary" to achieve "self-communion" as a way of divinely validating an otherwise crippled individuality. The spectacle of intimacy at Blithedale is excruciating because the valorizing of close personal relations is enshrined there as a new religious orthodoxy. His voyeurism is meant to initiate him into the new cult of intimacy, even as his belief in the self as its own god and priest excommunicates him. In general, the consoling and redemptive powers attributed to intimacy may be a response to a declining faith in the vitality of existing public religious institutions to shape a better world. Utopian reform confers on personal relations this new force—as such communities at Putney and Oneida legislated—dually spiritualizing and politicizing the life of intense emotions among others, a profane social life that Coverdale so deludedly considers profound. Westervelt exists, here to obstruct the fiction that the self can achieve its own communion, an individuality as false as the teeth in one's mouth, and later, to expose the very fraudulence, merely hinted at during this encounter of Coverdale's compromised conversion to the religion of intimacy.

Only at the close does Hawthorne return to Coverdale's passionate hatred for his own violated intimacy. When the poet confesses that he has all along been in love with Priscilla, it is as if he were trying to commune with an audience he knows he has cheated, and he must now make amends. All the time that he asked the reader to take him at his word, Coverdale knew that he was holding something back. Now, left alone after having been submerged in others' affairs, he finds that his desire to create intimacy is quickened. He prefaces his confession by calling himself a "poor and dim figure in my own narrative," the supporting character who barely makes his presence felt and who returns to give his version of the drama, the marginal character he suspects himself of being. What he confesses is intended to certify and elevate his story by finally bringing the reader into his confidence. His confession intends also to illuminate the proceedings he knows he has obscured by keeping his secret. Whether his notorious confession is a self-deceiving defense or a compulsive act of communication,[11] he tells his secret out of the voyeur's conviction that there is always something to be learned, a secret to be discovered—and that such knowledge may make all the difference in the reader's understanding of his story.

> Life, however, it must be owned, has come to rather an idle pass with me. Would my friends like to know what brought it thither? There is one secret—I have concealed it all along, and never meant to let the least whisper of it escape—one foolish little secret, which possibly may have had something to do with these inactive years of meridian manhood, with my bachelorship, with the unsatisfied retrospect that I fling back on

life, and my listless glance towards the future. Shall I reveal it? It is an absurd thing for a man in his afternoon—a man of the world, moreover, with these three white hairs in his brown mustache, and that deepening track of a crow's foot on each temple—an absurd thing ever to have happened, and quite the absurdest for an old bachelor, like me, to talk about. But it rises in my throat; so let it come.

I perceive, moreover, that the confession, brief as it shall be, will throw a gleam of light over my behavior throughout the foregoing incidents, and is, indeed, essential to the full understanding of my story. The reader, therefore, since I have disclosed so much, is entitled to this one word more. As I write it, he will charitably suppose me to blush, and turn away my face:—

I—I myself—was in love—with—PRISCILLA! (247)

Perhaps altogether too much importance is attached to this self-disclosure, by Coverdale, by Hawthorne, by readers who find the closure it entails more or less satisfying.[12] It may be that even after his "one foolish little secret" no longer pertains, if it ever did, Coverdale still believes that his love really affects the story he has told. For all the poet's choked embarrassment, the reader only learns that this has been a more personal involvement than the purely spectatorial interest that disguises Coverdale's impotent jealousy. However sincere the confession, some readers either discount it or do not need their suspicions confirmed. For others, the doubt still lingers that Coverdale could not possibly be imagined to love only Priscilla when he so obviously desires Zenobia: either the poet or Hawthorne, or both, needs to keep quiet the wish to touch, to consummate an attraction for the dark heroine, if only as a matter of convention.[13] Perhaps the ending fails to satisfy because this impulse is suppressed beyond Hawthorne's control.[14] Scarcely able to choose an appropriate title for his uncentered book, he now wishes to resolve its diffuseness of subject with a grandiloquent speech.

When nothing seems left to say, Coverdale confesses his "little secret" as a plea for the intimacy he has never enjoyed. Intimacy, he believes, can finally be achieved with a "charitably" forgiving reader, for until the reader learns the true state of Coverdale's feelings, he lacks a "full understanding" of the "foregoing incidents." But the story will not make much sense unless the reader also understands the emotional price exacted on the voyeur, a cost marked by the halting cadences and false starts that abruptly punctuate Coverdale's revelation. Then the reader will see that the voyeur's constant search for the proofs of intimacy in other people's lives expresses his doubly bound need for intimacy and desire for privacy, a conflict of desires hidden from himself that excludes him from achieving true sympathetic relations.

In this state of perpetually self-imposed removal from normal relations—intimate only with himself—Coverdale attains a semblance of intimacy if he can learn what others hold secret, as he tries to do, for example, when in his hermitage he struggles to overhear the conversation between Zenobia and Westervelt. His arduous prying stems from the guilty conviction that because he has a burdensome secret, so must others. By learning their hidden truths, the voyeur renews the animating power of his secret; by discovering others' secrets, the voyeur authenticates his own reality. And by learning others', the voyeur can preserve the privileged status of his own secret—the last word, he supposes, on the subject of intimacy—and thereby keep constant and alive the double bind in which he lives, the life of individuality and the illusion of possible intimacy with others. The "absurd thing" is that Coverdale conceives of his relation to others on the basis of his having a secret. In order to gain a "full understanding" of the untold passion beneath the story, the reader must also see that Coverdale does not define himself as a former utopian, a poet, or a perspicacious friend. Indeed, he does not even conceive of himself as a defeated lover as much as he does as someone who has a secret, without which his relations to others stop. The fact of Coverdale's having a secret, not the secret itself, has created and sustained his relations to others throughout. Once he tells his secret, there is, for him, nothing more to say.

Although Coverdale avers that he has "never meant to let the least whisper of it escape," there is no evidence that he succeeds in keeping his "foolish" secret. On the contrary, at least twice he broadly hints about it. First he bids a bird to tell Priscilla "that, if any mortal really cares for her, it is myself, and not even I, for her realities . . . but for the fancy-work with which I have idly decked her out!" (100). Here Coverdale tries to closet his sense of the truth by admitting to a foolish idealizing view of the seamstress, as if in exaggerating the truth he could nullify it. Yet as conditional as this confession is, later he comes still closer to letting the reader know how unmistakable is the inference to be drawn. When Coverdale observes Zenobia under the desolating power of her passion, the poet can hardly conceal his own anguish of love. So close is his identification that, even as he once complained about Westervelt, he feels no constraint when someone else is obviously in the midst of self-communion: "I never once dreamed of questioning my right to be there."

> It suits me not to explain what was the analogy I saw, or imagined, between Zenobia's situation and mine; nor, I believe, will the reader detect this one secret, hidden beneath many a revelation which perhaps concerned me less. In simple truth, however, as Zenobia leaned her forehead against the rock, shaken with a tearless agony, it seemed to me that the self-same pang, with hardly mitigated torment, leaped thrilling from her heart-strings to my own. Was it wrong, therefore, if I felt myself consecrated to the priesthood, by sympathy like this, and called upon to minister to this woman's affliction, so far as mortal could? (222)

Coverdale is so deeply moved by the image of this voluptuous woman rendered vulnerable that he conceives of himself as a priest of sympathy, though he really seems to enjoy, at a comfortable emotional distance, this spectacle of grief. In Zenobia, Coverdale sees the ravaging and paralyzing consequences of unrequited love, a plight that has a distinct "analogy" to his own unfulfilled longings for Priscilla. This analogy operates as a kind of transference, objectifying for the voyeur the vision of misery once love is pronounced, the humiliation that desire risks. The image of the distraught Zenobia confirms the similarity, in his mind, of their situations and allows him to rationalize his position as sympathetic.

"Heaven knows what an ache is in my soul!" (223). "This one secret" is what seems truly to involve him in the scene, the secret
that lies "hidden beneath many a revelation" until the close.[15] Really, though, "this one secret" is only Coverdale's helpless conviction that he even enjoys a capacity for the sort of intimacy Zenobia
finds so devastating, when of course he does not, except as the desire for the desire of another, recommended to his attention only
through some vicarious participation or voyeuristic appropriation.
A sympathetic reader might "detect" in Coverdale's allusions the
"least whisper" of the truth, but Coverdale's secret is really from
himself, his delusion. Even if the reader could take Coverdale at his
word, the final confession completes the narrative by making a
closure out of a problematic act of disclosure. This personal act
bespeaks the secrets of public life, for the "one secret" is not so
much the identity of Coverdale's beloved as it is the general social,
political, and cultural nature of his delusion.

The story of one man's secret-keeping as the key to selfhood
creates the foreground for Hawthorne's larger investigation of
cultural issues, as they appeared to him from his experience at
Brook Farm and on the basis of their public expression in Boston
lyceums and reading circles. For Coverdale's enterprise is stimulated by a dialectic between the individual psyche and new visions
of social organization. Beyond Coverdale's anxious response—the
voyeurism that Richard Sennett calls the "logical complement to
19th Century secularity,"[16]—Hawthorne's treatment of mesmerism, feminism, and philanthropy also clarifies how personal
secrets mirror public urgencies. Although finally indeterminate,
the characters' secrets find their ultimate expression in social attitudes, political and religious convictions. Coverdale's voyeurism
arises out of and is constructed by the social forces of change, and
its attendant disorder, which disrupts the placid life that the one-
time litterateur has led and to which he limply returns.

Complain as he does of ennui, and as cynical as he comes to be
about the utopian scheme, Coverdale first joins Blithedale in a
spirit of reform truer than Hawthorne's own practical interest in

Brook Farm. While the prospect of enjoying the free life of the mind surely engages him, Coverdale's is first of all an interest in social change. "Whatever else I may repent of, therefore, let it be reckoned neither among my sins nor follies, that I once had faith and force enough to form generous hopes of the world's destiny" (11). His desire is to breathe air "that had not been breathed, once and again! Air, that had not been spoken into words of falsehood, formality, and error, like all the air of the dusky city." Inauthentic as these convictions prove to be, they are mediated by a deep dissatisfaction with the current social circumstancing of individual fulfillment, as they seem in mid-century Boston. There one can observe how the poet may equate the dehumanizing "talk of an old conventionalism" with his own limited talents and production. The impulse to reform, even as it is rooted in good will, may find as profound a basis in self-disgust, one that attenuates itself by transforming social, economic, and political sources of degradation into a hopeful vision of the future.

Such feelings result not so much from Coverdale's belittled sense of being "no great affair" as a poet, but from the conviction that the order of institutions and values necessary to ratify the self is absent in society. Although the "greatest obstacle to being heroic" is to resist the "doubt whether one may not be going to prove oneself a fool," the commitment to social change, the "quest of a better life," is scarcely the "rubbish of the mind." So Coverdale defends himself from his own retrospective sense of his, and his compatriots', naivete. The self-deflating humor that marks Coverdale's descriptions of his original motives should not obscure the recognition that, however ambivalent or feeble his commitment, he refuses to relinquish the belief that it is "wiser . . . to follow out one day-dream to its natural consummation," even if that "vision" is "certain never to be consummated otherwise than by a failure" (10, 11). Indeed, the humor persists to guard against feelings of insufficiency by recommending to the poet's attention, and to ours, a less painful version of self-division than may have been originally felt. The urgency of reform can be understood, in Coverdale's case, as the demand to transform anxieties of the self into a program for public good. Such a transformation could override the fearful secret that the self, incapable as it may be of establishing right relations to others, can only be reconditioned through the reshaping of society and that, in itself, the self cannot inaugurate its own fulfillments, but is forever stalled. This state of self-disgust, then, is hidden under "many a revelation that perhaps concerned [the poet] less."

It is altogether appropriate that *Blithedale* not only ends as it does, in Coverdale's relentless effort to win sympathy, but also that it begins as it does, in Coverdale's divided reaction to a favor asked by a dim acquaintance, Old Moodie. Hawthorne's criticism of utopian fervor actually begins here, with Coverdale hesitant to grant a "very great favor," which a supplicant meekly means to ask, on the basis that the poet must make his preparations for improving the lot of humanity tomorrow. "Ready to do the old man any amount of kindness involving no special trouble to myself," Coverdale finds Moodie pathetic, clearly in need, but the poet's want of sympathy disheartens the old man. Coverdale's humanitarian interests are postponed from the start, while he can only offer, out of guilt, Hollingsworth's name as the "true philanthropist" to whom Moodie can turn. Implicit here is Hawthorne's ironic sense that the self, immersed as it is in its own vulnerabilities and blind to its own degradation, cannot act beyond its purposes for the public good, since the self is caught in a double bind of desire and denial, acting as the agent of corruption in the name of compassion, as Hollingsworth's career will later attest and as Coverdale's refusal puts in miniature. Even as Coverdale discourages the request, he becomes eager to know its nature. Coverdale's curiosity, sensitive to a dozen details in Moodie's appearance, is piqued by the old man's reluctance, thus making ironic the sense that the poet has cut himself off from knowing Moodie's secret, for "it was only through subsequent events that I ever arrived at a plausible conjecture as to what his business could have been" (7, 8). Although it asks too much of this moment in the narrative to argue that, from the outset, Coverdale disqualifies himself for real intimacy, still it can be seen that what ultimately ends in delusion also begins there.

The pressure of intimate life at Blithedale releases the poet from his illusory enthusiasm for reform, while the intensity of Coverdale's reaction to life among others arouses his interest in "turning the whole affair into a ballad" (223). Intimacy and reform are yoked together in his mind, and Hawthorne's, although neither the narrator nor the novelist makes explicit how the drama of personal life is the very foreground of the larger social enterprise. This connection, however, can be drawn from the implications of Coverdale's troubled response; dually thwarted in his desire for knowledge of intimate life and the pursuit of higher purposes, his chief means of participating in the community is, characteristically, to aestheticize the experience he observes.[17] Again, paradoxically but appropriately, Coverdale's way of involving himself with others is to withdraw from any close contact and enjoy the drama from the psychological distance of being an observer. As best he can, Coverdale casts the life unfolding before him into a romance, one that unintentionally reveals how irreconcilable are the aspirations of romance and the claims reality makes, how incoherent, finally, is the reality one would try to allegorize or reshape. The ultimate unknowable and inchoate nature of reality, the bewilderments it occasions, reassert how delusive are human efforts to mold it into patterns, quite as delusive as projects for reshaping society. Indeed, the deluded poet even knows that his efforts will fail, that "real life never arranges itself exactly like a romance" (104).

Although Coverdale's response to his marginal, unstable position at Blithedale is to see others as performing for an artist's benefit, that tendency is neither exclusively the special perception of the voyeur nor the general province of mid-century urban life, however much Coverdale's experience in both determines his reaction.[18] Instead, Hawthorne may well have drawn on the memory of the Brook Farmers' fondness for playacting, since masques and theatricals were the most popular entertainments there and a hallmark of the community.[19] When he came to characterize his interest in representing the "most romantic episode of his own life," Hawthorne reports in the preface, his concern was "merely to establish a theatre . . . where the creatures of his brain may play their phantasmagorical antics, without exposing them to too close a comparison with the actual events of real lives." Thus could

Blithedale achieve the "atmosphere of strange enchantment" that the "American romancer needs" (2, 3). In claiming this characteristic latitude, Hawthorne can bring together Coverdale's desperate need to aestheticize reality and the mystified, mystifying face through which the "fact" of daily life expresses itself as "essentially a day-dream" (2).

The need for this atmosphere may account, to some extent, for the vocabulary of the stage pervading the novel, yet there is also a sense in which the whole of the characters' experience is to be understood as a show, as a playing of parts. The language of the theater, for Coverdale and the other reformers, reveals the "experiment's most basic assumption," which according to Evan Carton is that "there exists an intellectually and practically realizable distinction between the artificial and the natural in human experience and relations."[20] In the novel, we see that the characters' desire to abrogate this distinction is the source of their projected achievement and their individual failures. The Blithedalers live so urgently and self-consciously according to an image of themselves that the distinctions between performance and life, role and self, are constantly blurred, suggesting their lack of any stabilizing rationale over their desires. Only the stalwart figure of Silas Foster, the one true farmer among them, reminds them of the difference between action and gesture, identity and part. Throughout the novel, Foster exists as Hawthorne's figure for a reality principle, dull as it may be; the Yankee farmer appears to the community as the solid, bedrock example of the life of working the land rather than the Transcendentalist cant that the communitarians would prefer to believe. For the Blithedalers, "the peril of our new way of life was not lest we should fail in becoming practical agriculturists, but that we should probably cease to be anything else" (65). Even as they try to be simple farmers, however, the utopians confuse hard work with the "spiritualization of labor." Labor, according to this misplaced sacralizing, "was to be our form of prayer and ceremonial worship."

Coverdale's worldly irony aside, we see here Hawthorne's criticism of defrauding real experience through the deluded commingling of the worlds of daydreaming and fact. Unlike Emerson in

"The American Scholar" or Thoreau in *Walden*, Hawthorne's narrator considers this blurring of the distinction between these two categories of perception a special danger for the very concept of identity. As Coverdale voices it, the "yeoman and the scholar" must be different, not only because "intellectual activity is incompatible with any large amount of bodily exercise," but also because these roles characterize "two distinct individuals, and can never be melted or welded into one substance" (66). Zenobia's characterization of the poet's dilemma reveals how role and self become so enmeshed that playacting is seen as a given, a necessary foundation for identity: "Ah, I see in my mind's eye, what sort of individual you are to be, two or three years hence! Grim Silas Foster is your prototype," whereupon she lengthily describes a model farmer's life, replete with conventional symbols and predictable images of domestic routine.

The Blithedalers' tendency toward self-dramatization proves crucial insofar as it suggests a division between public and private selves. This division is the discrepancy between desires and ideals, a duality that corresponds to unstable circumstances at large that the individual records. The very activity of reform, under this light, can be understood as a performance; the private self seeks to authenticate its hope for stability or salutary change by portraying and projecting its hypothesized solution to its turmoil. The theatricalized self means to win the sympathetic confirmation of its orchestrated victory over exigencies of desire, reforms it wants to legitimate as ideal. Thus by having its success in playing a role corroborated, the self dramatizes how anxiety-making conditions can be corrected or appeased. In Blithedale's case, the community presents its radical egalitarianism as a model for a new society, one that can replace the world of faded institutions. Even their commitment to putting on plays and masques is a predilection that suggests how the source of their amusement is also a response to their inspiration: the staging of a new order of society that will create an economic and social system wherein intimate life can proceed afresh. This theatricalizing can be both individual and communal. Yet even as the Blithedale community dramatizes its egalitarian imagery of reform, as self-consciously as the members drink from earthenware cups, they seem doomed only to reproduce their originating anxieties. Their staging of desire, like the voyeur's private dramatizing, makes nothing happen, since, like the voyeur, the Blithedalers neglect the mystery of experience by turning it into a subject to be plotted and resolved in due course.

Theatricality bears this special stamp on Blithedale itself, inasmuch as the community elicits and justifies Coverdale's recreation of its social scene. When he returns from Boston, his private view of Blithedale as a stage is vividly, cogently confirmed, as if his sense has been appropriated, magnified, and publicized. He finds his former compatriots now, as he enters the wood, in costume! This display is fully suitable. The voyeur's bewilderment has been intensified as he has passed among the deserted buildings of a seemingly abandoned stage where he had hoped to pry further into the affairs of his friends. Now in the forest, he finds all the Blithedalers in the middle of a masque, dressed variously as the goddess Diana, an Indian chief, Queen Zenobia, a Kentucky woodsman, a Bavarian broom-girl, Moll Pitcher, a gypsy fortune-teller, Jim Crow, a Shaker elder, Cavaliers, grim Puritans, Revolutionary officers, "Shepherds of Arcadia, and other allegorical figures from the Faerie Queen." Stimulating Coverdale's imagination, these folklore figures enhance the voyeur's commitment to seeing life as a theater for acting out "phantasmagorical antics" so that only the sight of Silas Foster, the image of obdurate fact, could "disenchant the scene" (210).

It seems merely a coincidence that Coverdale should return just when the community is enjoying a masquerade, but the scene also reflects the voyeur's perception that he is an audience of one watching an ever-unfolding panorama, here a catalogue of American culture, its European antecedents, and mythic models of heroism. Coverdale's "weird and fantastic" sense as he returns to Blithedale coincides with the self's private sense of public life and history, now projected disconcertingly before him. Coverdale himself could not have more forcefully willed this scene into being. As he makes his way to the farm, he entertains various "shifting fantasies" about how he will be received—conjectures that he compares to hallucinations—and draws the "ominous impression" that "some evil thing had befallen us, or was ready to befall" (207). The sight of the deserted community adds to his premonitions, and his surprising discovery of the revelers reinforces his theatricalizing of the events. This turn of the plot corresponds to the oneiric structure that Coverdale imagines. Finding the place empty and then seeing the members perform in the forest, as if on cue, fulfills the voyeur's wishes. Coverdale as poet could not have conjured the scene more precisely or completely; even when he gives himself away, the company still performs as if he were directing. They threaten to punish the voyeur, guilty as he knows himself to be, for his spying; once the secret of his voyeurism is revealed, he is rewarded with the execration he believes he deserves: "The whole fantastic rabble forthwith streamed off in pursuit of me, so that I was like a mad poet hunted by chimaeras" (211).

The collapsing of the distinction between real life and the *theatrium mundi* is further achieved when, following his escape, Coverdale stumbles into another tableau. Here he "intrude[s]" belatedly into the inviolable circle of privacy that he has imagined his friends to share.[21] As he comes upon Hollingsworth, Zenobia, and Priscilla, he finds "those who love, or those who hate, at some acme of their passion that puts them into a sphere of their own, where no other spirit can pretend to stand on equal ground with them" (213–14). His friends are removed from ordinary life and placed on a stage where secrets can be revealed. Now Coverdale may learn what he has been trying to guess throughout, and he is "affected with a species of terror" at the prospect. The vivid contrast between the masquerade and the private scene before him quickens the poet's realization that he has "no right to be or breathe there," for he sees what ensues between people when they think themselves unobserved. Hollingsworth in his everyday clothes, Priscilla, simply clad but for her calabash—slightly theatrical as usual—and Zenobia in characteristic high dress, all dramatize that this is no simple masquerade but the real life of intimate relations, from which Coverdale has always been separated and from which he now curiously "wished himself away." Coverdale's fear is that once he does learn their secrets, as now it seems he will, his relation to them is ended; his intimacy with them consists only in his searching imagination. Secretly, he is terrified at the prospect of having his desires met, for then he may have to confront the truth of desires that he wishes not to countenance.

To Coverdale, at Eliot's pulpit, the everyday life of concealed feelings and their theatricalized representation publicize a secret. As Zenobia tells him, "This long while past, you have been following up your game, groping for human emotions in the dark corners of the heart. Had you been here a little sooner, you might have seen them dragged into the daylight" (214). Coverdale knows that the subjects discussed in this "secret tribunal" are the ones that for months past have "kept my heart and my imagination idly feverish," the secrets of his three friends: "Zenobia's whole character and history; the true nature of her mysterious connection with Westervelt; her later purposes towards Hollingsworth, and reciprocally, his in reference to her; and, finally, the degree in which Zenobia had been cognizant of the plot against Priscilla, and what, at last, has been the real object of the scheme" (214). But Coverdale is again to be frustrated and left to his "adventurous conjectures"; instead of learning the truth, he is thrust into the role of "Judge Coverdale," presiding over Zenobia's trial of passion.

Hawthorne immediately compares this climactic scene to a dramatic episode in American history. Through Coverdale, he sees "in Hollingsworth all that an artist would desire for the grim portrait of a Puritan magistrate, holding inquest of life and death in a case of witchcraft" (214). Coverdale's aesthetic perception also historicizes the scene and thus imparts a social range and depth to its power of personal emotion. As in Hawthorne's other romances, the present tells a secret that the immediate past cannot and that the remote past can suggest only figuratively. In Zenobia Coverdale can see the "sorceress herself . . . fair enough to tempt Satan with a force reciprocal to his own," and in Priscilla "the pale victim, whose soul and body had been wasted by a witch's spells." All that remains for the artist to imagine is "a pile of fagots . . . heaped against the rock," a "hint of impending doom," which would have "completed the suggestive picture" of a witch about to be burned. While Hawthorne certainly knew that the Salem witches were hanged, he evokes a popular image of their prosecution at once to enliven the reader's sense of the ongoing drama and to suggest the cultural importance of Zenobia's tribunal. The image of Zenobia as a sort of outlaw emphasizes the relation between her personal affections—the lengths she may have taken to secure Hollingsworth—and her feminist values. By comparing Hollingsworth to a magistrate, Hawthorne also stresses how Zenobia's passion is a threat to the established order. Not only is there something unlawful about her love, but there may also be something unholy. In a very similar way, Emerson also understood the relation between history and reform when he observed that "the fertile forms of antinomianism among the elder Puritans seemed to have their match in the plenty of the new harvest of reform," including "projects that attacked the institution of marriage as the foundation of social ills."[22]

Here Coverdale aestheticizes this scene as reenacting the split between individual passion and social control. Zenobia's secret, now laid bare, is a menace to the existing order of affections and their uses, in a way analogous to the antinomian challenge to the Puritan community. Furthermore, by imagining Zenobia as a witch, Coverdale also captures the popular distortion of feminist sexuality. Thus in the historical framing of this scene, Coverdale controverts the threat Zenobia poses, giving it instead a melodramatic punishment, while demonstrating how a secret implies social issues. He does this, moreover, through Hawthorne's own historicizing: by setting this dramatic moment at Eliot's pulpit, Hawthorne also suggests the historical binding of the relatively tawdry drama of mid-century utopianism and the Puritans' quite different "errand into the wilderness."[23] In this, there also lies a more severe criticism than Emerson offers, since Hawthorne may at once be indicting a social and spiritual movement that has squandered any real, binding connection to the past, just as one may also see that the past has predicated the very anxieties that the present cannot resolve.

Coverdale's historically operative consciousness is awakened immediately prior to his intrusion. Fleeing from the masqueraders, he trips on a heap of moldy firewood and muses "in a fitful mood that swayed my mind." He becomes "quite lost in reverie," while reflecting on a long-dead woodsman and his family. The point of this incident, which Hawthorne is careful to include, is that it combines the poet's historicizing bent with the voyeur's penchant for aestheticizing a "scene." The effect of Coverdale's sprawl is similar to Hawthorne's meditation in "The Old Manse" on the "tradition" that Lowell told him of the New England youth who murders a British soldier. Both imbue history with an artistically projective capacity. Here Coverdale is stirred out of his reflections on the past only when he hears his friends calling him, but his consciousness of both history and theater has been so concentrated that the "scene" of the three together engages his fullest capacities to reconceive what he has missed and recover from its lingering passion the secrets of private life that, once again, he has been denied.

For Coverdale, history, theater, and art commingle to create a stage upon which secrets may be played out. The crucially close relation between history and art can be seen, according to Richard Sennett, in the mid-nineteenth century's demand for historical accuracy in theatrical production. The "passion for veracity in costume" was to relieve the increasing confusion about how one might know who and what another was. People "tried to find in the theater . . . a world where you could indeed be absolutely sure that people you saw were genuine. The actors really represented what they played," unlike life on the other side of the footlights, where "intimate knowledge" could no longer be communicated through clothes. In theater, "there was no possible deception, no act of deduction that might go wrong"; in the theater, "unlike the street, life was unshielded; it appeared as it was. . . ." Furthermore, the theater in the mid-century European capitals took on the social function of stylizing an activity that people could no longer do with habitual ease: in Balzac's Paris and Dickens's London, "society must depend on art to end mystification, to tell us a truth which men and women can otherwise arrive at only by a faulty process of deduction from miniaturized clues." While Sennett makes these remarks about urban centers which lend themselves to the "tyranny of intimacy," their relevance for Coverdale's Blithedale is especially illuminating, in spite of the necessary qualifications. As Sennett concludes, "the divisions between mystery, illusion, and deception on the one hand and truth on the other were in the mid-19th Century drawn into a peculiar form: authentic life, which requires no effort of decoding, appeared only under the aegis of stage art."[24]

The decoding of "authentic life" is precisely the voyeur's self-conceived challenge and mission, and Coverdale performs this task through his vigorous scrutiny of the drama in the present and through conjectures about the relation of the past to the present.[25] Thus does he seize upon his own imaginative renderings as the very essence of real life. The commingling of historical, aesthetic, social, and psychological associations visited upon him at his return represents a wish-fulfillment of which the voyeur is hardly conscious, but one so profoundly felt that the "pathway of that walk still runs along, with freshness through my memory" (205). Once he does encounter "the three together," his need for prying is all but met (he only has left to spy on Zenobia in her grief), and the narrative proceeds, without generating further digressions, interpolated tales, or frustrations, as if Hawthorne had finally granted Coverdale his wish. Of course, the urgency to learn these secrets prompts Coverdale back to Blithedale in the first place, for just prior to his return, he has witnessed Priscilla's performance in the village hall and Hollingsworth's retrieval of her.

Why the spectacle of the village hall should shake Coverdale, and why it predicates his return, first becomes apparent when we recall that spiritualists found the stage—like the voyeur's "mental stage"—as the most appropriate forum for their special enterprise of decoding authentic life. If the stage can bring secrets to light, without "generous sympathies" or thorough scrutiny, then spiritualists' use of the stage poses a dire threat to the voyeur. To the voyeur, their practice is a cheat; spiritualism tries to make occult the voyeur's earthly business. The spiritualist learns through "invisible agencies" what the voyeur must discover through "adventurous conjectures." Spiritualist endeavor makes unnecessary the voyeur's method and endangers his established order of relations. In the decade that Hawthorne called the "epoch of rapping spirits," spiritualism was a highly popular entertainment, if only because it professed to unearth the secrets of life, without Divine Revelation, and yield the clues to an improved life for the individual and society, or so Westervelt claims when "he spoke of a new era that was dawning upon the world; an era that would link soul to soul, and the present life to what we call futurity, with a closeness that should finally convert both worlds into one great mutually conscious brotherhood" (200). Social reformers were inevitably attracted to such claims: the cult of spiritualism "adopted the tone of millenial expectancy already familiar in various apocalyptic and utopian movements of the 1840s. . . . For the social reformers who flocked to the causes, spiritualism seemed to indicate that the spirits wanted to make themselves felt in earthly affairs and would, in fact, lead mankind to social regeneration."[26] The promises of spiritualism, however, easily lent themselves to the "mystic sensuality" that Coverdale deplores as the particularly inimical feature of "this singular age." All evidence of supernatural powers in human hands fills the poet with "horror and disgust" because, "if these things were to be believed, the individual soul was virtually annihilated" (198).

Just as Westervelt occasions an instant mistrust when Coverdale first meets him, posing as he does a risk to the voyeur's sense of individuality, so too is the safeguarding of identity the very stake at the village hall when Priscilla is about to perform. For Coverdale, the risk to his being is as historical and cultural as it is personal: "Alas, my countrymen, methinks we have fallen on an evil age! If these phenomena have not humbug at the bottom, so much the worse for us. What can they indicate, in a spiritual way, except that the soul of man is descending to a lower point than it has ever before reached. . . . We are pursuing a downward course, in the eternal march, and thus bring ourselves into the same range with beings whom death, in requital of their gross and evil lives, has degraded below humanity" (199). The debasing that Coverdale sees as imminent comes from surrendering the "idea of man's eternal responsibility," which spiritualists make "ridiculous" and "not worth acceptance." For Coverdale, this surrender of responsibility in the present life is an especially onerous temptation, because his individuality depends on a certain eternal vigilance over the ways individuals conduct themselves. Unnerving as this must be for Coverdale, all the more horrifying for the self is the danger of consorting with spirits, as he anticipates the spectacle of the Veiled Lady's performance. The idea that his secretly beloved is also the mediating agent for virtually annihilating the "individual soul" multiplies his dread: first, the spiritualist program sets itself against his own secret vocation; secondly, he is about to observe his beloved submit to this degradation; third, his own identity as the secret admirer is imperiled; fourth, Priscilla's powers also deepen the fear of loss of the self in love.

Although Coverdale's scorn may seem disproportionately vehement, the seriousness with which Westervelt's brand of spiritualism was practiced may well have merited this kind of contempt. Holding firm to orthodox Christian objections, Coverdale condemns those who would "hold intercourse" with the spirits, those who "stoop, and grovel," under the prostituting influence of a medium.[27] Coverdale's disdain, however, is not simply out of religious conviction. Like Hawthorne's anxiety over Sophia's visit to a hypnotist, Coverdale's fear is fixed on the ways that mesmerists intrude into intimate relations and threaten individuality. Particularly telling is the catalogue of possible trespasses that the voyeur lists as the consequences of mesmeric intervention: a maiden icily retreats from a lover's kiss, a recent widow digs up her husband's grave, a mother thrusts away her child—all profanations of intimacy. The threat of a mesmerist, like that of the voyeur, lies in the power to debase, to rob an individual of identity, for "human character was but soft wax in his hands." When Hollingsworth summons Priscilla from the stage, Coverdale is relieved that she escapes with her integrity, that she had "kept, as I religiously believe, her virgin reserve and sanctity of the soul throughout it all" (209). Despite Westervelt's manipulations, the Veiled Lady preserves her honor, saved precisely when, as the spectators imagine, "she was about to take flight into the invisible sphere, and to the society of spiritual being," or just when she is about to "hold intercourse" with the spirit world. By saving Priscilla when he does, Hollingsworth also keeps her pure, Coverdale thinks, for the poet. Still is she the nineteenth-century stereotype of a fair-haired virgin worthy of the voyeur's objectifying affections.

What is behind Coverdale's anxiety over Priscilla's purity? We later learn that it is his secret, but even at this point the reader knows that Coverdale's concern is not merely that "a bachelor always feels himself defrauded, when he knows, or suspects, that any woman of his acquaintance has given herself away," as he tells himself when he ponders the likelihood of Zenobia's sexual experience, and that once a woman has passed through the "gates of mystery," she has jeopardized her status in society and has lost the admiration of respectable men. Nor is Coverdale's concern merely protective, as it seems to him when he calls it his "duty" to keep Priscilla from the "catastrophe" of falling in love with Hollingsworth. Even though Hollingsworth rescues her from Westervelt, as far as Coverdale is concerned she is still in danger. And this concern is his secret. He rails against Priscilla's "mystic sensuality" both for religious reasons and for deeply personal ones. Not only must he argue against that which would annihilate the "individual soul," but also he must defend against the disclosure that he loves her and that he prizes her purity and integrity as only a fiancé can.

While he rages against the spiritual sickness of the age, his eloquence also serves to obstruct both the public disclosure of his own secret and his private reckoning of desire. For Priscilla's powers as a medium lie in her special perception of an individual's concealed truths: "Hidden things were visible to her (at least, so the people inferred from the obscure hints, escaping unawares out of her mouth), and silence was audible. And, in all the world, there was nothing so difficult to be endured, by those who had any dark secret to conceal, as the glance of Priscilla's timid and melancholy eyes" (187). Unlike a voyeur's victories, her success results from her faculty of seeing what cannot otherwise be seen, her knowing what ought to be unknowable—a talent especially troubling to the voyeur. Just as Dimmesdale needs to avoid the company of a physician whose training helps him to detect guilt, so should someone with a "dark secret" avoid the glance of a medium whose extrasensory perception, whose special power of sympathy, also discovers the concealed.

The appeal of spiritualism lies in the possibility that a world beyond the here and now is as knowable as the one in which a man has his "eternal responsibility." For Coverdale, the threat of spiritualism lies both in its implicit mockery of immortality and in its degradation of "our present life." If the spiritualist were any more than a "humbug," then life on earth would not demand eternal vigilance because, as Coverdale puts it, we would "thus bring ourselves into the same range with beings whom death . . . has degraded below humanity!" Were the secrets of the other life to be learned, how one lives in the present would make no difference. On the one hand, mesmerism challenges secular, democratic, humanistic values, and on the other, the fear of annihilating the "individual soul" is, for the voyeur, an impossible condition. The voyeur must believe that how one lives provides the key to what one is, and without a principle of individuation the voyeur's discovery of secrets is a meaningless venture. This very fear, that there really is a hidden life that cannot be known, is Coverdale's subject when he discusses with Zenobia the "unjustifiable stroke" of pulling down the shade she rightly suspects him of peering through:

> "I cannot call it a very wise [stroke]," returned I, with a secret bitterness, which, no doubt, Zenobia appreciated. "It is really impossible to hide anything, in this world, to say nothing of the next. All that we ought to ask, therefore, is, that the witnesses of our conduct, and the speculators on our motives, should be capable of taking the highest view which the circumstances of the case may admit. So much being secured, I, for one, would be most happy in feeling myself followed, everywhere, by an indefatigable human sympathy." (163)

Here the frustrated Coverdale expresses his conviction that everything can be seen, every secret may be learned, as long as one is alert enough to find the clues. So futile is the attempt to hide anything, the voyeur would like to believe, that one can only hope that one's "witnesses" and "speculators" are inclined to take a generous view. Any obstruction, such as the drawing of a curtain, is a threat to the voyeur. Coverdale's hatred for the spiritualists is thus directed at their attempt to learn the secrets of this world, not by observing closely but by gaining access to the other, where no secrets exist. According to Westervelt, Priscilla can hear not only such distant sounds as the "desert wind sweeping over the sands, as far off as Arabia," the grinding of icebergs in the polar seas, the "rustle of a leaf in an East Indian forest," but "the lowest whispered breath of the bashfullest maiden in the world, uttering the first confession of her love!" (202). It is a sound the bashful Coverdale would also note, and to his great relief, just when Westervelt makes this claim and to the mesmerist's "discomposure," Hollingsworth then mounts the platform and seizes Priscilla. Relieved as Coverdale is, he is also discomposed by her departure, for the poet must still guard her from ignominy, just as the voyeur must still guard his secret by uncovering the true nature of the relations among his friends. Without giving the reader any explanation at all, two days later Coverdale returns to Blithedale where he meets the masquerade.

Coverdale's fear of his secret's disclosure inspires his scorn for spiritualism, but beyond that fear lies the deeper secret that intimacy exists for the voyeur-poet only in the imagination. Thus his call to the dove to tell Priscilla that he loves her for the fancies with which he has idly bedecked her is unwittingly true. Furthermore, his relief when Hollingsworth saves Priscilla confirms the point. Coverdale's trepidation that his secret love might be exposed is allayed, his illusion of intimacy preserved, for had he witnessed the spectacle of Priscilla's final transformation, his love would have been diminished, shared with the audience, made vulgar, worthless, and disgusting to him. As Coverdale watches his rival whisk his beloved away, he is at least assured that she is safe from Westervelt who, as the image of the poet's darker self, would debase his sacralized love. Throughout the preliminaries to the performance, Coverdale imagines a horrifying version of his own desires as an alternative to his narcissistic idealizing of the seamstress, really Hawthorne's version of the conventional view of the female as both whore and goddess. For the poet, it is better that Priscilla is rescued by Hollingsworth rather than be humiliated by the mesmerist. As long as she remains a virgin, not to be publicly disgraced (in Coverdale's eyes) as some spiritualist trollop who communicates between this world and the other, promiscuously and for pay, Coverdale can still enjoy the illusion of his imagined intimacy. But the moment she emerges as the popular favorite, falling from the pedestal upon which he has placed her, she becomes disreputable. Then she becomes a woman of questionable honor to the poet, because she would not be the only one compromised; he could no longer imagine himself the forlorn lover of an innocent seamstress who once offered him the present of her elaborately embroidered purse, the novel's oft-remarked symbol of sexual promise and commerce.

In this regard, Hollingsworth's romantic intervention becomes preferable to Westervelt's purposes, allowing Coverdale to distance himself from his conflicting motives. Hollingsworth figures prominently in Coverdale's psychodrama as the very model of his desires, the exalted friend and rival who instructs the poet, first in the desire to become a reformer, then in the desire for Zenobia, and later, for Priscilla.[28] As Coverdale remarks, Hollingsworth is of a "much more solid character" than the poet. One may say, following René Girard, that Hollingsworth presents Coverdale with a model, one who is both exemplary and obstructive. Even though the two friends suffer an irreconcilable rupture, the philanthropist remains a crucial personage in Coverdale's psyche, especially with regard to approved sexual intimacy. Hollingsworth is the very image of the man of action, "purpose," desire. The philanthropist's self-possession and command of others seem to the poet-voyeur the necessary correction to the feelings of marginality that so generally paralyze him and turn him into a "tertiary" character. Hollingsworth may even be said to provide Coverdale with secrets. The poet sees Zenobia's great attraction to his friend, thus confirming her as a worthy object of desire. Moreover, Hollingsworth instructs Coverdale in the virtue of caring for the vulnerable Priscilla. Not only can the poet say that "Hollingsworth's behavior was certainly a great deal more creditable than mine," but also his friend's dictum that the company "not pry into her secrets" forbids Coverdale, temporarily, of his most individualizing trait. Coverdale finds himself bound to the double business of learning an identity from his model yet finding the model insuperable. Their rupture frees Coverdale to admit his suspicions about the project in the vivid form of leaving the community, but he retains Hollingsworth's example as a precept for deciding who is worthy of the poet's aspirations of love. For Coverdale, Hollingsworth consistently emerges as the person worthy of love, the male with whom women seek intimacy, the man who counteracts Westervelt's charm by making an equal demand on women's feelings of self-insufficiency, or in Priscilla's case, her complete lack of self. Appropriately, then, Hollingsworth rescues Priscilla, in Coverdale's scheme of things. Horrified as Coverdale is at Westervelt's purposes, the poet's general and impotent self-absorption can only be counterbalanced through the vision of Hollingsworth's staunchness. One may go still further and suggest that, for the voyeur, Hollingsworth's presence at the village hall is a psychological necessity. Hollingsworth's saving of Priscilla substitutes the poet's hero-worship for his own dreams of heroic action, thus allowing the poet a vengeance against one of his antagonists while preserving the delusion of later conquering the antagonistic aspect he attaches to Hollingsworth, the figure upon whom he otherwise depends for legitimating his desires. Thus his fantasy of love retains its purity and vitality.

Hawthorne's treatment of the effect that mid-century spiritualism had on the relation between the private and public self suggests why reformers found the movement appealing. By summoning voices from another world to answer the mysteries in the present one, spiritualism promised to absolve the difference between private self and public conduct. Under this condition, the "individual soul" would have neither secrets to keep nor advantages to attain. In distrusting this promise Hawthorne echoes Emerson, who believed that the integrity of the individual is really the key to reform, that the individual himself must be responsible for the difference between private and public selves: "When the individual is not *individual*, but is dual; when his thoughts look one way and his actions another; when his faith is traversed by his habits; when his will, enlightened by reason, is warped by his sense; when with one hand he rows and with the other backs water, what concert can be?"[29] However disregarded by spiritualists, the importance of the individual was at the center of such other reform projects as the call for sexual enlightenment. As attractive as utopians found the spiritualists' promise, even more compelling to them were the rights of women.[30]

The relation between feminism and intimacy shows how Zenobia's "secret," like Coverdale's, expresses itself in the tension between the challenge of public life and the demands of privacy. In more than one sense Zenobia's secret and the poet's share an "analogy"; their secrets are intertwined also to the extent that his confession develops out of her suicide, rather than out of his meeting with Hollingsworth and Priscilla. Once the carnal female of intelligence and imagination is removed, the narrative also loses its vitality. Westervelt ceases to be a part of the characters' lives—his past relation to Zenobia is no longer important; all Coverdale and Hollingsworth can do is drown themselves in their own self-reflective pools. The loss of Priscilla, Coverdale believes, should not cripple him, but it does, and in the same ways that he laments the tragedy of Zenobia's sense of futility:

> It was a woful thought, that a woman of Zenobia's diversified capacity should have fancied herself irretrievably defeated on the broad battle-field of life, and with no refuge, save to fall on her own sword, merely because Love had gone against her. It is nonsense, and a miserable wrong—the result, like so many others, of masculine egotism—that the success or failure of woman's existence should be made to depend wholly on the affections, and on one species of affection; while man has such a multitude of other chances, that this seems but an incident. For its own sake, if it will do no more, the world should throw open all its avenues to the passport of a woman's bleeding heart. (241)

Zenobia's suicide deadens the lives of the others: in the next chapter Coverdale records the spiritual death of the philanthropist who puts aside his scheme; in the last, the poet sings his own dirge. Without Zenobia, whose motor force of desire drives much of the narrative, Coverdale's own story becomes listless. Now that her impassionating energy, the force of desire Coverdale has both feared and exploited, is absent, nothing remains to fuel his own attenuated will. The impact of Zenobia's death also suggests that a culture that cannot provide possibilities of fulfillment for women of "diversified character," like Zenobia—or her prototype, Margaret Fuller—may grow as desiccated as Zenobia's survivors.

Zenobia's death dramatizes the horrible consequences of a secret which has come to light and which has not met a sufficiently sympathetic response. Avowed passionately yet received coldly, a secret thus made public explodes with its own annihilating power. Although the consequences are portrayed as psychological, they also implicate society, since a woman is seen as restricted in her status solely by managing matters of the heart. Zenobia tells Coverdale that, humiliated as she is when Hollingsworth scorns her and proves himself unworthy of her passion, a "woman in my position . . . feels scarcely at her ease among former friends. New faces—unaccustomed looks—those only can she tolerate. She would pine, among familiar scenes; she would be apt to blush, too, under the eyes that knew her secret" (225). Now that her secret is known, Zenobia vows to publicize it for the benefit of others, to make her secret the nation's business: "A woman in my position . . . would mortify herself, I suppose, with foolish notions of having sacrificed the honor of her sex, at the foot of proud, contumacious man. Poor womanhood, with its rights and wrongs! Here will be new matter for my course of lectures, at the idea of which you smiled, Mr. Coverdale, a month or two ago" (225–26).

These lectures are to be given on the rights and role of women. But instead of instructing society, Zenobia commits suicide. Yet before she does so, she tells Coverdale, perhaps as a warning, how isolating it is to have one's secret known; Zenobia threatens to retreat to a convent where she will hide her face "behind the black veil"—one of Hawthorne's favorite emblems for simultaneously concealing and expressing a secret.

Like Zenobia, Coverdale also desires to publicize his secret. If his revelation matters as much as the poet wishes his listeners to believe, it is because he can finally articulate his sense of his apprehensive relation to society. By proclaiming his abiding love for a woman who does not reciprocate his passion and whose sympathy lies elsewhere, Coverdale wants to bring the reader into a "full understanding" of his story. His confession bids for sympathy, but it also intends to be edifying. Why does Hawthorne conceive of telling this secret to be socially important? Why, we may ask, is this confession of an unfulfilled passion to be the last word in this romance about communal life and reform? Although Emerson had propounded that the "sentiment of love" "is the one remedy for all ills, the panacea of nature," Coverdale's fainthearted explanation cannot be confused with the philosopher's imperial dictum.[31]

The conventional answer to such questions is that Coverdale's admission confirms the dangers of the unpropped individualism implied in being a detached observer, the Hawthorne sinner who separates the faculties of mind and heart in pursuit of his purposes. Unpardonable sinners, like Coverdale, Hollingsworth, or Westervelt, are self-destructive; their practices disrupt rather than improve an already disturbed world of social relations. The reformers' means, like the voyeur's, are certain to obstruct their ends, especially if the lengths they take are as venal as Westervelt's or as self-promoting as Hollingsworth's. Indeed, the reformers' very connection to the mesmerist expresses their blindness to their own corruption, the inevitability of their failure: the novel documents how Hollingsworth's obsession to rehabilitate criminals and Zenobia's commitment to improve conditions for women are ultimately founded on a selfish and self-defeating set of principles which, Hawthorne tells us, turn inward on their purposes when they are applied too solipsistically. Ideals and motives, personae and desires are perpetually at odds. Instead of redeeming all criminals Hollingsworth has only to reform himself, or as Emerson cautions: "Our own orbit is all our task, and we need not assist the administration of the universe."[32] Instead of establishing new terms on which the relations between the sexes can flourish, Zenobia is felled by a woman's oldest traditional humiliation—rejection for another woman. These ponderous ironies suggest the unarticulated but pervasive secret of how social circumstances derive from an individualistically based need to keep and tell secrets, a tension between the desire for and dread of their disclosure.

Midway through *The Blithedale Romance*, when Coverdale retreats to his hermitage, a "hollow chamber, of rare seclusion" (98), he pauses to survey the idyllic landscape and to contemplate the noble intentions of the community's enterprise. On the one hand, the poet enjoys the vantage point usually reserved for an omniscient narrator, but on the other, the import of what he sees and hears must escape him. So privileged is his point of view that it encourages poetic and intellectual meditations: "It was an admirable place . . . in which the many tongues of Nature whispered mysteries, and seemed to ask only a little stronger puff of wind, to speak out the solution of its riddle" (99). Without the aid of spiritualists or reformers, the secret of how to live seems as if it can be coaxed out of the here and now.

The perception of this secret eludes Coverdale for the very same reason that it first of all seemed possible. This hermitage, Coverdale's "one exclusive possession, while I counted myself a brother of the socialists, . . . symbolized my individuality, and aided me in keeping it inviolate." His insistence on his individuality expresses the very distance that Coverdale has been careful to preserve throughout. Not only does it estrange him from the others, but his belief in the inviolability of the "individual soul," which underlies his hatred of the spiritualists, also keeps him at a remove from knowing the here and now any better. Even though his belief in the individual would seem to bring the voyeur closer, the need to keep his own individuality "inviolate" prohibits the intimate knowledge that seems so imminent when he is alone, prevents the "stronger puff of wind, to speak out the solution of [Nature's] riddle." Like the reformers' self-defeating methods, Coverdale's cherished individuality keeps him from realizing his dreams.

In the comfort of his detachment, when his thoughts turn to his rival Hollingsworth's project, Coverdale grows skeptical over the scheme: "And why, when there is enough else to do, should we waste our strength in dragging home the ponderous load of his philanthropic absurdities? At my height above the earth, the whole matter looked ridiculous!" (100). However inclined he may be to see the grandiose scheme as an absurdity, his jealousy is also awakened by his realization that the "baulked philanthropist had the battle-spirit in his heart," while the poet does not. For then he flings a message to Priscilla to be carried by a passing bird:

> Tell her . . . that her fragile thread of life has inextricably knotted itself with other and tougher threads, and most likely it will be broken. Tell her that Zenobia will not long be her friend. Say that Hollingsworth's heart is on fire with his own purpose, but icy for all human affection; and that, if she has given him her love, it is like casting a flower into a sepulchre. And say, that if any mortal really cares for her, it is myself; and not even I, for her realities . . . but for the fancy-work with which I have idly decked her out! (100)

Susceptible of the most enlivening influences as he sits in his perch, Coverdale cannot but connect his distrust of Hollingsworth and his desire for Priscilla. Still, without the "stronger puff of wind," the poet must couch his desire for intimacy in the "fancy-work" of his imagination, the aestheticizing of his desire, rather than admit the reality of his yearning either to the reader or to himself, or both.

These commingled perceptions lead to a more telling one. Under the "sensual influence" of the sun at its zenith, Coverdale sees now, as for the first time, the futility of the Blithedale romance: "I suddenly found myself possessed by a mood of disbelief in moral beauty or heroism, and a conviction of the folly of attempting to benefit the world. Our especial scheme of reform, which, from my observatory, I could take in with the bodily eye, looked so ridiculous that it was impossible not to laugh aloud" (101). Coverdale is especially ready to make this conjecture because of his isolation and the pressure of his desire, both of which ensure his frustration.

What he sees he sees clearly enough, but his vantage point distorts the evidence for his conclusion.

Confirmation comes when the poet stipulates that the "joke is a little too heavy. If I were wise, I should get out of the scrape, with all diligence, and then laugh at my companions for remaining in it!" Then, in a completely uncanny moment, Coverdale hears the very laugh that he would have, and he hears it with "perfect distinctness" as the "peculiar laugh" of Westervelt, who appears with Zenobia as if by magic. The laugh that seemed impossible for Coverdale to resist is now the laugh he cannot tolerate: "It brought my thoughts back to our recent interview. I recognized, as chiefly due to this man's influence, the sceptical and sneering view which, just now, had filled my mental vision in regard to all life's better purposes." Coverdale settles, or displaces, the authority for his "mental vision" onto Westervelt rather than admit that his jealous hatred for Hollingsworth underlies his scorn for "life's better purposes." Coverdale's complex reaction to Hollingsworth comes, in large part, from his disappointed expectations as well as his perception of his friend's hypocrisy. Once again, Emerson articulates plainly what Coverdale leaves unsaid. The voice in "New England Reformers" could be, at this juncture, the voyeur's. For unlike Hawthorne, Coverdale believes, with Emerson, that the secret of private and public happiness can be known and can be told:

> As every man at heart wishes the best and not inferior society, wishes to be convicted of his error and to come to himself—so he wishes that the same healing should not stop his thought, but should penetrate his will or active power. . . . What he most wishes is to be lifted to some higher platform, that he may see beyond to his present fear the trans-Alpine good, so that his fear, his coldness, his custom may be broken up like fragments of ice, melted and carried away in the great stream of good will. . . . We desire to be made great; we desire to be touched with that fire which shall command this ice to stream, and make our existence a benefit. If therefore we start objections to your project, O friend of the slave, or friend of the

poor or of the race, understand well that it is because we wish to drive you and to drive us into your measures. We wish to hear ourselves confuted. We are haunted with a belief that you have a secret which it would highliest advantage us to learn, and we should force you to impart it to us, though it should bring us to prison or to worse extremity.[33]

Furthermore, Coverdale cannot admit that his complicated response to the philanthropist so affects him and his views, for then he must also acknowledge that his desire for Priscilla is "for her realities," not for her appeal to his imagination.

By emerging to take on Coverdale's suppressed anxiety over Hollingsworth, Westervelt performs a critical function in the poet's psychodrama. Westervelt officiates at unholy ceremonies of entry into another world and presides over the profaning of Coverdale's vision of intimacy, while Hollingsworth intractably stands for an allegiance to "purpose," a firmness that not only angers and shames the poet in his fear of marginality, but also helps to win the philanthropist sexual success with the very women Coverdale considers worthiest of speculation. Both Hollingsworth and Westervelt seem to twin what is divided in Coverdale—a belief in individuality and the desire for intimacy—and thus are twins themselves, the villainous bastard and the favored prince. To the keenly observant Coverdale, their hypocrisies ought to be easily exposed, but, as we see, the women take no notice of Coverdale's pathetic efforts to debunk his doubles. In a sense, Coverdale uses one to vanquish the other. At the village hall, when love is at stake, Coverdale needs to have Hollingsworth emerge. Here, to undo the strength of Hollingsworth's mastery, Coverdale seizes on Westervelt's corrosive skepticism to steady his own.

In finding Westervelt's "influence" as the source of his dissatisfaction, Coverdale raises rather than devalues this darker self's symbolic proportions and makes the mesmerist into a suitably blameworthy provocateur. Westervelt's cynicism is unbearable because it reminds him too much of his own capacity to take the lowest rather than "the highest view which the circumstances of the case may admit" (163). As Coverdale reflects, "the Professor's

tone represented that of worldly society at large, where a cold scepticism smothers what it can of our spiritual aspirations, and makes
the rest ridiculous. I detested this kind of man, and all the more,
because a part of my nature, showed itself responsive to him" (101–
2). By "responsive" Hawthorne does not mean merely sensitive but
sympathetic, intimately affinitive. And this sympathy is what
binds him to Westervelt, even as late as the mesmerist's assessment of Zenobia's wasted career. His description of the mesmerist
might just as easily apply to himself: "Nature thrusts some of us
into the world miserably incomplete, on the emotional side, with
hardly any sensibilities, except what pertains to animals. No passion, save of the senses; no holy tenderness, nor the delicacy that
results from this. Externally, they bear a close resemblance to other
men, and have perhaps all save the finest grace" (103). When
Zenobia and Westervelt approach, it is altogether appropriate, from
Coverdale's point of view, that they be discussing Zenobia's past
connection to Westervelt and Priscilla's present connection to Hollingsworth: "A breeze stirred after them, and awoke the leafy
tongues of the surrounding trees, which forthwith began to babble,
as if innumerable gossips had all at once got wind of Zenobia's
secret" (105). Disappointed in his eavesdropping and spying, Coverdale still does not learn all "Zenobia's secrets," because in spite of
the voyeur's effort to aestheticize reality, "real life never arranges
itself exactly like a romance" (104).

What amuses Coverdale as he sits in his hermitage is precisely
the "sceptical and sneering view" that he attributes to Westervelt.
Out of his reluctance to accept this tendency in himself, Coverdale
tries to defuse the threat of admitting his contradictory reactions
to the project of social reform. Even at the very end, he hears the
echo of Westervelt's laugh and remains ambivalent: at the same
time as he tenderly reminisces about "our beautiful scheme," he
also self-mockingly suggests that he is too world-weary to care. But
this pose is also uncomfortable: "Yet, were there any cause, in this
whole chaos of human struggle, worth a sane man's dying for, and
which my death would benefit, then—provided, however, the effort
did not involve an unreasonable amount of trouble—methinks I
might be bold to offer up my life" (246). While readers may hear

echoes of Hawthorne's description of Holgrave's "error" and "enthusiasm" for reform, Coverdale's irony reflects more than skepticism. The tension of his ambivalence, seen in his apposition, signifies the very double bind that the aside was intended to undo, for
Coverdale has just renounced any such interest: "As regards
human progress (in spite of my irrepressible yearnings over the
Blithedale reminiscences,) let them believe in it who can, and aid
in it who choose!" Although he offers an exclamation, again his
conflict is suppressed by embedding an opposing desire within a
statement of resolve.

Perhaps in an effort to appease the anxiety that besets him—"in
these years that are darkening around me. . . . More and more, I
feel that we had struck upon what ought to have been a truth"—
Coverdale indulges in a joke which keeps him from identifying too
closely with his "former associates," keeps him from admitting
that in some part he still shares their romantic desire to develop
the power to change the order of society, keeps "these last two or
three pages for my individual and sole behoof." This joke, about
Kossuth's campaign for Hungarian rights, seems much lighter than
the "heavy" one that earlier occurs to him when it erupts out of his
hatred for Hollingsworth and is projected onto the community as a
whole. Freud would consider this kind of joke different from those
that express "the disguised aggressiveness . . . directed against
people." These jokes have wider social applications and attack "institutions, people in their capacity as vehicles for institutions, dog-
mas of morality or religion, views of life which enjoy so much respect that objections to them can only be made under the mask of a
joke and indeed of a joke concealed by its facade."[34]

The joke that Coverdale makes, that he "would gladly be [Kos-
suth's] man, for one brave rush upon the levelled bayonets," provided that the battlefield was pitched "within an easy ride of my
abode," "on a mild, sunny morning, after breakfast," fairly well
corresponds to the sense of life that underlies the conclusion. To see
how subtle this joke is, how deeply buried lies the secret it conceals,
let us examine Coverdale's confession once again, for then the social
implication of his secret can be better understood. At the close,

Coverdale believes that he has "Nothing, nothing, nothing!" to say. Sickened at the death of Zenobia, he leaves Blithedale to enjoy a life that has passed, "I was going to say, happily—but, at all events, tolerably enough." Giving up his poetry, he pursues a life of harmless pleasures, of ease, of such little trouble as he jokingly stipulates that he "should be loth to pledge" himself. "Being well to do in the world, and having nobody but myself to care for, I live very much at my ease, and fare sumptuously every day." The "beautiful scheme of a noble and unselfish life" that "might endure for generations, and be perfected, as the ages rolled away, into the system of a people, and a world" is now supplanted by Coverdale's halfhearted carpe diem, a call for modest private pleasure in the face of moral and social challenges. The Blithedale community, no longer a "ridiculous" project, now seems utopian in the best sense of the word; it promises a social arrangement that might make men and women happier. Coverdale quells the fear of having misspent his life, quiets his "new hostility," and suppresses the memory of the actual selfishness of Zenobia and Hollingsworth that caused him so much pain, by making a joke about his cultivated and detached pursuit of individual wants and preferences. Freud describes the underlying message of Coverdale's kind of joke in an analysis that touches upon the novel so directly that I must quote at length. Underlying such jokes is a doubt, both psychological and social: "I will gladly renounce all methods of satisfaction proscribed by society, but am I certain that society will reward this renunciation by offering me one of the permitted methods—even after a certain amount of postponement? What these jokes whisper may be said aloud: that the wishes and desires of men have a right to make themselves acceptable alongside of exacting and ruthless morality." Then in a criticism of the social cost that self-promotion incurs, Freud defines the "conflict" and offers this startling assessment of the need for reform: since the "art of healing has not gone further in making our life safe and so long as social arrangements do no more to make it more enjoyable," it will be "impossible" to stifle our desire to rebel against the "demands of morality," as such jokes suggest.

Every honest man will end by making this admission, at least to himself. The decision in this conflict can only be reached by the roundabout path of fresh insight. One must bind one's own life to that of others so closely and be able to identify oneself with others so intimately that the brevity of one's own life can be overcome; and one must not fulfil the demands of one's own needs illegitimately, but must leave them unfulfilled, because only the continuance of so many unfulfilled demands can develop the power to change the order of society. But not every personal need can be postponed in this way and transferred to other people, and there is no general and final solution of the conflict.

We now know the name that must be given to jokes like those that we last interpreted. They are *cynical* jokes and what they disguise are cynicisms.[35]

Just as Coverdale's tendency toward cynical humor has earlier prodded him to attribute the "sceptical and sneering" influence to Westervelt, now Coverdale must apologize for his insisting on the individualist's preferences before "life's better purposes" by saying that he "exaggerate[s]" his own "defects." Yet rather than leave the reader with this vision of himself as a man who chooses worldly pleasures, however modest, over reformist principles, Coverdale tries to explain how his lack of social "purpose" (as Hollingsworth calls it) "has rendered my whole life an emptiness." His extenuation is, of course, his disappointment in love, but even he must consider this "an absurd thing . . . an absurd thing ever to have happened, and quite the absurdest for an old bachelor . . . to talk about."

In blaming the essential absurdity of his circumstances—his "unsatisfied retrospect . . . and listless glance toward the future"—on his hopeless love, Coverdale tries "illegitimately" to fulfill his demands on life. He reveals that his cynical choice of individuality above intimacy dooms him still to yearn for intimacy, wanting its consolations but fearful of its price: the normal depreciation of the self, which for Coverdale means the relinquishment of the voyeurism that Zenobia once condemns in him as "monstrous scepticism in regard to any conscience or any wisdom, except one's own; a most irreverent propensity to thrust Providence aside, and substitute one's self in its awful place." Still choosing individuality, Coverdale remains, like Hollingsworth, a "self-beginning and self-ending piece of mechanism" (218). His confession of his "one foolish little secret" is also his request for confirmation that his ending is complete and for consolation over disguising and withholding the completeness of his own absorption in the self. Zenobia's description of the hypocritical philanthropist now reads for the delusions of the voyeur: "It is all self! . . . You have embodied yourself in a project. You are a better masquerader than the witches and gypsies yonder; for your disguise is self-deception" (218).

In this final gesture of asking the reader's forgiveness, Coverdale persists selfishly in trying to achieve, with the reader, his lost possibility of intimacy. Yet this sense of self-absorption has been seen before in the novel. It is the disqualifying attribute of Theodore, the young man of Zenobia's legend whose failure of faith in the beauty that lies behind the veil leads him to the misery of a doomed Romantic quest. Rather than submit to the presence of secrets, he lifts the veil as a result of his normal notion of the individual power to know. The veil allures him but denies his desire for determinacy and curses him with the hint of what he might have had but what now can be only imagined. Although the relation between Theodore and the Veiled Lady may be "broadly understood" as signifying the very "problem of romance," so also does the young man's reaction suggest the failed relation between secrets and sympathy.[36] Rather than sympathize with the Veiled Lady's sense of individuating mystery— the integrity of the soul, in Hawthorne's view—Theodore asserts his own self-reliant and self-damning power to see and to know. Attracted as he is by the rumor of the Veiled Lady's beauty, he also mistrusts the spiritualist claptrap governing the Veiled Lady's reservation. Thus he is led, according to Zenobia's legend, to violate the self of another and exiles himself, like Coverdale, from intimate life. Theodore's sin of pride and the self-absorption of desire exclude him, just as surely as the veil repels him.

Zenobia's legend, like Coverdale's confessing his "foolish little secret," like *The Blithedale Romance* itself, reveals how the self is ensnared in this fundamental duality. That tension can be understood, I have argued, as disclosing the secrets of "this singular age," the crisis of individuality and the complex terms of intimacy that structure both the project and defeat of social regeneration. Zenobia's tale makes explicit what Coverdale's confession leaves implicit: how in the theater of reform and the politics of love, individual response is socially and historically grounded. In *The Marble Faun*, Hawthorne turns to this question of how sympathy may finally be achieved, how a manifold rhetoric of secrecy shapes a reader's response.

CHAPTER FOUR

The Marble Faun: Sympathy and the Secret of Art

In the postscript to his last romance, Hawthorne imagines himself at Saint Peter's conversing with his characters in the fancy that they "might safely utter here the secrets which it would be perilous even to whisper on lower earth."[1] No doubt, the author provides this whimsy to tease those readers who demanded that the mysteries to which the novel repeatedly alludes be explained at last. Annoyed as he must have been, Hawthorne could not resist the chance to demonstrate, however playfully, "that some laws and proprieties . . . should be implicitly and insensibly acknowledged" (463). Rather than give "further elucidations" of such "romantic mysteries" as Donatello's furry ears or Miriam's last name, Hawthorne refuses to offer even "one word of explanation" or proof. His reluctance to illuminate "several dark recesses" of the plot attests to his faith that his romance could demonstrate how art shapes moral transformation, a process that depends on recognizing the ambiguous, sometimes indeterminate character of experience. Hawthorne's refusal to explain is of a piece with his declining to give often-crucial information throughout. Moreover, his reluctance comes from a Romantic conviction that a work must be "suggestive," thereby involving the reader in effecting its resolutions. Thus "secrets" need not be specified, as long as the reader's "apprehensive sympathy" is called upon in the process of interpretation. Under such rhetorical circumstances can the reader also participate in the moral educations that the romance observes, the "transformations" that give Hawthorne's last novel its original title.

In *The Marble Faun*, as nowhere else in the canon, Hawthorne persistently raises the issue of how sympathetic apprehension is a necessary condition of reception.[2] Nowhere else is the writer's subject so self-consciously the nature of art, its workings and effects. Afraid that he had lost his ideal reader during the eight-year lapse in production following the publication of *Blithedale*, Hawthorne turns to the issue of reception as his explicit subject in the preface, where he describes his worry that he will not find again a reader who is an "all-sympathizing critic," "that unseen brother of the soul," who would be "more comprehensive of his purposes, more appreciative of his success, more indulgent of his shortcomings" than the inappropriate reader he nervously anticipates. Caught as Hawthorne was between the aesthetic need to obscure how narrative communicates the "laws and proprieties" of moral life and his desire to make explicit their truth, Hawthorne directs his attention to an ideal of sympathy as an imperative for both aesthetic and social experience. It becomes a fundamental article of faith, so vigorously insisted upon that the novel may even suffer from Hawthorne's urgent sense of its redemptive powers.[3] If we consult contemporary taste and ask why this novel's appeal has diminished, although it was once his most popular, it may be for the reason that the response Hawthorne wants is but historically conditioned, even as he conceives of it as timeless and transcultural.

Although Hawthorne always fretted over the public's understanding of his work, his years in Europe, especially those in Italy where he trooped from galleries and museums to monuments and cathedrals, quickened his interest in the general question of how art is apprehended and appreciated, how it brings the viewer out of the self and into the artist's sphere. Perhaps surprised by his own reaction to vivid Italian works, Hawthorne found himself increasingly curious about the transaction art achieves. As a result of his immersion in speculations about both the creative and interpretative process, the novel that evolved is replete with travelogue descriptions and meditations on the works he saw.[4] Indeed, part of *The Marble Faun*'s initial success was owed to its guidebook appeal. Like so many other travelers, Hawthorne did not forbear to give his American audience a grand tour, describing the treasures that awaited them while defining the influences that had been exerted on him. By instructing his readers in the merits and subtleties in the works he saw, Hawthorne might have also supposed that he could teach readers how best to respond to his novel.

Less sure of his form, anxious that only the foreign could provide recognizable romance conventions, Hawthorne wished to allay his fears that his powers had diminished or that his audience had forgotten him. So he undertook, by recounting his reflections, to explain how art does not serve to make all clear. In this purpose, he was aided by his assumption that readers would be fairly familiar with the masterpieces he cited, while he could also count on readers' interest in his subject of Americans in Europe and their willingness to have their understanding enlarged. Such readers might be ready to respond to the work's opacities, might be willing to encounter the romance's setting of mystified particulars. Readers could learn, as Hilda explains to Kenyon, that "there is a class of spectators whose sympathy will help them to see the Perfect, through a mist of imperfection. Nobody . . . ought to read poetry, or look at pictures of statues, who cannot find a great deal more in them than the poet or artist actually expressed. Their highest merit is their suggestiveness" (379).

Here Hawthorne uses a conversation about art and reception as an exemplary scene of interpretation to remind readers of their own position in regard to the text. First, he stresses the need for sympathy in discovering the clearest and most complete senses of what the artist "actually expressed." Sympathy penetrates the "mist of imperfection" surrounding a work, the inexactly executed representational details, the lacunae of insufficiently rendered intentions. Sympathy permits the reader or viewer to find "a great deal more," a condition for interpretation that Hawthorne sees as twofold, since it derives from both the lively spiritual kinship a reader may have and from the ways that a text's "suggestiveness" enhances the reader's capacity for sympathy. Thus the respondent is not caught forever in the limitations of the self: a work can mediate between creator and critic, prevailing upon the latter to go beyond merely personal categories, for the "great deal more" is generated through the confrontation with what the artist "actually expressed." Even masterpieces, Hawthorne tells us, require of "the spectator a surrender of himself, in due proportion with the miracle which has been wrought." Like these spectators, readers can also respond by using their "own resources of sensibility and imagination" in "helping out" an artist (335). Respondents contribute their help not out of their own purposes but out of respect for the "miracle" of an artist's fulfilled conception. Sympathy, then, is to be seen as objectifying this "miracle," not transforming it into the interpreter's subject. This "helping out," for Hawthorne, is the collaborative activity of finding a work's most resonant possibilities, most precise attainments of perfection, the fulfillment of a work's suggestiveness, the apprehension of its deepest "secrets."

One painting was particularly suggestive for Hawthorne during his Italian sojourn, so much so that he made the portrait a crucial element in his own work's "mist of imperfection." Among the many transcriptions from his notebooks, Hawthorne copies his impressions from his first as well as "farewell look" at the painting that may have meant the most to him: the Beatrice Cenci once attributed to Guido Reni. Scholars have already described the painting's integral role in the novel's moral and psychological themes, but its relevance to Hawthorne's sense of aesthetic reaction needs to be elaborated, because, as his own response reveals, reception hinges on the sympathetic effort to appropriate a work's secrets of theme, method, and purpose.[5] So overpowering is Hawthorne's reaction to the portrait—"the very saddest painting that ever was painted, or conceived"—that he finds the girl's expression too elusive, "as being humanized by some terrible fate, and gazing at me out of a remote and inaccessible region where she was frightened to be alone, but where no sympathy could reach her."[6] The portrait's unaccountable effect entranced Hawthorne "as if the picture had a life and consciousness of its own, and were resolved not to betray its secret of grief or guilt" (F&IN, 520). But as fascinating as he finds the painting, he notes that he was finally glad to leave it because "it so

perplexed and troubled me not to be able to get hold of its secret"
(F&IN, 521).

The Beatrice's suggestiveness is itself a leitmotif in the novel. For
Hilda, her ability to sympathize with the painting proves her talents
as a copyist; she alone of Italy's legion of imitators can capture its
"vanishing charm of sorrow" (F&IN, 521). For Miriam, not only is the
painting intimately associated with her own past, but through her
"painful sympathy," along with "her passionate wish and struggle to
penetrate poor Beatrice's mystery," she seems, for a moment, to resemble the portrait, whose "secret" hints at Miriam's own. As one
reader has already observed, "the most important function of the
Cenci archetype lies in the portrait itself, which serves as a paradigm
of Hawthorne's own romance art—an art that reveals the secret soul
of (in this case) woman to the perceptive eye."[7]

The painting's affective powers are just as interesting as its thematic implications in that the former show Hawthorne's view that
aesthetic reception is determined by apprehending, or at least acknowledging, the presence of secrets. The circumstances that
cloud the Beatrice's secret were well known in the nineteenth century. As the popular tradition had it, the dark-haired beauty had
been raped by her father, who may have killed her mother, and then
she collaborated in his own murder. The story was made still more
familiar through Shelley's verse drama (1819). The "secret of guilt
or grief" could not, however, be more precisely determined. On first
seeing the portrait, Hawthorne wished that "it were possible for
some spectator, of deep sensibility, to see the figure without knowing anything of its subject of history; for no doubt we bring all our
knowledge of the Cenci tragedy to the interpretation of the picture" (F&IN, 93). The spectator cannot perceive her secret, armed
with the legend. The more one knows about the family history, the
less suggestive, the more demystified, the painting actually is, and
the less sympathy the spectator can bring to bear. Response is
framed within the already-received information; the viewer, aware
of the terms and insufficiently bewildered, is not compelled to
search the painting further or to probe one's reactions more deeply.
When Hawthorne alludes to Miriam's crime as similarly notori-

ous, he keeps that secret undefined, except to observe it as something already a matter of public record. Naming that earlier crime would limit the other characters'—and by analogy, the reader's—sympathetic response. The viewer of the painting, like the reader of the novel, must discern the secret by a "sort of intuition" (F&IN, 92). For Hawthorne, this special power of perception comes from a heightened sense of psychological understanding, one that even engages history, to supply meaning when the sense of the truth is missing.[8]

Hawthorne's conviction that the portrait of this dark lady has some secret to tell is a distinctly literary view—and a commonplace one at that. The idea that a literary work conceals a secret to be learned, as Wolfgang Iser argues, is the dominant form of nineteenth-century reception. Although literary response had always been geared to some extent to the recovery of a message, the nineteenth century observed literature as taking on a "functional importance" in disclosing "solutions" that "religious, social, and scientific systems" could either no longer or not yet provide. At a time when the "hierarchy of thought systems" was not as stable as once it had been, literary representation was now seen as counterbalancing the "increasing complexity and numbers of such systems and the resultant clashes between them." Literature came to be considered as encompassing "all existing theories and explanations" and offering "solutions" wherever other systems flagged. According to Iser,

> It was only natural . . . for readers to seek messages in literature, for fiction could offer them precisely the orientation they felt they needed in view of the problems left behind by the various systems of the age. Carlyle's view that "Literature, as far as it is Literature, is an 'apocalypse of Nature,' a revealing of the 'open secret' " was in no way out of the ordinary. The critic in James's "The Figure in the Carpet" is also in search of the "open secret," and from it can only be the message that will ratify the claim of the book as a work of art.[9]

Although Iser uses the example of James to show the "negation of historical norms" in aesthetic reception, this description of the re-

lation between fiction and secrets points to a plausible, normative
mid-century value for response. One can accede to Iser's broad
claims and still resist the historical line of demarcation he draws
for the beginning of the twentieth century, especially since James
conceived of the "open secret" in "The Figure in the Carpet" as
nothing less than the "Author's secret."[10]

From the beginning, *The Marble Faun* makes vivid the sense
that a work of art has secrets to express, as Hawthorne describes
the effect he wishes to achieve. In the image (that James later dramatically appropriated, transformed, and made famous) of a tapestry, Hawthorne pictured his romance as having threads that readers
should not examine too closely, lest the figure that these threads
create lose its charm.[11] The image is so critical that it comes to
Hawthorne in both the first chapter and the last (before he added
the postscript). Hawthorne's value for charm is both radically subjective and historically conditioned; the implied reader that his
narrative is to shape needs to be alive to both senses. For it is as
charm that Hawthorne conceives of the effect to be wrought upon a
reader: "that state of feeling which is experienced oftenest at
Rome . . . a vague sense of ponderous remembrances . . . that the
present moment is pressed down or crowded out, and our individual affairs and interests are but half as real, here, as elsewhere"
(6). Thus Hawthorne intends that readers submit to a "state of feeling" even as that state is susceptible of being historically animated.
Herein also lies the novel's affinity for the parable, its self-conscious sense of being about fortunate falls and possibilities of grace.
To the extent that parables are the narrative forms that most concentrate the act of simultaneously hinting at and obscuring a secret, while but partially defining how a secret may be appropriated,
they rely on a listener or reader who can bring at once a personal
sense—"a sort of intuition"—and a historically grounded ideal of
interpretation—Christian doctrine, typological convention—that
the narrative strategies excite. In this sense is all of Hawthorne's
fiction twice-told, reverting to history and appealing to or creating
a "mood" for the reader's involvement. Thus the narrative presents
itself as a tapestry "into which are woven some airy and unsub-
stantial threads, intermixed with others, twisted out of the com-

monest stuff of human existence," so that the "evanescent and visionary alike" are knit together. Herein lies Hawthorne's dual sense of the fleeting or ephemeral character of concrete daily experience enmeshed with fantastic or illusory qualities. This intermingling, Hawthorne hoped, would allow the reader to apprehend a text by bringing to it a unifying grasp of both the "commonest stuff" and thoroughly subjective dimensions.

The Italian backdrop of Hawthorne's tapestry, with its exotic senses of mystery and history, then "may not seem so widely different from the texture of our own lives." In this milieu, Hawthorne wanted to find the aura of strangeness that he believed necessary for romance and absent in America where there was "no shadow," "no mystery," "no gloomy wrong" (3). There, scarcely a year before the Civil War, Hawthorne could uncomprehendingly write that only a "commonplace prosperity" abounded, illuminating all that needs to be left implicit and insensible if romance were to flourish. Rome seemed to Hawthorne to resolve his "recurring dilemma between novel and romance" because its picturesqueness and antiquity could combine with its elusive mystery to provide a place where the Actual and the Imaginary might meet, where Hawthorne might make its quality of estrangement seem everyday.[12] Yet for many readers, in the last 130 years, Hawthorne's weaving together the "commonest stuff" and its otherworldly analogue cannot work. "We simply do not believe that . . . any literal reality can satisfy the supernatural requirement Hawthorne has placed on his situation, and we can believe that the terror remains unspeakable only because the author dare not speak lest it evaporate before the breath of reality he cannot make impressive enough. So we never find out the details."[13] Readers never find out the details, just as Hawthorne cannot seize the secret of the Beatrice, because the necessary range of details is precisely what is in question. Readers can examine the historical record only so far before it shrinks, whereupon they must rely on an intuition, one based on the sympathy a secret arouses.[14] While one may argue that in *The Marble Faun* the author gives all too few details, we may also see that by keeping the fundamental facts obscure, Hawthorne means both to raise the reader's subjective faculties of response and to emphasize, since all cannot be told, that real experience is too mysterious, too myriad and complex, intractably resisting the effort to shape it according to one point of view, and that art can and should prove this point.

Fallacious as this may be as a theory of imitation, it aims to engage the reader by activating inferential processes. Hence Hawthorne implores "kindly Readers" not to inspect the "wrong side of the tapestry," for then they would see through the mystifications contrived out of the author's obvious artifices; the romance would lose its spell, its power to charm. Hawthorne asks these "kindly Readers" to "accept" any "brilliant or beautiful, or even tolerable effect" and to resist "tearing the web apart, with the idle purpose of discovering how its threads have been knit together." A narrative, for Hawthorne, is a "fragile handiwork, more easily rent than mended," whether it is "history or romance." The reader must recognize that "the actual experience of even the most ordinary life is full of events that never explain themselves, either as regards their origins or their tendency" (455).

Hawthorne's anxiety of representation is not that readers will "violate" the text, "to tear it, perhaps to change it," as Edgar Dryden writes of examining this tapestry.[15] Hawthorne is less concerned about signification than he is about scrutiny: to inspect the workings of the tapestry (a procedure different from seeking its meaning), Hawthorne fears, is to become too conscious of its technique, in the same way that scrutinizing a sculpture can dissipate its effect by making the viewer too aware of its materials, too comfortable with its contours, less aware of its details, more at ease with its strangeness, and thus less involved in apprehending its secrets. At risk is the objectivity of the object if the viewer sees it as the product of a maker's hand rather than an autonomous signifier. In one of the novel's initial conversations about art, Hilda complains that too long a familiarity with a "beautiful statue" spoils the spectator's inclination to be charmed and transforms a sculpture into "corroded and discolored stone." Kenyon retorts that the same holds true of painting: "It is the spectator's mood that transfigures the Transfiguration itself. I defy any painter to move and elevate me without my consent and assistance" (17). In this context of shaping response, Kenyon and Hilda's perceptions suggest Hawthorne's appeal that readers suspend their rage to know and submit instead to the novelist's romance materials, like the Roman backdrop, in order to feel the work's effect. The reader's "mood" should not be too hastily dismissed as integral to interpretation, for the effective disclosure of secrets, *The Marble Faun* stipulates, requires a willingness to receive them. The eliciting of this willingness proves the artist's power of charm, which is the force of bringing a reader out of the self and into a "communal space."[16]

In winning this consent, in enlisting this assistance, Hawthorne uses the image of the tapestry to suggest how secrets may be learned. As the feature of ordinary life distinguished by its mysteriousness, the secret is bound together with what is known, perhaps in the same way that a tapestry's simple designs are woven into a larger, more elaborate, less traceable pattern. The more closely this pattern is examined, the more difficult does it become to observe the figure's components. As Hilda protests during an argument over Donatello's "faunship" and his wonderful resemblance to the statue: "It annoys me very much . . . this inclination, which most people have to explain away the wonder and mystery out of everything" (104). The penchant to demystify distances the viewer who must instead see a work "with the eye of faith." The sense here is that art reveals its secrets when the spectator's mood appropriately matches the one that the work aims to achieve. The passion to "explain away" the otherness that romance wishes to establish betrays both the work and the viewer. For the "depth and tenderness of . . . sympathy" lie in this "self-surrender" of fixed, prejudiced critical faculties. The "adequate perception" of art, "like all revelations of a better life," requires a "gifted simplicity of vision" (335). When, for example, Kenyon is distressed by Hilda's failure to keep their appointment at the Vatican galleries, he hurries past the "treasures and marvels"; they leave him indifferent. Missing the "delicious sort of mutual aid" which often brings out "the inner mystery of a work of genius," Kenyon sees nothing "he had not seen a thousand times before, and more perfectly than now." Only the Laocoön group impresses the troubled lover; especially for its theme, the "long fierce struggle of man, involved in the knotted entanglement of Errour and Evil." Although the sculptor cannot resist making a critical evaluation to explain why he is moved, Hawthorne tells the reader, "in truth, it was his mood of unwonted despondency that made him so sensitive to the terrible magnificence, as well as to the sad moral of this work" (391–92).

Just as the Pantheon—"the central point of the labyrinthine intricacies of the modern city"—presents itself to the "bewildered stranger, when he is in search of other objects" (456), so may a work of art yield its effect and direct one out of moral complexities when an observer is least aware. When Kenyon, Miriam, and Donatello happen to glance up at the statue of Pope Julius, the "majestic figure" seems to bless the repentant pair: "There is a singular effect . . . when out of the midst of engrossing thought and deep absorption, we suddenly look up, and catch a glimpse of external objects. We seem, at such moments, to look farther and deeper into them, than by any premeditated observation; it is as if they meet our eyes alive and with all their meaning on the surface, but grow again inanimate and inscrutable, the instant they become aware of our glances" (323–24). This description of how one seizes a work's hidden meaning suggests that secrets are to be known by chance, not through hard-headed, clear-eyed inspection. Viewers discover these otherwise undisclosed facets of a work serendipitously, by an even-casual glance propitiously timed. Here Hawthorne's mystifications endow a work of art with a peculiar self-consciousness, one that can be dismantled when taken by surprise, as if the viewer or reader needs to experience an uncanny moment when the work's repressed meanings are exposed. "Premeditated observation" proves futile, for the secrets will not reveal themselves according to our fixed principles of interpretation; the richer experience of art, Hawthorne wants to remind the reader, comes largely by the accident of the reader's psychological, social, historical preparation in meeting a text's potentialities. In the same way, the "peculiar expression" of the Beatrice "eludes a straightforward glance and can only be caught by side glimpses, or when the eye falls upon it casually, as it were, and without thinking to discover anything; as if the picture had a life and consciousness of its own, and were resolved not to betray its secret of guilt or grief, though it wears the full expression of it when it imagines itself unseen" (F&IN, 520).

Fortuitous glimpses and random glances may catch a work of art in expressing its "secret," but these moments of perception are also subject to a reader's or viewer's mood. Response comes from one's readiness and willingness to be surprised; only then does the reader escape the normal, prescribed attitudes that actually discourage the sharing of a secret, in Hawthorne's scheme of reception. Mood makes the interpreter vulnerable, while making a work's secret accessible. And once a reader learns the secret infusing a work, the secret convictions in one's own haunted mind are brought closer to articulation; their resistance to suppression is more forcefully provoked.

In social experience, this uncanny revelation of secrets also results from an element of surprise. Even the spoken word, like a chance look, can create an effect, however inadvertent, that reveals the presence of a secret:

> Nothing is more unaccountable than the spell that often lurks in a spoken word. A thought may be present to the mind, so distinctly that no utterance could make it more so; and two minds may be conscious of the same thought, in which one or both take the profoundest interest; but as long as it remains unspoken, their familiar talk flows quietly over the hidden idea, as a rivulet may sparkle and dimple over something sunken in its bed. But, speak the word; and it is like bringing up a drowned body out of the deepest pool of the rivulet, which has been aware of the horrible secret, all along, in spite of its smiling surface. (228–29)

The "smiling surface" of social life, like the polish of a text, covers the world of secrets, drowned bodies (like Zenobia's) which can even gruesomely emerge to break the surface clarity, coherence, and purport of experience or a text. The residual evidence of secret crime or sin or agony—the drowned body—returns, needing only a mild pressure to claim a reader's attention. When Kenyon speaks Miriam's name, it throws Donatello into a "ghastly emotion" and reminds him of the secret he shares with her. As he has just informed the sculptor who wants to carve his bust: "You may take me if you have the power . . . and if you can see what makes me shrink from you, you are welcome to put it into the bust. It is not my will, but my necessity to avoid men's eyes." Donatello's "anger or terrour" is as much having heard Miriam's name unexpectedly from someone's lips as it is the fear of having his "horrible secret" found out, captured through Kenyon's art. Kenyon's reference to her (and her failure to uncover the Count's ear, with all the symbolic weight that this detail bears) recalls the horror of his crime, as Kenyon momentarily portrays it in plaster molding.

For Hawthorne, art reveals such secrets, but they can be known only through "side glimpses," random apprehensions. His early notebook entries attest to his conviction that the artist even casually finds mysteries inhering in ordinary life and that the business of the artist is to take this latency by surprise. Whether the artist chances to conceive of making literal pictures out of figurative expressions or fancifully observes a town's business from the point of view of a water pump, common experience can be transformed into something fantastic and thus made to unveil the secrets it bids the artist to seize.[17] Art distinguishes and discloses the mysterious, the otherworldly senses suffusing literal life and, in turn, makes these senses alive to someone else, if the reader's mood, at its most suggestible, is brought into sympathy with the writer's. To this purpose, Rome seemed to Hawthorne a particularly suitable setting. Not only did the novelist find a world "naturally invested with an atmosphere half-mysterious but definitely real . . . a world in which time—eternity, the past, the present—was manifest and observable," but he also could use its rich tradition of art: "in choosing the most famous, the most conventional, the most frequently discussed objects, he was choosing things that were already both actual and romantic, that, because of their traditional connotations, existed in both the real world and Faery land."[18]

Throughout The Marble Faun, secrets are woven into the tapestry of its narrative. Whether Hawthorne records the speculations over Miriam's antecedents or the notion of her relation to the model or Donatello's heritage—even the "secret" of his family's powerfully intoxicating wine—the writer offers plausible interpretations as if to suggest that such secrets need not have murky causes but merely follow from a lack of hard evidence to explain their apparent mystery. Hawthorne gives commonsensical reasons to compete with the mysterious ones he has prompted. The seemingly plausible understanding, however, is never verified as likelier than the interpretations that the characters assign. Instead, the effect of a weakly demystifying account emphasizes that the Actual and the Imaginary are always commingled. Hawthorne leaves open whether Miriam's crime is really as dark as incest and murder; the model need not be the monk of Memmius's legend but may be a beggar, a common thief, or a crazy person; Donatello's forebears may have been a "merry and kindly race of people," not fauns; the "secret" of their quick extinction may have been nothing more puzzling than the fault of the air at Monte Beni; the wine itself loses its secret appeal, becomes "disenchanted both of its fragrance and flavor," if lingered over too long or drunk too carelessly.

By presenting commonplace rationales, even as he holds out the possibility of romantic ones, Hawthorne elaborates the formula of alternatives and invokes the reader's capacity for wonder. Then the reader can experience the confusion between explicable life and its secrets. Hawthorne intends to create a mood wherein readers can be their most apprehensive and thus most capable of seeing through the screen that ordinary life imposes: "At no time are people so sedulously careful to keep their trifling appointments, attend to their ordinary occupations, and thus put a common-place aspect on life, as when conscious of some secret that, if suspected, would make them look monstrous in the general eye. Yet how tame and wearisome is the impression of ordinary things, in contrast with such a face!" (178). The contrast that a secret reveals between the ordinary and the mysterious is the very impression Hawthorne wishes to leave, the effect to establish, the mood to impart. Under such influences, readers will grasp what is "implicitly and insensibly" true, while they relinquish the need to guess, in a way analogous to Hilda's final acceptance of ambiguity as a fundamental condition of moral experience.

By exploiting what is undisclosed, Hawthorne enlivens his sense that the secret itself is less telling than the transformations it generates. Each character, we see, is meant to undergo a process of moral change, and, except for Kenyon's, this process is stimulated by keeping some kind of secret. These transformations coalesce to form the novel's process of resolution, as the secrets that can come to light do, even as the secrets that cannot, like the final assignment of guilt, do not. Hawthorne keeps such details obscure rather than invent ways of exposing them because their opacity allows the characters at once to seem ordinary enough that the reader may sympathize with their circumstances, yet different enough that readers can escape a certain narcissism and extend their sympathy to include the characters' transformations. Thus sympathy operates dynamically: it begins as an approximate identification and can still be exercised to bring readers into an even finer sense of their identities.[19] For readers to make this leap of sympathy, their own moral imaginations need not be fixed on the differentiae—the secret, individuating facts about the characters. To sympathize most intimately, readers need to see the characters' experience as both generalizable and analogous to their own. In effecting this analogy between the characters' moral issues and the lessons that readers are to learn, Hawthorne did not feel as confident as did such Victorian contemporaries as Dickens or Thackeray in assuming a shared ground of social particulars with his reader.[20] Justified or not in this conviction, he turns to a particularity of references that he could safely assume: he at least felt assured that readers shared the genteel attitudes toward the artworks he describes as part of the novel's guidebook attractions. Through this schema, Hawthorne makes aesthetic experience play the prominent role of instructing his readers in moral experience. While this imposing of aesthetic experience over moral issues has seemed too loose a fit for the novel's formalist readers, we may also see that, for Hawthorne, the rift between art and life is exactly what he means to narrow.

The dualistic opposition between aesthetic and moral concerns is resolved through sympathy, a resolution resulting from the efficacy with which sympathy can secure a secret or prepare a reader to be surprised, having been immersed (Hawthorne hoped) in the life of mystery and consciousness of guilt that Rome would provide. Drawing from the characters' conversations about art, their reflections on the hidden implications of a painting or a statue, absorbing Hawthorne's interests in the artworks he sees, readers can submit to the novel's treatment of aesthetic experience, familiar as they are made, with the necessary mood for appreciation. Through this kind of reciprocating apprehension, readers may also learn of their own moral lives, for when Hawthorne calls his novel a tapestry, asking readers to dispense with their usual sense of how narrative unfolds, he asks that they turn away from inspecting the individual pattern and toward beholding the entirety. If the resolutions seem nominal or contrived—the effect of the spell, lost—perhaps the moral imagination that Hawthorne asks of his readers does not provide a rationale to reward any reader's indulgence, except to stress the depth of the Count's fall. Similarly, Hilda's willful vision of innocent hopefulness in the face of unanswered, unanswerable moral questions may too closely resemble Hawthorne's contemporaneous readers' normal, unextended views. Nor does Hilda's vision seem to justify the novel's premeditated indeterminacy. Requiring the readers to further their sympathy seems to gain them no deeper knowledge of moral questions.[21]

Hawthorne's insistence on the ultimate unknowableness of some secrets, in art and life, ought not to be peremptorily explained away as an effort to import mystery where there need be none or to offer "vague Gothic elements which remind us of unspeakable and unholy terror."[22] Like the vision of moral clarity at the end of Seven Gables, the optimism at the close of The Marble Faun represents the force of Hawthorne's faith in the power of sympathy to approach the necessary secrets. Edgar Dryden suggests that here, as at the end of Seven Gables, the enchantment of love is substituted for an "unequivocal interpretation of the novel's meaning."[23] Yet we must also suppose that an "unequivocal interpretation" would break the spell that Hawthorne then says is the measure of the book's success. The author's declining to offer his own conclusive reading, however, does not necessarily amount to encouraging interpretations to proliferate or to making the novel a de-historicized exemplum of interpretation.[24]

In leaving key facts indeterminate, Hawthorne means to prod the reader's unpursued possibilities of understanding. Thus he explains Miriam's confession of the "terrible event" in her past, the "frightful and mysterious circumstances of which will recur to many minds, but of which few or none could have found for themselves a satisfactory explanation" (431). Hawthorne implies, then, that even if we knew all the facts, we would not know any more precisely what to do with them. A "satisfactory explanation," like an "unequivocal interpretation," is elusive, and not merely because the necessary details cannot be known, since readers are also unable to make comprehensible all the senses of the facts that they do know. Even as the "mysterious circumstances" remain opaque, their lesson for the reader need not be obscure: "It only concerns the present narrative, inasmuch as the suspicion of being at least an accomplice in the crime fell darkly and directly upon Miriam herself." While it makes a great deal of difference whether, in fact, Miriam is guilty of some horrendous misdeed in the past, her culpability is not really the issue at this point. That she is implicated in a notorious crime, no longer under the protection of social codes demanding that a woman act to avoid the suggestion of misconduct, ensures the potency of the reference and galvanizes a range of associations quite beyond local sources or temporal references. The reader, then and now, may bring a more general notion of infamous crimes in response to the aspersions made against Miriam and her role in "one of the most dreadful and mysterious events that have occurred in the present century" (467).[25] Hawthorne alludes here to the Praslin murder case, but whether readers get this clue and use their knowledge of that scandal to fill in the blanks that Hawthorne leaves is not so much the point as is the author's raising an everyday reference of a dreadful mystery. Just as Hawthorne could presume that his readers would be familiar with particular artworks, so could he also suppose that the reader, like Kenyon, would "most assuredly remember" at least the "nature of the troubles." Here Hawthorne might be having some sort of joke, in the conceivably exaggerated sense of expecting readers to have the command of details surrounding the case. So Hawthorne strengthens the analogy between the characters' experience and the readers' by emphasizing the mysterious aspect intrinsic to ordinary reality and by reminding readers how the "commonest stuff" is interwoven with the things which, literally, cannot be known, though they may be approximately educed. The reference to Miriam's past, then, is not some key by which perfect sense can be made of her career; rather than guide the reader to hidden meaning, the allusion signifies that the "nature of the troubles," not the details, can satisfactorily explain, even if this is not the satisfaction of an "unequivocal interpretation." The secret itself is less important than the reality of moral experience to which it points.

Again and again in the novel Hawthorne states explicitly the moral and social cost of merely being implicated in guilt. These consequences may have resulted from "no crime," but from "only one of those fatalities which are among the most insoluble riddles propounded to our mortal comprehension; the fatal decree by which every crime is made to be the agony of many innocent persons, as well as the single guilty one" (93). One's association with guilt-provoking "fatalities" need not be direct or intimate. Instead, "many innocent persons" are entangled in a crime's implications, while the network created is both complex and involving. Innocence exists only beyond the horizon of guilt, Hawthorne suggests. The fact of mere being is, in a sense, a "fatal decree," one that makes innocent bystanders and impartial observers part of the "insoluble riddle" of human responsibility and culpability. Although here Hawthorne resists an easy, universalized sense of complicity, the answer to the riddle can be seen later in Hilda's own tacit, if unwilling, sympathetic partnership with the "agony" of the criminal. To this extent, Hawthorne implies, human beings are always the accessories in any crime, if only after the fact.

This sense of being implicated is especially telling for the narrative framework in which Hawthorne involves the reader. For Hawthorne, the "actor" in "some specific misfortune" or "great crime" becomes an "alien in the world" who "interposes a wholly unsympathetic medium betwixt himself and those whom he yearns to meet." One may wish to suppose that these remarks resonate with the guilt of a father and husband who feels intensely the sorrow of having endangered his child and wife by exposing them to an unhealthy Italian climate.[26] Or the remarks might express the guilt of an author who interposes himself between his text and its readers, "those whom he yearns to meet," by making his work into the "unsympathetic medium" of a willfully obscured narrative. In either case, Hawthorne tries to overcome the resulting "moral estrangement" that a writer suffers in relation to a projected audience by creating still another fiction.

The "actor" in "some specific misfortune" or "great crime" communicates his secret of guilt or innocence in "but a few vague whisperings," of which the narrator can only report the substance. Hawthorne's special fondness for this image should not obscure the recognition that such whispering is the conventional voice for the confiding of secrets. Because these "mystic utterances" in themselves offer no coherent story, the writer-reporter must try to bring them together as a "continuous scene." Thus Hawthorne recurs to a fundamental fiction of himself as an artist: he who recovers and refurbishes the fragmentary evidence, thereby telling a tale, as for the second time, through an imaginative, though perhaps inaccurate, recasting. In this, creating a narrative is likened to "a task resembling in its perplexity that of gathering up and piecing together the fragments of a letter which has been torn and scattered to the winds." For Hawthorne, the ramifications of this undertaking cast doubt on the very enterprise of mimetic story telling: "Many words of deep significance—many entire sentences, and those possibly the most important ones—have flown too far on the winged breeze to be recovered. If we insert our own conjectural amendments, we perhaps give a purport utterly at variance with the true one. Yet, unless we attempt something, in this way, there must remain an unsightly gap, and a lack of continuousness and dependence in our narrative" (92–93).

The writer offers his experience of piecing together meaning out of the irrecoverable and cautions the reader that the "purport" may not match the original letter-writer's intentions. On one hand, this posture is akin to the pose of being the editor of *The Scarlet Letter*, a playful disavowing of real authorship and true authority; on the other, this description of his method is Hawthorne's justifying of a problematic omniscience: everything that can be known is known, but not everything can be known. The "conjectural amendments" are made to avert discontinuity and to overcome the indeterminate or secret. First compared to a tapestry of "fragile handiwork," suggesting a unity and coherence between components and the sum, narrative is redefined as disunified and discontinuous, an incompletely reassembled letter, made up of torn and scattered fragments that need to be reconstituted through conjectures. Fearing an "unsightly gap," longing for the completeness and continuity that missing sentences and words—"possibly the most important"—would provide, the writer creates fictions, interpretative acts of conjecture, to sustain perhaps both sequence of event and logical "dependence" of cause and effect. As Frank Kermode explains this demand for narrative continuity, "a passion for sequence may result in the suppression of a secret."[27] Hawthorne's description of creating narratives out of previously written texts now in irremediable disarray, however, stipulates that out of a fear of discontinuity, the writer make some "amendment" through which a secret may be learned. This amendment comes from the writer's own sympathetic reading of a supposed story, which, in the image of this example, is likened to the act of writing itself. Thus Hawthorne means to combine both his anxieties about his fiction as letters to the world, which never get received intact, and his commitment to fiction as defying the illusion of a continuous, directly observable world, where all secrets, motives, or explanatory details can be learned. "An unsightly gap" is the rift between experience and report wherein secrets remain.

Yet for all the deconstructive possibilities to be gleaned from this image of writing, consider also the rhetoric of signification at work: only "possibly" are the missing elements the "most important"; conceivably, they are not. In that possibility does Hawthorne validate the conviction that only the little we do know of reality, imbued as it is with the coloration of the Imaginary, counts. If "perhaps" the "purport" is at "variance" with the "true" meaning of the letter, then conceivably, the reconstructed version really matches the original missive. Consider also the strength of "unless" the writer "attempt something, in this way" as a condition rather than an imperative for overcoming the fear of aporia—the unsightly gaps—which the act of imaginative reconstruction assuages. The letter serves as a metonymy for the act of reaching an audience, an act that Hawthorne fears will be interrupted or interfered with. Yet even as the image of the patched-up letter may be a self-consuming one, revealing Hawthorne's anxiety over completing a correspondence, his own retreat from an "intercourse with the world," it also remains an image of artifice rather than the literal activity it seems to reflect—a metonymy superimposed upon a metaphor. Redoubling its effect, the letter-as-image for writing further indicates how the effort to create a seemingly seamless narrative risks, compromises, and falsifies the writer's acknowledging of secrets, like that of the suspect who does not speak out but who can only communicate a secret through a "few vague whisperings."

While the description of reconstructing a destroyed letter discloses the writer's response to the anxiety-provoking "lack of continuance and dependence in our narrative," perhaps just as important is it also an image of the reader's function. To whom was the fictive letter originally addressed? Who has torn it up? Why must the writer put it back together again? Hawthorne's image of the writer suggests how writers are inevitably readers, even if readers are not generally writers. The "conjectural amendments" that he makes signal the reader's response, as Hawthorne wants to shape it, to a world of intrinsic mystery. Hawthorne provides a model for readers to reassemble, out of their own imaginations, a writer's purposes, if only to apprehend what has been omitted or, at least, to recognize that the omitted, the indeterminate, the unacknowledged, the destroyed, the hidden, the lost, are less an issue than the narrative strategies which a secret excites. Hawthorne, we see, takes up both positions: literally, the fearful author of a text that may not reach its audience, and figuratively, the reader whose text has been interfered with or impaired. In this dual image, Hawthorne suggests that divergent as are the reader's and writer's tasks of correspondence, they are also conjugate. Readers follow an author's "conjectural amendments" which also structure their own.

These amendments are presented, as they are about Miriam's secret relation to the model, in order to overcome the "chill remoteness of [alienated beings'] positions" beyond the reach of sympathy. Unlike the friends who withdraw from Miriam, readers must extend their sympathy, according to Hawthorne, so that they may meet an "alien in the world," that they may come to know the image of their otherness. For dogged as Miriam is by this "sinister personage," she grows so removed from Hilda and Kenyon's sphere that she can only hint "at an intangible confession, such as persons with overburthened hearts often make to children or dumb animals, or to holes in the earth, where they think their secrets may be at once revealed and buried" (65). But if Miriam's distance now, like Parson Hooper's, precludes the very gesture of sympathy that she needs, and if the extremity of her remoteness discourages Kenyon when Miriam seeks his "brotherly counsel," Hawthorne means for readers to learn from the benefit of Kenyon's bad example and to exercise their sympathy for her plight.

To this purpose, Hawthorne provides the reader with an example of the relation between the need to confess a secret and the desire for sympathetic response. This model takes the dramatic form of Miriam's meeting with Kenyon at his studio, a scene mediated through her reaction to his Cleopatra, so that rhetorical transaction is part of the scene's vividness. In a restless and melancholy mood, Miriam visits Kenyon, whose sculpture of Cleopatra, and the secrets of female psychology it supposedly captures, encourages Miriam's passionate identification with the African queen and excites her to share her secret with its creator. The sculpture mixes up femininity with "all those seemingly discordant elements" of womanhood and renders a wholly complex Romantic figure of a female: the "secret" of its composition lies in Kenyon's grasping the exotic "shadow of darkness and evil" rather than the sunny goodness of his beloved Hilda. Such moral understanding as infuses the Cleopatra works like a spell on Miriam and incites her to cry out for sympathy: " 'Oh, my friend,' she cried, with sudden passion, 'will you be my friend indeed? I am lonely, lonely, lonely! There is a secret in my heart that burns me!—that tortures me! Sometimes, I fear to go mad of it! Sometimes, I hope to die of it!

But neither of the two happens. Ah, if I could but whisper it to only one human soul! And you—you see far into womanhood! You receive it widely into your large view! Perhaps—perhaps—but Heaven only knows—you might understand me! Oh, let me speak!' " (128).

Kenyon's reluctance to sympathize results from his fear that he might thus have to hear the girl's confession. First he tells himself that he is merely observing the conventions of friendship. But the "reserve and alarm" that Miriam notices really protect him from sanctioning the personal tie that the distraught Miriam yearns for: "The more her secret struggled and fought to be told, the more certain would it be to change all former relations that had subsisted between herself and the friend to whom she might reveal it. Unless he could give her all the sympathy, and just the kind of sympathy, that the occasion required, Miriam would hate him, by-and-by, and herself still more, if he would let her speak" (129). Unprepared as he is to meet her "pent-up heart," when Kenyon does offer his sympathy, he is rebuked for his insincerity and unresponsiveness, "cold and pitiless as [his] own marble."

The details of Chapter Fourteen, "Cleopatra," are so telling that the circumstances of this conversation encapsulate the novel's treatment of moral, social, and aesthetic experience. Miriam's response to the Cleopatra—"fierce, voluptuous, passionate, tender, wicked, terrible, and full of poisonous and rapturous enchantment"—quickens her desire to confess, especially as she now perceives the sculptor to understand a woman's moral burdens. The spell that the sculpture casts makes her want to confess and leads her to compare herself to Hilda, although she has scarcely any of the copyist's "ethereal" qualities. Moved as Miriam is by the Cleopatra's expression of "profound, gloomy, heavily revolving thought," viewing the sculpture occasions "a glance into her past life and present emergencies." Even in the anger of her disappointment, Miriam still wishes to convince Kenyon of her innocence: "You can do nothing for me, unless you petrify me into a marble companion for your Cleopatra there; and I am not of her sisterhood, I do assure you." For to be of her sisterhood, Miriam fantasizes, is perhaps to try to "overcome [Kenyon] with her fury or her love? Were you not afraid to touch her, as she grew more and more towards hot life beneath your hand?" Even if one discounts the sensuality obviously suffused in her questions, Miriam's later recognition of the inappropriateness of her appeal cannot be dismissed. Asking for too much sympathy, or the wrong kind, from a friend is an inappropriate appeal, "Unless I had his heart for my own, (and that is Hilda's, nor would I steal it from her,) it should never be the treasure-place of my secret." When Miriam detects Kenyon's reluctance, his hesitancy thwarts her desire to share her secret, "the gush of passion that was thus turned back upon her." Her rejoinder then is that instead of the man of feeling for whom she momentarily mistakes him—under the spell of his production, in the urgency of her mood—the sculptor is only good for making statues, plaster casts of passion. The spell of art wanes; marble returns to stone and no longer seems like flesh.

Art's enchantment urges Miriam to confide her secret, but this mood is too weakly reciprocated. Kenyon cannot or refuses to respond in kind because, "conscious of it or no," he knows he does not love her. Frightened, as perhaps anyone would be, to take up the burden that Miriam would present him, he falters into conventional expressions of friendship whose sympathy cannot bridge the distance Miriam yearns to close. In spite of the artistry that permits him to create his Cleopatra—"I know not how it came about at last. I kindled a great fire in my mind, and threw in the material"—he cannot yet sympathize with the living embodiment of the female psychology he has just rendered concrete. Although he is clearly attracted to Miriam, Kenyon is forbidden by temperament and by the socially conventional choice between a dark and fair heroine of romance to provide the sympathy that Miriam demands. Just as Coverdale cannot provide the sympathy for Zenobia in an almost identical exchange, Kenyon reacts with "reserve and alarm" out of the justifiable fear that Miriam demands too much, a fear that also answers to his own squeamishness. It is, however, more than a matter of decorum that secrets are to be expressed, without being openly stated: Hawthorne's self-deprecating jokes about boring the reader of the prefaces by being too personal remind us that one must rely on another's "apprehensive sympathy."

The reader must sympathize, but it is the writer's task to win that response by being subtle, not excessive. In the face of any normal human limitation, the conditions that Miriam places on her confession ensure her failure, and Kenyon's. Just as Miriam's murderous intent is later communicated to Donatello in a glance, so too is conveyed Kenyon's want of sympathy that seems to kill: "Obscure as it was, when Miriam looked into [Kenyon's] eyes, she detected it there at once" (129).

In this failure of sympathy by which Hawthorne obstructs the disclosure of Miriam's secret, an analogy between Kenyon and the reader must also be drawn: like the sculptor, the reader has not yet been prepared to understand the moral lesson of being implicated in universal guilt, as Hawthorne later notes of Kenyon's response to the Laocoön. Once under the influence of Hawthorne's Cleopatra—the image of the overwrought but defiant Miriam—the reader may begin to see that sympathetic apprehension is not merely the business of lovers but the interpretative temperament that permits a friend to hear confessions. Then the reader might be, as Hawthorne wished in the preface, "that one congenial friend . . . closer and kinder than a brother," "that friend of friends," "that unseen brother of the soul" (1, 2). First presenting in Miriam's aesthetic response a model of how to experience a work of art, Hawthorne then provides a model of how not to respond to a friend's "pent-up heart."

■ The tragic effect, in this novel, of Kenyon's hesitant moment is that Miriam's secret remains undisclosed and thus precipitates the dire events which follow, though it also predicates the supposedly redemptive process of moral transformation that Hilda undergoes. As in *The Scarlet Letter*, *Seven Gables*, and *The Blithedale Romance*, an obstructed confession sustains the spell that a secret conjures, under which the reader learns the novel's moral lessons. Once aborted or deflected, these incomplete confessions figure as Hawthorne's means of keeping constant the air of enchantment or spell that a secret provokes. Dimmesdale's partial confession, Holgrave's interpolated tale, Coverdale's address to a bird, are all concerned to uphold the conviction that, left unsaid, a secret can promulgate the aura of mystery. In *The Marble Faun*, this spell works its effect from the beginning: Hawthorne's treatment of Miriam's secret exemplifies the privileged status of mystery in the plot and serves to instruct the reader in apprehending how to live with "insoluble riddles."

This secret is first suggested when the company puzzles over the riddle of Donatello's startling resemblance to the Faun of Praxiteles. So removed is the young count from their ordinary experience that he does not even know his own age, an unselfconsciousness that prompts Miriam to wish for an equal state of ignorance or, at least, "to forget one day of all my life" (15). First by having Miriam mitigate the remark, then by disparaging her sincerity in calling the comment the kind of talk *artistes* will make "between jest and earnest," Hawthorne calls attention very early to Miriam's burdensome secret. The reader soon learns also that there is an "ambiguity" about this dark heroine which ensures her acceptance in Rome though it would exclude her elsewhere. Thus substantiating the appropriateness of the setting as a place where mystery flourishes and is even welcomed, Hawthorne then offers both commonplace and fantastic speculations, neither of which adequately fixes the cause of the young woman's shadowy circumstances, only to conclude that she was "plucked up out of a mystery, and had its roots still clinging to her" (23).

These roots become visible when the specter appears, personifying the secret of her past. The model himself articulates his mysterious connection to her: "She came to me when I sought her not. She has called me forth, and must abide the consequences of my reappearance in the world" (31). Whether he is regarded as the image of unregenerate sin that the legend of Memmius suggests or as the "return of the repressed," the model's grip on Miriam is so powerful that the reader sees her—even when the characters cannot—kneeling to him in supplication. He is, in one critic's judgment, the "ultimate portmanteau figure who combines Hawthorne's cognate interests in myth and psychology. In him the notion of a shadowy racial memory glides imperceptibly into Miriam's own 'subterranean reminiscences,' uniting to form the single idea of that dark interior world of primitive consciousness which inspires both nightmare and art. No more, it is frequently suggested, than a creation of Miriam's own brooding imagination, the model is somehow responsible for her initiation into both unspeakable sexual knowledge and the secrets of her craft."[28]

Furthermore, he is the model to be executed—in both senses of the phrase—as another reader has put it.[29] The embodiment of mystery, the model glides through the centuries as he seems to slip through the streets of Rome, making his appearance by surprise, or whim, or compulsion. In this exotic city, he is the still-stronger counterpoint to ordinary reality and inspires "monstrous fictions" that observers supply to account for his hold on Miriam. His very presence requires interpretative acts of a fabricating imagination to subdue the threat he implies. The monstrosity of the readings, in turn, reflects the horror that the spectators perceive in his relation to Miriam. Readers also become engaged in this process of interpreting this clandestine relation because they must then interpret Miriam's "wilder fables" that she offers in "explanation of the mystery" (33).

While Miriam's "romantic fantasies" portend a "disastrous result from her connection with her ill-omened attendant," they are offered to forestall her confidants' curiosity as well as to express her own anxiety. Under the cover of their "melancholy sort of playfulness," they suggest Miriam's own secret. In the two versions, seemingly plausible pacts result in completely improbable outcomes beyond "any which German ingenuity or Italian superstition had contrived." These fairy tales are concerned to put the mystery within the scope of ordinary experience: in the first, the model promises to teach Miriam a "long lost but invaluable secret of old Roman fresco-painting," which would place Miriam at the "head of modern art." This Faustian agreement is sealed by the artist's pledge to "return with him to sightless gloom." In the second, Miriam offers a "soberer" account that changes the secret from art to religion. She and the model wrestle in a controversy over Christian faith, in which Miriam "had even staked her own salvation." As if to lessen the importance of these allegories, which are Hawthorne's own "monstrous fictions," the author intercedes by suggesting that there really is "no demand for so much rumor and speculation," that the relation can be explained "without going many steps beyond the limits of probability." Readers might accept instead the altogether pedestrian interpretation that the model has no connection with her past and might be some beggar or criminal or, as Miriam later admits, lunatic. Yet in its suggestion that no secret exists, this too-reasonable interpretation cannot execute the model, cannot dispel his power, except by a representation so insistently literal that the force he seems to wield disintegrates. If there were no secret, or if its nature could be so plausibly determined, the model would no longer be the other—the monstrous aspect of the self that continues to resurface in society and that realistic representation tries to make tame.[30]

Romantic fables as they are, Miriam's explanations reveal how secrets communicate Hawthorne's combined value for artistic achievement, social conduct, and moral transformation. The human figure whose very presence implies Miriam's secret knows the infallible formula, otherwise hidden from the uninitiated, that could establish the painter's prowess and fame. Here Hawthorne asserts his characteristic sense of an artist's search for the deepest secret to his or her craft, for once Miriam possesses the prescription, she (like Owen Warland of "The Artist of the Beautiful") can produce the truly rarefied: "the most beautiful and lovely designs" for frescoes. This chance to win the otherwise ungraspable is worth the risk of "sightless gloom," especially since the secret is to be plied for spiritual instruction. As Hawthorne later observes of the Sodoma fresco at Siena: "This hallowed work of genius shows what pictorial art, devoutly exercised, might effect in behalf of religious truth; involving . . . deeper mysteries of Revelation, and bringing them closer to man's heart, and making him tenderer to be impressed by them, than the most eloquent words of preacher or prophet" (340). In Miriam's account, the artist, having learned the secret of seeing, must give up vision and resign oneself to despair, as if the achievement of "unrivalled excellence" is the devil's bargain. The knowledge of this secret power of sight, paradoxically, results in blindness. Elevating as this vision may be, so also is it debasing or incriminating.

The duality that this secret supports is emphasized again in Miriam's second account. There she prophesies that she must return to the catacombs if she loses her religious debate with the "Man-Demon." This fable subordinates any allegory of the artist to one of Hawthorne's fundamental human situations, the state of the soul. For implied in Miriam's secret connection to the model is the question of whether the soul can prevail once it is encumbered with doubt. Like Young Goodman Brown, Miriam becomes engaged, through her own imagining, in a controversy over the value of faith; and if Christian faith is defeated, Miriam must again bid "an eternal farewell to the sun," including the light of God's grace. Once doubt supplants faith, as Kenyon dares later only to suggest and must quickly deny, sin becomes socialized and no longer seems "such a dreadful blackness in the universe" but "merely an element of human education." Miriam's failure to convert the "old infidel" means her return to "penal gloom," as she describes to Hilda her fears that the model will triumph. Here it is critical to recognize, however, the duality made psychologically appropriate in this address to the copyist. Miriam's account is told to the one person who has yet to experience a secular perception of guilt; as the figure completely committed to Christian faith, though at this point untested, Hilda personifies virtue beyond question. From this exchange, the reader can infer that Miriam, without such virtue, cannot persuade the model out of his "errors" because he personifies her own secret lack of faith.

These fables suggest how Miriam's secret stimulates fictions which also define the problems of artistic achievement and moral transformation that structure *The Marble Faun*. Just as Hawthorne's final resolutions seem insubstantial, so these fail to convince Miriam's confidants. Nor do they disburden her of her secret. Their effect is to leave her in a "brooding melancholy" and "moody passion." Although her "morbid symptoms" are "generously interpreted" by Hilda and Kenyon as having "sufficient cause in the stimulating and exhaustive influences of imaginative art," especially practiced in Rome, such an interpretation can explain neither the model's influence nor the stories' effect upon the young painter. As the naive Donatello perceives by "one of those instructive, unreasoning antipathies . . . which generally prove more trustworthy than the acutest insight into character" (36), Miriam's trouble lies in the "shadow of her model"—her secret. In the next chapter Hawthorne will hint that this secret may be related to the "mysterious force" of the Cenci portrait, but whether her secret is one of incest or murder, sexuality or complicity, doubt or pride, such guesses are less important than its actual presence and fiction-making function. And Donatello's response demonstrates that, however generously her friends interpret Miriam's plight, however plausibly the narrator accounts for her secret, the secret still works its spell.

The analogy between the characters' responses and the reader's underlines the importance of sympathy. As in the example of Kenyon's reluctance, the confession of a secret not met with sympathy can lead to tragedy. Hilda and Kenyon inadequately account for Miriam's profound depression; Donatello's ingenuous ill-will is too much the lover's hatred to recognize her despair. None of these responses raise the moral awareness of the agent. In spite of the easy intimacy among the artists, Hilda and Kenyon sympathize with Miriam's plight up to the point at which they can disengage themselves from her despondency, as their later reactions show. Donatello's animal fidelity, which unleashes his antipathy, merely shows that "he was of a nature so remarkably genial and joyous, so simply happy, that he might well afford to have something subtracted from his comfort, and make tolerable shift to live upon what remained." His involvement here begins and ends while his own happiness is at stake. He cannot yet respond out of a complex moral awareness because he has not yet sinned or repented. At this early juncture, neither form of response can be sympathetic enough. As Hilda later learns when she endures her own "terrible secret" of knowing about the murder: "It was that dismal certainty of the existence of evil in the world, which (though we may fancy ourselves fully assured of the sad mystery, long before) never becomes a portion of our practical belief until it takes substance and reality from the sin of some guide, whom we have deeply trusted and revered, or some friend whom we have dearly loved" (328).

In the sense that only those with their own "hideous secret," like

Parson Hooper or Hester Prynne, can recognize and sympathize with the hidden misery of others, the reader too must be brought to sympathy and, to do so, must follow and surpass the example of the characters. Hilda's transformation from self-righteous prudishness to prudent righteousness directly results from her growing understanding of her participation in others' guilt. Her knowledge of the murder weighs so heavily upon her that she becomes, in her own eyes, as guilty as Miriam or Donatello. "To this innocent and tender girl, holding the knowledge was almost the same as if she had participated in the guilt. . . . she felt her own spotlessness impugned" (329). To the degree that Hilda is transformed, her moral education results from the "dreadful secret" of knowing evil in her own life and of "partaking the human nature of those who could perpetrate such deeds." This understanding brings the copyist to sympathy with Miriam, just as Miriam is brought to sympathy with Donatello. The painter's, however, is the less vicariously learned. When Kenyon informs her that the pained and bewildered Donatello is undergoing "a wonderful process" of achieving moral complexity, Miriam avows her personal responsibility for his education: "Who else can perform the task? Who else has the tender sympathy which he requires? Who else, save only me—a woman, a sharer in the same dread secret, a partaker in one identical guilt— could meet him on such terms of intimate equality as the case demands? With this object before me, I might feel a right to live! Without it, it is a shame for me to have lived so long!" (282–83).

Isolated as Hilda feels, swearing that she will "perish under this terrible secret," her transformation is not complete until she communicates the terror that her new knowledge has wrought upon her. She longs for the sympathy to help her say it: "Had there been but a single friend—or not a friend since friends were no longer to be confided in, after Miriam had betrayed her trust—but, had there been any calm, wise mind, any sympathizing intelligence, or, if not these, any dull, half-listening ear into which she might have flung the dreadful secret, as into an echoless cavern—what a relief would have ensued!" (329). So completely does her secret lead her to withdraw into the self and so pronounced is her own need for sympathy that Hilda loses the "depth and tenderness of sympathy" on which

her excellent copying depended. When art no longer yields its secrets to her, she loses her reverence for it: "Heretofore, her sympathy went deeply into a picture, yet seemed to have a depth which it
was inadequate to sound; . . . Not that she gave up all Art as worthless; only, it had lost its consecration" (341). In her "awful loneliness," in such "great need of sympathy" as she hoped to find in
Kenyon, Hilda turns from art and finds in a quasi-religious experience of sympathy the comfort of confessing her secret.

Secular as her confession is, Hilda learns from her visits to the
Catholic shrines that here she might find spiritual correspondence
and consolation: "If the worshipper had his individual petition to
offer, his own heart-secret to whisper below his breath, there were
divine auditors ever ready to receive it from his lips; and what encouraged him still more, these auditors had not always been divine,
but kept, within their heavenly memories, the tender humility of a
human experience" (346). In the human power of sympathy then,
not through art or religion, but out of the "tender humility" of
being mortal, Hilda discovers that "there was an ear for what the
overburthened heart might have to murmur, speak in what native
tongue it would" (356). Ironically, it is Hilda's delicate apprehension of art that helps to bring this consciousness into being. When
she recognizes that the Italian masters' Madonnas are but the "flat-
tered portrait of an earthly beauty," not the celestial representation
of individual inspiration, Catholicism, Hawthorne tells us, loses a
convert. Yet it is her perception of art that affirms Hilda's Puritan
sense of the ultimately human responsibility to endure whatever
"glorious trial" Providence puts in her way.

Hilda's perception of the merely mortal applies as much to the
confessional as to painting. Unable to abide the prospect that the
models of holy figures are mere people, neither can she ask absolution from another person. It is this awareness of the distinctly
human capacity for sympathy that makes the confessional so ken-
otic for her. She responds to a human voice: "It spoke soothingly; it
encouraged her; it led her on by apposite questions that seemed to
be suggested by a great and tender interest, and acted like magne-
tism in attracting the girl's confidence in this unseen friend" (357).
Hawthorne stresses the very humanity of the priest even as he oth-

erwise implies a Jesuitism. Insofar as he is a priest, his religious sympathy is "confined exclusively to the members of the one true Church," but to the extent that his sympathy makes Hilda's confession possible, he is a "mortal man." Indeed, as both he and Hilda repeat, he is a "countryman" of this "daughter of the Puritans." Yet he is also a citizen of the world, a man whose face was "strikingly characterized by benevolence. It bore marks of thought, however, and penetrative insight" (358). If the model is Miriam's secret personified, the priest is Hilda's figure of sympathy. In spite of the "blessed privileges" and "unspeakable advantages" of the Church, Hilda confesses her secret as a result of the human power of sympathy by which it was elicited and with which it was received. She comes to the confessional "a motherless girl" who has "only God to take care of me, and be my closest friend" and finds in the priest, not absolution, but the contact with humanity, the absence of which has driven her to despair. Just as secrets may present themselves by surprise, as when Hilda looks up and witnesses a murder, so too can sympathy disclose itself, as when Hilda looks up and sees the inscription PRO ANGLICA LINGUA and its promise of sympathy—"It was the word in season!"—under the varnish of religious accoutrements.

In contrast to Miriam's earlier aborted effort to reveal her secret to Kenyon, this human experience at the confessional ultimately leads Hilda to confess her "terrible secret" and conclude that there is an imperative need for sympathy within the "close bond of friendship." Although she still cannot acknowledge that evil and good coexist within the same idea, she learns that she must be sympathetic, especially in the face of an "intimate" friend's wrongdoing:

> For in these unions of hearts, (call them marriage, or whatever else,) we take each other for better, for worse. Availing ourselves of our friend's intimate affection, we pledge our own as to be relied upon in every emergency. And what sadder, more desperate emergency could there be, than had befallen Miriam! Who more need the tender succour of the innocent, than wretches stained with guilt! And, must a selfish care for the spotlessness of our own garments keep us from pressing the guilty one close

to our hearts, wherein, for the very reason that we are innocent, lies their securest refuge from further ill! (385)

Whether an act can be interfused with "Right" and "Wrong" is "all a mystery to me, and must remain so," Hilda protests in the hope that she might never understand this commingling. The pressures of making ethical decisions, like those on pure women as the moral arbiters in mid-century America, force Hilda to "trust in a simple girl's heart" (as she tells her confessor), not in a casuistry she can neither follow nor afford. But rather than smile along with Kenyon at her systematically healthy-minded, "unworldly and impracticable theory," the reader may draw another analogy and affirm, with Hilda, that "this is my faith; and I should be led astray if you could persuade me to give it up" (384). Hawthorne thereupon continues to persuade the reader of the naivete in Hilda's theory at the same time that he also persuades the reader to submit to her faith. Few readers now are likely to find the copyist to be much more than the allegorical vessel of purity for which she so unabashedly stands. Nor does the historical recognition that her exaggeration would not, and did not, grate on Hawthorne's mid-century readers really convince us that her characterization is any less wobbly than it seems to be, even if we recognize in her situation the plight of the simple American girl that James would make so dramatic. Hawthorne anticipates the reader's skepticism—it may have been his own—and has Kenyon vent that frustration with Hilda's faith in the religion of friendship. That Kenyon lays aside his casuistry to marry his image of purity signifies Hawthorne's intention that readers forget, under the spell of romance, their worldliness and practicality and embrace Hilda's faith, the necessary belief in the compelling virtue of sympathy in a world as intrinsically mysterious as the one Hawthorne's Roman setting reflects.

Hilda's willingness to live with mystery and act with sympathy is the necessary course in a life where secrets reveal how little may be known or understood. As if to stress this lesson, Hawthorne seems to withdraw and chides Hilda's faith by calling her conviction mere fancy. He even seems to patronize her limited model of response by protesting that, in this belief in the "close bond of friendship," Hilda is "misled by her feelings"—just as the priest has warned her of confusing "right-feelings and foolish inferences." At once Hawthorne calls attention to the faith one must place in a simple girl's heart and provides a qualified model for the reader. Hawthorne cannot "unhesitatingly adopt" Hilda's view, and neither should the reader, who must sympathize with all the characters' guilty secrets in their turn: Miriam's dark passions, Donatello's murderous vitality, Kenyon's worldly skepticism. Without this sense of complexity, the reader cannot become Hawthorne's "friend of friends." Then, no matter how subtle one's moral distinctions, the reader still can also respond to the truth of a pure girl's heart. At the close of the novel, Hilda accepts Miriam's wedding gift, "the symbol of as sad a mystery as any that Miriam attached to the separate gems." Tempered by her acceptance of mystery, Hilda's "hopeful soul" is brought into sympathy with Donatello and Miriam, and she realizes that intimacy confers its own morality: "The idea stubbornly came back, that the tie between Miriam and herself had been real, the affection true, and that therefore the implied compact was not to be shaken off" (386).

In the same way Hawthorne asks the reader to accept the kept secrets in the novel and see the nature of the response the author intends, his own "implied compact": art without sympathetic apprehension is incomplete. Hilda's experience of sorrow and the flowering of sympathy encourage her to take a "deeper look into the heart of things." Although she loses the "devout sympathy" that once enabled her to possess an old master's general idea, now "Instructed by sorrow, she felt that there is something beyond almost all which pictorial genius has produced" (375). What she discovers, what the reader also learns, is that, without sympathetic apprehension, art cannot "soften and sweeten the lives of its worshippers. . . . It cannot comfort the heart in affliction; it grows dim when the shadow is upon us." Art, "of its own potency . . . has no such effect" (340). Without sympathy, the gentle reading that Hawthorne begs of his "one congenial friend," his art is but ordinary words on the page, its secret life unseen, the community between writer and reader never established.

CHAPTER FIVE

Hawthorne's James and the Power of Sympathy

Hawthorne's sense that disclosing secrets requires the reader's sympathy especially pertains to his problems in completing his last projected romances. His failure to define a controlling secret or to organize a plot by which a central secret can be disclosed marks the decline of his imaginative powers. For the fragments do not reveal a narrative logic for their completion: the secrets underlying the proposed narratives are too circumscribed by the lines of plot Hawthorne had laid to allow sympathetic apprehension, or too much is left to a reader's intuition. In one version or another of his American claimant plans, for example, Hawthorne discloses a secret merely as an elucidated mystery. This transparent reliance on gothic conventions led Hawthorne to grow dissatisfied with his procedures as strained and even silly. The projected shape of these narratives, however, imitates a form with which this study has made us familiar: a secret antedates the action and stimulates the plot; its disclosure gives the narrative a structure and that organization is either aided by sympathetic apprehension or impeded by an absence or a misuse of that opportunity.

The extent to which Hawthorne's failure centers on discovering a form for disclosing a secret can be seen, initially, in his projected romance about an American's journey to England. Before he began *The Marble Faun*, Hawthorne was intrigued by the possibilities, suggested to him in his experiences as consul to Liverpool, of this transatlantic tale, but the "international" theme proved too unmanageable. In his notebooks he records how a "secret" underlies the proposed narrative: "In my Romance, the original emigrant to America may have carried away with him a family secret, whereby it was in his power, had he chosen, to have brought about the ruin of the family. This secret he transmits to his American progeny, by whom it is inherited throughout the intervening generations. At last, the hero of the Romance comes to England, and finds, that by means of this secret, he still has it in his power to procure the downfall of the family."[1] Hawthorne's first sketch of the romance repeats, virtually verbatim, the notebook entry, but in the second study, he begins to see the problems he will face: "A murder shall have been committed; a blood-stain, that keeps freshening out of the floor yet, at due times. But then the family secret, partially lost;—what can that be? Something, I am afraid, that has reference to property; no this secret must typify the hereditary disposition of the family. It shall seem as if dead men still were active agents. How? How? I don't know, really. Horror! Horror!"[2] The writer's "horror" results from the realization that this integral aspect of his conception is missing, as it was not in *Seven Gables*, of which this description should have reminded him. Hawthorne's not knowing the "secret" or how to "typify" it might also have alarmed him as the first signs that his powers were waning. Why the novelist never completed this story is a matter of speculation, yet the several explanations to be conjectured all point to his avowed difficulty in defining a secret and creating the appropriate form of disclosure.[3] That failure can be seen by considering questions of Hawthorne's psychology, the romance mode, cultural circumstances, audience, and the interrelation among these categories.

After the winter of 1859, Hawthorne was spent. It is impossible to overestimate the effect that Una's illness had on her father. Julian suggests that Hawthorne was never the same man after the ordeal of having his daughter near death and his wife gravely ill. His son reports that during this benighted season Hawthorne developed a croak in his voice, which he was to have for the rest of his life.[4] It is easy to imagine how sharply Hawthorne, always keen to see himself as a loving father and devoted husband, would have blamed himself for submitting his family to the dangerous Roman climate. In this sense, the fragments attest to his old doubt that his practices of art could not lead to anything harmonious or salutary; his guilt about being a mere "idler" might have redoubled. (Conceivably, if Hawthorne's croak suggests an anxiety about speaking which is echoed in the stifling of his authorial voice, his fears may even have seemed to him paralyzing.) Mere conjecture as this is, his last fragments—*Septimius Felton* and *The Dolliver Romance*— have come to be called *The Elixer of Life* manuscripts, since these works are preoccupied with finding a secret for saving lives at risk. In his last years Hawthorne may have become convinced of what he suspected in his youth—writing was a perilous business, one that then seemed to endanger his sanity and, now, his family's welfare. Just as the "secret" of Hawthorne's dismissal from the Custom House could have spurred him to avenge himself against the forces of humiliation by creating his most finished work, so might the effect of nearly bringing his family to disaster entail a psychological necessity of proving himself a failure.

If Hawthorne's failure can be understood as his inability to construct an imaginative triumph over his perceived faults, this self-dissatisfaction readily extends to his understanding of his previous ways of doing things, including his treatment of romance narrative. Unlike *Seven Gables*, the aborted romances reveal a lost faith in fusing a symbol or image with a moral or a determinate secret that supports a host of indeterminacies. The romance convention of an overarching symbol now seemed too labored either to hint at secrets or to beseech sympathy. As Yvor Winters suggests, the last efforts have "all the machinery . . . and mannerisms of the allegorist" without the "substance of his communication": "We have the hushed, the tense and confidential manner, on the part of the narrator, of one who imparts a grave secret, but the words are inaudible."[5] The "formula of alternative possibilities" could only work as long as Hawthorne was committed to a symbolic mode that contained the variety of secrets to which it gave rise. The symbolic spiders, footprints, elixers, and poisons were no longer adequate for the range of secrets they were supposed to determine. Hawthorne is left only with the "horror" of indeterminacy, whereas before, his method of representation could invoke secrets that were both knowable and not.

It can also be argued that Hawthorne's unworkable symbols do not function as a form of disclosure, because the "circumstances of the time in which he lived and his fundamental inability to take either the bloody footprints or the elixer of life as serious and important images forced Hawthorne into hasty improvisations which he substituted for the tough mental labor of years gone by."[6] Certainly, the Civil War would have tested his faith in romance. While some writers during and after the war maintained their confidence in this narrative form, Hawthorne, having spent the preceding seven years abroad, was more unprepared than many for the turmoil. The spectacle of America enjoying a "broad and simple daylight" in all its "common-place prosperity" had obviously darkened, taxing Hawthorne's confidence in his judgment of these circumstances and the secrets they suggested. The secrets to be revealed in the tensions between Old World and New, as projected in the American claimant romance, now must have seemed too dim a reflection of the most urgent national circumstances he witnessed in America. If *The Blithedale Romance* demonstrates how "even without social pressures, the socialized psyche would reconstruct the old order," the world Hawthorne now faced was too challenging to believe that the old order needed only to be reshaped, that a new order was not necessary.[7] Similarly, the split in the Democratic party would have further worried his sense of his relation to the populace. Immediately following the attack on Fort Sumter, he put aside his work on the American claimant romance.[8]

Hawthorne could also have come to believe that readers were no longer interested in the questions that his last romances entail. Readers were certainly cool in their response to *Our Old Home*, although much of its unpopularity stemmed from political considerations. Dedicated to the man who appointed him consul, the work was all but ensured a poor reception, hated as Franklin Pierce was in the North for his policy of conciliation. Hawthorne believed that his friendship with Pierce canceled any need for public discretion, and this conviction may have strengthened his sense that he had lost touch with his time and his audience. Telling secrets requires, as in *The Marble Faun*, the will to believe that one's audience can be made, or already is, sufficiently sympathetic, and it would be quite understandable if Hawthorne had come to think that he could no longer instruct his readers, that he could not meet them on intimate ground, so distant had they become. Hawthorne may not only have doubted whether he could still rely on his readers, but he also must have wondered whether he had anything else to impart, any secrets to tell, even if he could find the right form of disclosure and could marshal a reader's sympathy. With no secrets to tell, he must have known his career to be at its end.

Hawthorne was unknowingly to find the reader who would be his "one congenial friend" when, shortly before the author's death, an aspiring novelist, Henry James, spent a summer reading through the romancer's works. James would reassemble Hawthorne's literary remains and reshape the American claimant tale into "A Passionate Pilgrim" among several other stories and novels, including one of his own uncompleted works, *The Sense of the Past*. Just as Hawthorne represented himself as reading and enlarging upon Surveyor Pue's posthumous papers, so would James find in Hawthorne's writings an American literary past that needed to be read and that offered the young novelist the occasion to confront the fate of American letters.

In what follows, we will see how Hawthorne's value for secrets and sympathy sheds light on some of the developments in James's career. Moreover, James's reading of Hawthorne can be placed in a kind of intertextual relation to his own fiction and critical writings, for in the ways James comes to "appreciate" Hawthorne, his own achievement is clarified. Seeing James this way will also help us to observe the interest of secrets and sympathy beyond Hawthorne.

■ This study of Hawthorne has been primarily concerned with the implications of the ways he keeps and tells secrets in his novels. Only occasionally have the procedures of other writers or the general function of secrets in fiction explicitly entered the discussion. In examining the concern for secrets that one writer entertains, I do not suggest that Hawthorne alone exploits the secret or prizes sympathy as the necessary ground of reception, although he alone sees the necessity of combining the recognition of a secret with a call for sympathy. Hawthorne's example of bringing these two principles together shows how fundamental these terms are, especially for other nineteenth-century American authors, including Melville, Fuller, Poe, Thoreau, and Whitman, among Hawthorne's contemporaries. British authors also warrant comparison: Mary Shelley, Charlotte Brontë, George Eliot, and Thomas Carlyle, among many others. Yet perhaps James, above all, is the writer through whom the broader implications of secrets and sympathy are revealed for nineteenth-century fiction. He is an appropriate choice, not merely because of the long critical condition of viewing him under the Hawthorne aspect, but also because his treatment of secrets and sympathy, in large part, completes the nineteenth-century normative values so central to Hawthorne.

Secrets, we have seen, propel the plots of Hawthorne's novels, while their compromised articulation intensifies the reader's sympathetic involvement. Occasionally, explicit scenes of telling or learning secrets make the value for sympathy overt. Yet even implicitly, the relation between secrets and sympathy crystallizes the various issues of Hawthorne's novels, often creating a starting point for critical discussion. Sometimes, the characters harbor secrets; often, a mystery eludes them. All the novels, like much of the short fiction, chronicle the experience of confronting the half-known life that the right application of sympathy can illuminate or change. The relation Hawthorne creates between secrets and sympathy is fraught with his characteristic concerns: the "deeper psychology," the anxiety of interpreting history, the play of language, the distinction between novel and romance, the ambiguities of social life and dangers of intimacy, the challenges to the soul, the unresolved contradictions in the American character, the problematic conflicts in the drama of American political life. Central to Hawthorne's view of the workings and effects of art, the twin concerns of secrets and sympathy pervade his sense of the New England mind, in its Puritan formulation and Romantic variations. The relation, as we have seen, underlies Hawthorne's understanding of mesmerism and reform as surely as it does the nature of sin and the necessity in the present to correct the sins of the past. In addition, the dynamic relation between secrets and sympathy defines Hawthorne's circle of communion between writer and reader, and that communion is achieved insofar as rhetorical, psychological, and cultural issues coalesce as a function of genre. That communion, moreover, must be enjoyed apprehensively, since the many efforts to elicit sympathy are met by almost as many retreats. The relation between secrets and sympathy establishes the intimate ground where Hawthorne initiates his "intercourse with the world," even as it permits him to renege.

Recognizing the existence of this relation does not mean seeing Hawthorne simply as a mid-century moralist who teaches that sympathy can redeem the lonely, unmoored individual, as the treatment of a "monstrous secret" might suggest in "Egotism; or, The Bosom-Serpent" and "The Christmas Banquet"—the two surviving tales of Hawthorne's projected collection, "Allegories of the Heart." Instead, Hawthorne is concerned to criticize the easy senses in which sympathy is invoked and to show how closely this faculty of response resembles its obverse, antipathy. As complex as the secret is—some obviously need to be told and can be; others clearly must not be said or cannot, while others have their meanings evaporate upon disclosure—sympathy is no less manifold. Sympathy can be imagined as "perfect," though in practice it cannot or should not or need not be. Sometimes sympathy is salutary in its incompleteness; sometimes, damning. Like Chillingworth's, it can be scientific or reductive, but also, like Phoebe's, it can be freeing and uplifting. Like Donatello's, it might even be an animal passion, yet, like Coverdale's, sympathy can be cultivated and studied. It can lead to communality, like Hester's, or to isolation, like Zenobia's. It can bring one more fully into the apprehension of art, but it can also lead to misunderstanding, however well-intended. In short, the power of sympathy defines a Hawthorne character morally, to be sure, but also socially, politically, and psychologically. Readers also are measured through the sympathy they exercise, since it distinguishes their own fitness of response, in Hawthorne's critical framework. Testing readers as he does, Hawthorne requires them to refine and extend their powers so that readers grasp the "objectivity" of his enterprise, the extent to which his characters' concerns anticipate, textualize, and clarify a reader's.

We need not preserve an image of a melancholy Hawthorne to see how in the privacy of his contemplations of a soul's secrets, he means to elucidate and objectify a citizenry's. His concern, throughout the short fiction and the novels, is to bring almost to light the secrets a nation has sought to evade. From his earliest writings, like "Alice Doane's Appeal," he means to counter the American tendency to acquit itself of accountability in the present for the excesses of the past by bringing his readers into sympathy. He means for his American readership also to see how the secret abuses of the past linger putrefyingly into the present, as in "Roger Malvin's Burial," where a suppressed secret generates destruction in the name of protection in the present.[9] In the late sketch, "Main-Street," American history is treated as a procession of secrets, the true import of which can be disclosed only with "a little aid from the spectator's imagination."[10] The "aid" Hawthorne wants to enlist is the sympathetic recognition of participating in a national blindness to corruption. Democrat that he is, Hawthorne takes some comfort in the heart of the multitude, but he never loses sight of our darkest secret, as a populace, that American ideals, as in "My Kinsman, Major Molineux," are readily commingled with their distortion and debasement, perhaps the unifying political theme of his novels. As his catalogue of historical sins in "Main-Street" suggests and as the responses of the audience confirm, this condition is both past and present, a contradiction resulting from the gap between secret truths and the country's all-too-complacent sympathy. This contradiction is destined to perpetuate itself, in a culture whose citizens demand back their money from the showman who would give them the truth. The spectators cannot forgive him the vision of antipathy—of hatred, cruelty, corruption, and violence—he has revealed by the simple turn of a crank. The sympathy he asks for, in order to bring his fragmentary show into coherence, is exactly what the overweening spectators deny, just as it has been wanting in the past.

Sympathy, as the faculty of relating writer and reader to each other, individuals together, and private self to the polity, proves quite as fundamental to James, who sees this principle of response as part of a still larger value for "appreciation." Indeed, James found Hawthorne's use of *sympathy* annoyingly vague, as he complained in his biography of the novelist, but it was a vagueness to which he himself succumbed throughout his career. Four years before *Hawthorne*, Rowland Mallet, the stable yet supple New England reportorial consciousness in *Roderick Hudson*, characterizes himself as the apt observer of "a hideous, mocking mystery," since "Without flattering myself, I may say I'm cursed with sympathy—I mean as an active faculty, the last of fond follies, the last of my own."[11] Indeed, sympathy bespeaks the very "secret" that James called an American writer's "joke" when he describes in his *Hawthorne* the "consolation" for American writers. After his famous account of the things absent in American life that James believed a novelist needs as a "fund of suggestion," he appends this stipulation to his affidavit of America's bankruptcy: "The American knows that a good deal remains; what it is that remains—that is his secret, his joke, as one may say. It would be cruel . . . to deny him the consolation of his national gift, that 'American humour' of which of late years we have heard so much."[12] This passage has been quoted so often that it is surprising how rare are the efforts to define James's sense. What is this "secret" that is also a "joke," and why does James, even in condescension, connect Hawthorne to the local colorists and regionalists then coming to attention most notably for their wit? The "secret" is not the ponderous "joke" that "in popular democracy the customary and characteristic institutions that have traditionally embodied cultural, social, and ethical values are missing from the scene, and yet the values themselves, and the attitudes that derive from and serve to maintain them, remain very much part of the national experience."[13] James conflates the open-endedness of secrets with the closed dimension of jokes by turning the American writer's "consolation" into some private irony, one that may well be lost on the English reading public, but one that Hawthorne would share.

James never does say what this "secret" is, though he follows the "terrible denudation" by praising Hawthorne's "democratic strain" and "relish for the commoner stuff of human nature," the "thoroughly American" "vagueness of his sense of social distinctions" that inspires his "imaginative interest and contemplative curiosity." Under this aspect, Hawthorne does deserve a qualified inclusion among the new writers, at least to the extent that he joins in their puncturing of elitist assumptions or in their conviction that an easy social assimilation is nothing more than a sham or confidence game. For James, Hawthorne shares with such writers an observably American "readiness" to forget social rank if a "moral or intellectual sensation were to be gained by it" (*EL*, 354). In putting the case to an English audience, James refers to the American friendliness that had already become legendary, just as he wishes to disabuse those readers for whom Hawthorne is terminally "a dusky and malarious genius." So James is at pains to distinguish Hawthorne's "easy and natural feeling about all his unconventional fellow-mortals," "one of the points of his character which his reader comes most to appreciate." The implications that James characteristically finds in this seemingly native, spontaneous interest in other people's variety and peculiarities are especially suggestive: Hawthorne's interest in others underscores a rhetorical necessity of sympathy, since it generates the "fund of suggestion" that American life can provide its writers. Such an interest—a "democratic strain in his composition"—fills the void for those "who possess in a strong degree the story-telling faculty." Thus in defining the Americanness of Hawthorne as an author, James naturally categorizes his own: an emphasis on other people, the relations to be observed, the "moral and intellectual sensation" this interest stimulates.[14]

The discussion of James's complex reaction to Hawthorne has been long and valuable. Although questions of sources and explicit influence comprise the traditional interests, more recently scholars have pursued farther-reaching issues. In the past, the subject of

James's relation to Hawthorne often began and ended with James's critical biography, when, in fact, as Richard Brodhead and Hyatt Waggoner have shown, James returned, substantively, to thinking about Hawthorne during the period of his final development.[15] The wealth of commentary on *Hawthorne* seems to accept that James's purpose in that study is to assuage, undo, and free himself from some mentor-protégé relation, really a condition that could apply to several other novelist-precursors: Balzac, Eliot, and Turgenev. The preponderant attention to *Hawthorne*, a work written under some duress, dulls readers to the truth that James never does get over his American forerunner.[16] Yet there is no need to suggest that James was obsessed with Hawthorne, consciously or not modeling himself upon and distancing himself from this figure of priority. That would sensationalize what is really more of a commonplace: James continued to find in Hawthorne an instructive example, one he could test himself against, especially during the last twenty years of his career—in an introduction for the Warner's Library, in a letter sent for a centenary celebration, in *The American Scene*, and in his autobiographical volumes. Again and again James returned to Hawthorne with "clinging consistency," to redefine his identity as a novelist, to ascertain his own relation to America, and, in part, to clarify his own strategies of fiction. The mistake, then, is to minimize, as James did not, Hawthorne's enduring effect by maximizing the seemingly mythic drama of confrontation and liberation *Hawthorne* has been supposed to enact.[17]

The revelance of Hawthorne for James, in this study, is to be found in the continuities and variations in the linking of secrets and sympathy. It impoverishes the discussion of such relations in narrative discourse, however, to suppose that James patterned his treatment of secrets on Hawthorne's example or that the procedures of inference in James's fiction find their source in Hawthorne's special senses of sympathy. On the contrary, the relation between secrets and sympathy in Hawthorne reveals how James, out of his own psychology, exactions of genre, understanding of cultural issues, and value for the reader, develops his own rhetoric of secrecy. This rhetoric includes Hawthorne's but also extends it. "Sympathy" remains a key word, but its special senses are embraced as "appreciation"; "apprehension" becomes "curiosity" or "penetration." As we will see, the increments of meaning to be understood in these gradations will require the still broader vocabulary of "objectivity" and "subjectivity."

In the preface to *The Princess Casamassima*, James defines the importance of an artist's command of secrets, which he considers the implicit meanings of experience that a novel must capture and communicate. As James addresses anyone who would write a novel, "that if you haven't, for fiction, the root of the matter in you, haven't the sense of life and the penetrating imagination, you are a fool in the very presence of the revealed and assured; but that if you *are* so armed you are not really helpless, not without your resource, even before mysteries abysmal."[18] In James criticism, this passage is a locus classicus for the novelist's aesthetic of going beyond preliminary awareness, and, by implication, for the reader who would be one of those upon whom nothing is lost. The "penetrating imagination," a phrase freighted with valorizing associations many readers can find objectionable, is also to signify James's acute desire to probe the source of one's bewilderments, one's confrontations with the secret—"mysteries abysmal" (a similarly troubled construction). Less often recalled is that James uses the term, some thirty years before, in *Hawthorne*, when he extols Hawthorne's "delicate and penetrating imagination" as "always at play, always entertaining itself in a game of hide and seek."[19] Hawthorne's sport is conducted in the "region in which it seemed . . . that the game could but be played—among the shadows and substructions, the dark-based pillars and supports of our moral nature" (*EL*, 340).

James characterizes Hawthorne's treatment of a secret as child's play, though later, in describing his own mission, he reserves the phrase to suggest his own, more adult endeavor of "precisely" producing the effect of "our not knowing, of society's not knowing, but only guessing and suspecting and trying to ignore, what 'goes on' irreconcileably, subversively beneath the vast, smug surface" (*EW*, 1102). Beyond the younger James's need to infantilize Hawthorne, especially in the context of describing the older writer's "period of incubation," is the mature James's need to discover a relation between a realist imperative and "penetrating" vision, an imagination which delves beneath and beyond what we may legitimately know but from which, for one reason or another, we are excluded. James's Hawthorne finds this faculty in penetrating the "dusky" regions of the moral imagination; Hawthorne's James, in the netherworld of intimate relations as well as political and social life.

However bedimmed, vague, and sultry one's knowledge of that milieu, says James, the knowledge that comes from penetrating is no less privileged than careful research. The "penetrating imagination" perceives the secrets of how a class of people lives, seizes on all "that we never can directly know," and transforms such information into "things we cannot possibly *not* know, sooner or later, in one way or another," the realms of knowledge that distinguish romance's dominion and the world that the real represents.[20] James's sense of how this knowledge is reached is more plainly, if crudely, articulated in a much earlier statement, where he explains that any American realist needs a "*grasping* imagination" if the "face and nature of civilization in this our country" "will yield its secrets."[21] Like the "grasping imagination," the "penetrating" one provides a vivifying means of verification, a superior mode of apprehension that gives the writer entry into the world of secrets. In much the same way, James affirms the interest of such corroboration in "The Art of Fiction," where he argues (at about the same time he is at work on *The Princess*) for the suggestiveness of impressions as constituting experience. Yet his tone in the preface to *The Princess* is significantly different from the sane passion animating the earlier set of fiction's constitutive principles. Here he promulgates the ordinances of the penetrating imagination with a grandiloquence that means to suppress an anxiety more urgent than a novelist's fear of not knowing the world he has taken it upon himself to report, a world that James saw as more ambiguous and uncertain than the life of society that Hawthorne confronted.

Why James so insists on the power of the novelist's vision to pierce the dark abyss of secrets can be understood, again, in his treatment of Hawthorne, for in the same context that he first assigns this "delicate" power to Hawthorne, he ascribes to it values perfectly consonant with the characteristic reticence of the Jamesian artist: "Beneath the movement and ripple of his imagination . . . lay directly his personal affections. These were solid and strong, but according to my impression, they had the place very much to themselves" (EL, 340). Hawthorne's "personal affections"—his life of feelings and desires—are what "goes on" beneath the ripples that his imagination casts, the moral hide-and-seek he plays, the secrets he finds and those he veils. James's "impression" is of the lonely freedom of those feelings; these exist, for James, undetected, unplumbed, unconstrained. It is not enough to observe, however, that James is obviously writing himself in Hawthorne's place; when he defends the sketchy knowledge his own penetrating imagination gleans, he inevitably makes the question into one of an "artistic position" in place of an emotional one: "I couldn't deal with that positive quantity for itself—my subject had another too exacting side" (EW, 1101). This "too exacting" dimension, suggested throughout the preface as James's intense identification with the hero, Hyacinth Robinson, becomes so exasperating that he speaks of his potential failure to "piece together a proper semblance of" Hyacinth's politics and "affiliations" as an embarrassment. The shame is not just a realist's betrayal of his purposes, but also of James's not making use of his "advantages," his knowledge of the life of "personal affections" his character embodies.[22]

The intensity of James's response is again suggested in his previous description of Hawthorne, but with the important difference of James's contradistinguishing of himself as a social, rather than moral, observer. In haunting the great city, "and by this habit to penetrate it, imaginatively," James claims to find a novelist's "authentic" information: "That was to be informed, that was to pull wires, that was to open doors, that positively was to groan at times under the weight of one's accumulations" (EW, 1101). In this adult version of a realist's hide-and-seek, the novelist searches for that object of knowledge which presumably will complete him, the search providing a structure of identity, in the same way that a penetrating imagination becomes the conduit of social knowledge and understanding. In the same vein of privileging his endeavor over Hawthorne's, even when the phrasing is consistent, James discredits the Zolaesque habit of taking literal notes, the practice of a student or an apprentice in mastering the techniques or secrets of a profession: "If one was to undertake to tell tales and to report with truth on the human scene, it could be but because 'notes' had been from the cradle the ineluctable consequence of one's greatest inward energy: to take them was as natural as to look, to think, to feel, to recognise, to remember, as to perform any act of understanding. The play of energy had been continuous and couldn't change" (EW, 1101). Here James names five functions of the imagination's means of penetrating secrets, and these fairly well schematize the play of his "greatest inward energy" as a novelist: looking, thinking, feeling, recognizing, and remembering.

Several of James's most famous plots turn on this question of taking imaginative note in apprehending a withheld secret, one that is only to be learned through a character's intensely apprehensive concern to look, think, feel, recognize, and remember. From Isabel Archer's meditative vigil to Maggie Verver's response to a scene on a balcony, James's characters continually provide examples for readers of grasping an abysmal mystery. One merely needs to recall the import of secrets in such works as *The American, The Princess Casamassima, The Turn of the Screw, What Maisie Knew, The Sacred Fount,* "The Beast in the Jungle," *The Ambassadors, The Wings of the Dove,* and *The Golden Bowl* to recollect how the forms of their disclosure relate centrally to the development of plots and the resolutions attained. In "The Science of Criticism" (1891; 1893), James explicitly defines how readers are to apprehend these secrets when he explains how a critic performs the "sympathetic" office of being "infinitely curious" in order to "penetrate" a writer's purposes. The language that James finds is more like Hawthorne's than he can have intended, insofar as James sees the critic as the "real helper of the artist, a torch-bearing outrider, the interpreter, the brother."[23]

At the prospect of finding an ideal reader, James is moved "to pay almost any homage": "When one considers the noble figure completely equipped—armed *cap-à-pie* in sympathy and curiosity—

one falls in love with the apparition" (EL, 98). To embody this spirit, James then conjures the image of the critic as a "knight," "sacrificial in his function," "ready to lend himself, to project himself and steep himself, to feel and feel till he understands so well what he can say . . . to be infinitely curious and incorrigibly patient, and yet plastic and inflammable and determinable." The critic, for James, becomes the artist's "valuable instrument" to the extent that "he is sentient and restless, just in proportion as he reacts, reciprocates and penetrates." In being "patient" and "plastic," the critic must be willing to take the shape a novelist determines and to be susceptible of illuminating sparks. Like Hawthorne's critical reader, James's must enjoy an even "sacrificial" "sympathy," yet also be "infinitely curious," an attending spirit, "armed" head-to-foot with these capacities. In distinguishing "curiosity" as one of the reader's necessary faculties, however, James also points to the ways that Hawthornean "sympathy" is to be extended and enlarged. The Jamesian difference is that "curiosity" makes readers react and reciprocate, just as "sympathy" makes them "sentient and restless."

James stresses this broadened sense of response by describing the critic's task of immersing oneself in "impressions": "The more he is saturated . . . the more he can give out" (EL, 99). James considers this endeavor "heroic, for it is immensely vicarious." The success of the critic depends on being "indefatigably supple"—a "formidable order," since the critic has "to understand for others, to answer for them; he is always under arms." Moreover, the critic's sympathy comes from being "closely connected with life"—"doubly." The critic "deals with life at second-hand as well as at first, that is, he deals with the experience of others, which he resolves into his own," just as, first hand, the critic makes the "uncompromising swarm of authors" "as vivid and free as the novelist makes *his* puppets" (EL, 99). The close, double connection to life that James speaks of requires the critic, through sympathy and curiosity, to enter into a writer's vision and technique so completely that he makes the writer's object his own. In this, he must be sympathetic, must objectify the works of these "clamorous children of history," yet he must also make these works his subject, subjectify these works, as the novelist does in creating his own characters. This task, as we shall see, is the appropriating function of curiosity, which, for James, signifies how readers bring themselves into any act of critical "appreciation," but a tendency Hawthorne professes to discourage, even as he elicits the response. Critical readers are then "always under arms," always torn between two opposing yet complementary impulses, "resolving the experience of others into their own"—subjectifying the text—and dealing "with life at second-hand"—objectifying the work—being both curious for themselves and sympathetic with the "uncompromising swarm of others."

For all the high praise James affords the critical endeavor in "The Science of Criticism," the true "critical sense" is "so far from frequent that it is absolutely rare" (EL, 98). The dominant tendency of the essay is to correct the impression that criticism is "a new and flourishing industry," instead of a practice too often "puerile and untutored," replete with "vulgarity," "crudity," "stupidity." For the most part, James is responding to the criticism spawned by the necessities of the periodicals and their voracious consumption of ideas and art, a rampant consumerism that irritated James even worse than it did Hawthorne. A few years following "The Science of Criticism"—after James suffered his embarrassment as a playwright—he returned to the business of criticism, making it the background for the story that is best known as his most fully executed meditation on the operations of fiction and of critical response, "The Figure in the Carpet" (1896), where James's version of the relation between secrets and sympathy becomes the tale's explicit subject and even supersedes Hawthorne's conception.[24]

In the preface to "The Figure in the Carpet," James speaks of his desire in the story "to reinstate analytic appreciation" in the criticism of fiction. He conceived of the tale as the comic spectacle of "some artist whose most characteristic intention . . . should have taken all vainly for granted the public . . . exercise of penetration."[25] The "charming idea" was to see the writer, with "so much spent intensity and so much baffled calculation," left "wholly alone, amid a chattering, unperceiving world, with the thing he most wanted to do" (EW, 1235), although readers now find the question of the critic's failure to be the rewarding source of inquiry. By this time, no reader can take up the story with the naive hope of guessing Hugh Vereker's "very beautiful and valuable, very interesting and justly remunerative secret." Whatever the "Author's secret" is—the "undiscovered, not to say undiscoverable, secret" (EW, 1234)—it may only come to the critic who is "admiring, inquisitive, sympathetic, mystified, skeptical," a Jamesian ideal reader strikingly akin to Hawthorne's.[26] James admits to being fascinated by the challenge this story represents and sees it as the occasion to strike some "truce" between "close or analytic appreciation" and "this odd numbness of the general sensibility, which seemed ever to condemn it" (EW, 1234). The genesis for the tale came to him during the autumn of 1895, a special year in his biography since it begins with the humiliation at the premiere of *Guy Domville*. That ordeal, as we know, resulted in a period of ferocious concentration, when James vows to "make some masterpieces" and records the ideas for *The Turn of the Screw*, "The Beast in the Jungle," and *The Ambassadors*, along with *The Awkward Age, What Maisie Knew*, "The Friends of the Friends," "Glasses," " 'Europe,' " "The Given Case," "Miss Gunton of Poughkeepsie," "Covering End," even as he adumbrates his sketches for *The Wings of the Dove* and *The Golden Bowl* and is already writing "The Next Time" and *The Spoils of Poynton*. It was perhaps the most febrile year in James's life and a year during which the relation between the subtleties of his art and public reception was constantly on his mind.[27]

"The Figure in the Carpet" is given first place in the collection of tales published one year after his debacle, a grouping he called *Embarrassments*. This emphasis suggests how James understands the relation between secrets and sympathy as the warding off or defense against embarrassment, the attenuated version of humiliation at having one's secret discovered, having the source of one's disappointment publicized. As the other stories in the collection— "Glasses," "The Next Time," "The Friends of the Friends"—also suggest, embarrassment entails the fundamental fear of having one's secret sense of oneself involuntarily made obvious or having the life of "private affections" degraded and of being diminished on that account. Each story details how one character or another futilely tries to parry the advent or return of a failure; each tries to uphold some secret ideal of success—commercial, artistic, marital, social, sexual—that is inevitably frustrated, a failure made mortifyingly public in some cases, but at the very least made all too vivid to oneself. For James, embarrassment also provides a social context for the sometimes personal, sometimes rhetorical activity of hiding one's own secrets or pursuing others'. In one case, "Glasses," the very fear of being found wanting leads to a virtually complete blindness and a nearly total inversion of the character's desires.[28]

Whatever else this story suggests, "The Figure in the Carpet" can be read within the context of secrets and critical appreciation. Capturing Hugh Vereker's "secret" promises professional success for the narrator-critic, but learning it also comes to mean amatory success for George Corvick and promises artistic success for his widow, financial success for the lovers who can count on the generosity of Gwendolyn Orme's rich mother and marry, once they know the author's secret. The secret, it emerges, is never to be known by anyone outside the intensest bonds of sympathy. Indeed, the very fact that Corvick is in love, as the narrator is not, "may help him," according to Vereker. That love is not so much a question of the secret of adult sexuality as it is of the close communication between two people—lover to beloved, reader to writer.[29] Vereker's "little secret," he explains, is not his work's "esoteric meaning," but "its only meaning," the "very soul and core" of his fiction that readers need to appreciate.[30]

While Vereker never says what the secret is, he does explain what it isn't. More important than the "buried treasure" is the wasted expenditure of critical reading; it makes no difference to Vereker whether critics praise or derogate his fiction since they all miss the "exquisite scheme." They fail to grasp the implied coherence in and among his works, the "very string . . . that my pearls are strung on." Their limitation, we see, is alternately one of curiosity and sympathy, for only when the critic is armed with both can a writer's fiction be penetrated, in James's sense, a value that can also be traced to his enthusiasm for Sainte-Beuve.[31] Only when the critic possesses both, sympathy and curiosity in balance, as Corvick eventually does, can a work's secrets be known. Upon Corvick's death, the "secret" of Vereker's work becomes Gwendolyn Orme's very "life," as it has been transmitted from her husband. With the humiliating hunger of ungratified curiosity and the obtuseness of insufficient sympathy, the narrator later approaches Orme's widower and prosaic second husband, Drayton Deane, for information about the "secret," and finds himself vindicated that she has not shared it with Deane, just as Deane is disturbed by this suggestion of "her want of trust." This turn of events should, at the last, give the narrator a final clue that the secret is that his curiosity alone does not suffice but must be joined by sympathy, yet this is exactly the knowledge from which his mean-spirited pleasure disqualifies him. The narrator's want of sympathy precludes his ever learning the secret, just as this kind of lapse distances the narrator of *The Sacred Fount* in his exercise of curiosity, because, paradoxically, the narrator-critic is sympathetic enough, in a preliminary way, to have entered the bewildering morass in the first place. Like another of James's Coverdalean observers who would turn himself into a Westervelt, the narrator-scholar of "The Aspern Papers," the narrator-critic of this story desperately contemplates marrying the woman he supposes to hold the secret, so distorted and distorting is his notion of sympathy. Of this aim, however, he stops short and sees how in "that way madness lay!"

Obsessed as the critic is, his curiosity alone will not "initiate" him into Vereker's secret. When he asks Vereker whether the writer might "just a trifle" "assist the critic," the novelist responds that "assist" is what he has done "with every stroke of my pen": "I've shouted my intention in his great blank face!" The critic persists, claiming that there must be "initiation"—the writer installing the worthy or instructing the willing in some kind of secret association. Vereker retorts, "What else . . . is criticism supposed to be?" but this effort of "initiation": "Besides, the critic just isn't a plain man: If he were, pray, what would he be doing in his neighbor's garden? . . . and the very *raison d'être* of all of you is that you're little demons of subtlety. If my great affair's a secret, that's only because it's a secret in spite of itself—the amazing event has

made it one. I not only never took the smallest precaution to keep
it so, but never dreamed of any such accident. If I had I shouldn't in
advance have had the heart to go on" (15:232). The critic, according
to Vereker, must work "in his neighbor's garden," a construction
that suggests James's twofold sense of appreciation, since it splits
the critic's selves, the "helper" who performs, out of sympathy, for
another and one of those "little demons of subtlety" who has his
own reason for being. At the same time, Vereker's anger records his
disappointment that his secret has not been culled, since it was
never his intention to have it so obscured. That disappointment is
James's recognition that a critic's two offices are not so easily combined, the "amazing" consequence of the critic's divided labors.
This division is the rift between sympathy and curiosity, a gap in
which secrets reside in spite of themselves and one that James
means to narrow by reinstating a value for "analytic appreciation."

The conversation between Vereker and the critic, like so many in
James's stories of writers suffering the embarrassment of working
for an uncomprehending, inadequately sympathetic and insufficiently curious reading public, is animated by the intense desire for
"initiation," an intensity that harbingers a fear equally pressing.
That anxiety is the fear of invasion, of a public's seizing of a text,
often represented, as in "The Death of a Lion"—where a text is
actually lost—as the public's appropriating the writer's very being.
To combat this possibility, James enlarges Hawthorne's concept of
sympathy to include its complement, curiosity—the root impulse
of appropriation—and meld them into the practice of "close" or
"analytic appreciation." For Hawthorne, curiosity leads to vio-
lations, sometimes unpardonable sins. What allows James to collapse these operations is the value he places on the "penetrating
imagination" he first attributes to Hawthorne as a moral faculty
and later reserves for himself and his own psychological and social
realism. Analytic appreciation supposes a condition in which sympathy and curiosity can be brought into some kind of dialectical
balance, however mythical. Hawthornean divisions between heart
and head can be mended: The drive, which is curiosity's, to appropriate a work and its secrets, to transform it into the reader's property, to make it into the reader's subject by prompting the reader to

textualize the self, is met by its antithesis, sympathy. The reader's curiosity must be brought into accord with the writer's purposes, the sympathy that corroborates the writer's object—in both senses of the word, aim and construction.[32]

Sympathy, as we have seen especially in Hawthorne's letter to Sophia, refers to a reader's intuiting the writer's themes and purposes and complying with his strategies in representing the "objectivity" of the work. Readers corroborate that vision as universal, seeing it as signifying "what is common to human nature," not "peculiar" to Hawthorne or, by implication, any individual reader. Hawthorne argues that he can "sympathize" with others, can represent what is objectively true about readers' human nature, transform their lives into objective reality, can objectify them, while the opposite rarely obtains. To sympathize, according to Hawthorne's scheme, is to preserve the creator's object as *his* subjectification; the work may not be appropriated for the reader's own themes and purposes. To appropriate is to subjectify, to turn the work into a reader's own code of needs, desires, illusions. Rather than comply or sympathize with the writer, the appropriating reader penetrates the haze of mystification, slashes through the writer's indirection, and establishes the work as the reader's own, one that fulfills a reader's intentions. Hawthorne's "involuntary reserve" marks his resistance to being so appropriated, veiling himself as the textualized subject, without "pouring [him]self out—presumably safe from the risk of self-exposure or even self-voiding. Insofar as readers "sympathize" with him, they see the work as Hawthorne does: the objectified version of his own subjectification. To the extent, however, that readers see themselves as participating in what is "peculiar" to Hawthorne, they are invading the text, subsuming it as their subject, transmuting Hawthorne's work into something of their own. Sympathy, as this study of Hawthorne's sense of the word suggests, effects the reader's complicity in the writer's purposes of objectifying the world of experience that fiction exhibits, a function of upholding a novel or story's illusion of autonomy, its fabricated reality and freedom from historical norms, the same kind of historicity out of which sympathy, as a category of response, emerges and which it unintentionally sustains. For James, "appreciation" is the means of bringing objective and subjective categories together for the reader, just as a writer must be ready to receive impressions and know the fullness of their truth.

When James later refines his sense of what it means to criticize, the dual operations are one in his mind. In the preface to *What Maisie Knew,* he describes the task of the telegraph clerk of "In the Cage" (1898) as involving the "acuter vision" of "this most beset of critics," the "student of great cities" (as he suggested of himself when he articulated the "wisdom" of having a "penetrating imagination" in the preface to *The Princess*): "To criticise is to appreciate, to appropriate, to take intellectual possession, to establish in fine a relation with the criticised thing and make it one's own" (*EW,* 1169). If we consider that the telegraph clerk is cast as both compositor and critic, that she is both sympathetic, in the senses of remembering the right message and objectifying, and curious, in the sense of bringing herself into the drama and subjectifying, the simultaneity of these concerns seems to be achieved. That simultaneity, however, is more of a wish than practicable end, if it is true that readers are guided sometimes more by one, less by the other of these faculties. Apprehensive and kind as readers might be, their "appreciation," as Hawthorne believed, is not and never should be complete.

In the later stages of James's career, the writer's incorporating of the divided labors of author and critic is given ample testimony in his prefaces, essays, and especially letters to other writers who submitted their work to him and to whom he protests that reading is but the invitation, for him, to rewrite a work and give it "rounded objectivity."[33] Similarly, in the late novels, as several scholars have shown, language becomes a medium dually constructive and critical, especially insofar as the characters' conversations work as ever-emerging, dramatized fusions of subjectifying and objectifying impulses.[34] In some respects, this development in James can be seen in his developing relation to Hawthorne, even as James augments his sense—and Hawthorne's—of sympathy and secrets. Thematizing Hawthorne's example only throws into high relief one of the several, variegated, richly associated, complex, and intersecting routes by which James arrives at his final development, but it is a thematic proposition that helps James himself to observe his development.

In his critical introduction to Hawthorne's works, written also in 1896 and published in 1897, James's reading of Hawthorne changes subtly yet significantly insofar as he begins to situate Hawthorne's art "on a serious social and moral ground."[35] Here, James socializes the context of Hawthorne's emotional and moral "hide-and-seek," now describing his predecessor's imagination as grasping "a life of the spirit more complex than anything that met the merest eye of sense." "It was a question of looking behind and beneath for the suggestive idea, the artistic motive. . . . This ingenuity grew alert and irrepressible as it maneuvered for the back view and turned up the under side of common aspects,—the laws secretly broken, the dark corners, the closed rooms, the skeletons in the cupboard and at the feast. It made . . . a mystery and a glamour where there were otherwise none very ready to its hand."[36] "Looking behind and beneath" is James's version of Hawthorne's value for sympathy as Jamesian penetration, even to the extent of positing the "closed rooms" into which his own penetration was "imaginatively" "to open the doors." Hawthorne's "ingenuity" is as "irrepressible" as James's own "continuous" "inward energy," especially now that Hawthorne's vision is directed not on the "shadows and substructions" of "our moral nature," but on the whole world of "common aspects."

James associates Hawthorne's power of "looking behind and beneath" as the necessary manner of discovering the "latent romance of New England." For James, Hawthorne's "distinguished mark" is that through "looking behind and beneath" the "common tasks and small conditions" in all their "general grimness," Hawthorne discovers a world animated by the "secret play of the Puritan faith," the "ingrained sense of sin, of evil, and of responsibility" (EL, 459). This way of seeing has been crucial for James throughout his career; now he concedes that Hawthorne's "looking behind and beneath"—a phrase James would have used as a distinctly American idiom—is a response to the secrets of social circumstances rather than the life of "personal affections" he previously designated as Hawthorne's domain. While James still must emphasize how Hawthorne's way of "looking" serves romance, that imagination is presumably foundational for any novelist. As James writes in "The Art of Fiction" just before his pronouncement that the novelist writes from experience and that impressions *are* experience, "The power to guess the unseen from the seen, to trace the implications of things, to judge the whole piece by the pattern, the condition of feeling life so completely that you are well on your way to knowing any particular corner of it—this cluster of gifts may almost be said to constitute experience."[37] Not only are the vocabularies in the two essays in accord, but they also suggest the step, in James's mind, by which the "tapestry" of *The Marble Faun* becomes the figure in the carpet—the "whole piece" revealed in the "pattern."

When, in 1904, James writes to celebrate the Hawthorne Centenary at Salem, he resumes his praise of Hawthorne's "admirable and instinctive" tendency to "look behind," but with an important difference from either of his previous assessments. Perhaps under the influence of an audience presumably self-conscious with civic pride, James connects Hawthorne's way of seeing, not merely to the secret mind and heart—the "life within the life," as Hawthorne called it—but to the realities of "old and sunny Salem."[38] Now James says that Hawthorne has borne the test of time because he sees "the interest behind the interest, of things, as continuous with the very life we are leading, or that we were leading—and you, at Salem, certainly were leading—round about him and under his eyes." Such an aspect is the "romantic side," but one which a real world affirms. Hawthorne saw the "interest behind the interest" as "continuous with the life" led in Salem, "saw it in the very application of the spectator's, the poet's mood, in the kind of reflection the things we know best and see oftenest may make in our minds" (*EL*, 470, 471). Rather than a texture all too thin to support a novelist, James sees in his retrospective of "this blissfully homogeneous community of the forties and fifties" a world of "streets and corners and doorways" "*waiting* to bestow their reward" on the romancer, who is alive to their secret potential for fiction. Perhaps under the pressure of saying something ingratiatingly grandiose for the occasion, but also as a result of his continuing evolution, James pauses to praise the very stones Hawthorne trod. He does so by way of characterizing the "interest behind the interest" as concrete: *Seven Gables, The Blithedale Romance, The Marble Faun* are "singularly fruitful examples of the real as distinguished from the artificial romantic note," a reality to be found in the way Hawthorne "had read the romantic effect into the most usual and contemporary things"—*Seven Gables*—and "in the parti-coloured, angular, audible, traceable Real, the New England earnest, aspiring, reforming Real, scattered in a few frame-houses over stony fields"—*Blithedale* (EL, 471, 472). Thus James finally locates Hawthorne's romance-writing in a world of solidly specifiable reality, the interest behind the interest of Hawthorne's concern for secrets and sympathy. Hawthorne's "very freedom of the spell remains all the while truth to the objects observed," "not a shower of counterfeit notes," but an "artistic economy which understands *values* and uses them" (EL, 472).

James seems ready to conclude his relation to Hawthorne at the close of this letter, for he distinguishes him as a 'classic' and announces that Hawthorne, having 'passed' his examination, "may be left to the light and the ages." In fact, he begins the letter with the desire to be "objective" in his assessment, objectivity, not merely in the service of "cold criticism," but also to defend himself against "a certain tenderness of envy." When, several months later, James visits Salem and sees for himself how little "homogeneous" the town now is, he also comes to see how little "objective" he has been in the letter or his previous writings, how little in sympathy he has been, how much the secrets of Hawthorne's fiction elude him. Before we discuss that realization, however, we need to consider why and how James could have believed his relation to Hawthorne was finished.

James writes this letter shortly after he completed *The Golden Bowl*, the culmination of his three years' work that also produced *The Ambassadors* and *The Wings of the Dove*. Hawthorne's influence on these works easily can be overestimated, but it ought not to be discounted merely as James's elaborating of the symbolic mode, the sentient observer, or the "international" theme, though the implications of James's efforts have telling connections, which

have been well remarked, to Hawthorne's example. The presence
of Hawthorne found in these novels is a negating one, for in these
works James undermines both sympathy as an interpretative norm
and the secret as a compositional resource. This case might be
made for any of the three novels, all of which take up the question
of "how mysteries within the works merge with the complications
of the novel process itself."[39] Rather than examine all three, the
argument can be educed, in a preliminary way, out of the novel that
may be the least Hawthornean of the three, *The Wings of the Dove,*
in its treatment of secrets and sympathy.[40]

Two "secrets" dominate *The Wings of the Dove,* Milly's actual
illness and the engagement between Kate and Merton. Both are
pieces of information that the characters consciously withhold
from each other; both are to be coaxed out of obfuscated evidence.
Both "secrets" have a suffocating effect on the characters themselves, the basic fact of their existences that seems most to define
them in the others' eyes. Kate and Merton conceal "our secret" "of
being as we are" from Milly, while Milly is "fiercely shy about so
personal a secret" as her illness with regard to all, but especially
Merton.[41] Kate and Merton have to proceed throughout on the
basis of "refinements . . . of consciousness, of sensation, of appreciation" between them, while Milly has to meet the "face of sympathy," to struggle against the "machinations of sympathy," to tolerate "sighing sympathy" and "amiable sympathy" until her end.
Kate penetrates Milly's secret when she divines that Milly must
really be ill and in love with Merton after Milly misses the dinner
at Maud Lowder's. Similarly, "Milly expressed to Susan Shepherd
more than once that Kate had some secret, some smothered
trouble" that, according to "Milly's subtle guess," "implied" "some
probably eminent male interest," at least as the "secret" could be
known "by the admiring eye of friendship."

Up to the point of Milly's death, these "secrets" organize the
narrative, as James shifts attention from one to the other to show
how entangling they are. Once Lord Mark tells Milly the truth and
once Merton inadvertently corroborates it by pretending no necessity to deny it, the "secrets" are finally clotted in a way that ultimately makes them irrelevant. In turning "her face to the wall,"

Milly negates the creative and destructive properties of Kate and Merton's plot and subsumes them into a plan of her own. Yet Milly's "secret" is also overturned. It isn't so much the case that her "obscure" disease is so unrealistic that readers find themselves within the confines of Hawthornean romance, but that Milly's illness, as she recognizes, is everyone's "secret"—that one could live if one would, would live if one could. Milly's illness merely objectifies her "secret": clearly, she is the object of sympathy, in the sense of compassion to be sure, but also in the ways in which she is transformed into an object—of Kate and Merton's desire, of Susan Stringham's interpretations. To sympathize with Milly is to corroborate the self as an object, as Merton is led to do by the close, even though it is the anxiety of identity he has felt throughout as an embarrassment and the fear against which he continually struggles. What Milly's secret signifies is the way that the self cannot resist, actually wants, objectification but simultaneously demands to see itself fully as a subject, fully capable of realizing its desires, as Milly can do only after her death, when Merton truly falls in love with her and Kate is defeated. Thus Milly moves from object—the self as chronically bewildered, inauthentic, unshaped—to subject—the self as integrated, fulfilled, and possessed of itself, a traditional plot of growth and development, one that Hawthorne also adopts for the "transformations" in The Marble Faun.[42]

Kate and Merton's development observes the reverse plot as the self moves from the illusion of being its own subject to the recognition of its objectified cast. Merton's love for Kate can be understood as a mediating of the self, since she, in all her seeming high self-possession, is seen as the worthy projection of selfhood that he, in all his marginality, feels himself to be missing. Her "talent for living" impresses him, just as his capacity for moral thought appeals to her. Kate, however, no more deserves the distinction of having achieved selfhood than Merton does, since she, from the start, knows how fully capable she is of vacating the illusion of selfhood in her willingness to surrender herself, including her love for Merton, and become the object of her father's wishes. Kate's love for Merton, as the self's seeking the other, operates to the extent that she sees Merton as the subject worthy of desire. In turn, Kate sees

Milly, and in her "poetic versions" leads Merton to see Milly, as merely an object—the fabulously wealthy American girl—to be appropriated for their ends, the figure objectified as a "dove," in the same way that Susan Stringham sees Milly as a "princess"—the objectified presence who confers on others "the real thing."

Just as Milly's money makes her the object of Susan's fiction-making ends, so also are her millions the currency of selfhood Kate means to use for her own desire to live in the "great world," her one alternative to seeing herself as a nullity who exists merely to content others, the very alternative Merton forbids her if she is going to have him, now that he has come under Milly's influence. The novel closes on this dilemma of choosing between a vision of the self as its own agent, capable of purposes and desires, or a vision of the self as the repository of others' wishes, the illusion of itself as its own determining agent forever dispelled. This division is really to be understood as the essence of Milly's secret, a consciousness of the self as object, existing only to die, versus a vision of the self as wanting to live, of having desires met and dreams fulfilled. In the sense that Kate sees this choice as Milly's legacy—"She did it *for* us"—she comes to be aware that "we shall never be again as we were," that is, fully believing in the illusion of themselves as subjects who share "our secret" of being "as we are," absolutely in love.

How Kate and Merton are so transformed is to be observed in their succumbing to Milly's way of seeing, of objectifying herself. As James early on describes Milly's personality, we also see that Milly counts something as a text to be appreciated: According to novelist Susan Stringham, "She worked—and seemingly quite without design—upon the sympathy, the curiosity, the fancy of her associates. . . . She exceeded, escaped measure, was surprising only because *they* were so far from great" (19:116). Working upon the "sympathy," "the curiosity" of others, Milly becomes the fiction *par excellence*, beckoning a critic to react, reciprocate, to be "sentient and restless," if only to match Milly's own "high restlessness." Yet even before Milly fully possesses her "secret," she is distinct and different from others, the test of their success and failure, and, as James characterizes it, different from herself. The terms of her representation stress this point, especially when she stares at the Bronzino portrait, seeing in it a subject—one that is also object—from which she is compelled to differentiate herself. For Milly sees in the portrait what others see in her: her own perceived lack and her own ideal, an object of curiosity and sympathy. When she announces, "I shall never be better than this" (19:221), she is sincere in both senses: an assessment of herself as having achieved a social ideal at Matcham, but an admission to herself of the desire to be aestheticized into an object—of admiration, of love. In this contradiction of purposes—of loving and of being loved, of living for oneself and of being appropriated, of working on one's "sympathy" and "curiosity"—she is supposedly appreciated, when Kate proclaims Milly "satisfied" in "having . . . realised her passion. She wanted nothing more. She has had *all* she wanted" (20:332).

Milly's "peace" with Merton, as Kate ironically puts it, "is what I've worked for" and leads her to the "hideous" conclusion that "we've not failed" (20:332–33). Kate is still under the illusion of the self as its own determining agent, with secrets to keep, secrets worth keeping, a self that succeeds or fails in its purposes. What Kate has "worked for," she earlier describes as *their* way of appreciating Milly" (20:38), but only at the close is that appreciation complete. Then Kate fully sees how Milly truly has realized her passion, in the image that gives the novel its title. Kate observes that now Milly's wings "cover us": "she died for you then that you might understand her. . . . And I do now. . . . I used to call her, in my stupidity . . . a dove. Well she stretched out her wings, and it was to *that* they reached." Thus Kate realizes that her first formulation of Milly as a dove is merely the result of seeing herself as the active subject, Milly as the objectified other; at the close, Kate comes to see that Milly, in her death, emerges as the subject, Kate and Merton, the objectified selves left as they are, covered by Milly's wings, never again to be as they were. Kate's great "talent for living," which has defined her otherness from Milly, is undermined, her "secret" voided, while Milly's dovelike status—her invitation to victimage—ascends, in all its mastery.[43]

What Kate and Merton do to Milly and her "secret" is what unsympathetic readers do to narratives; they "appropriate" a text that they fail to "appreciate." On the other hand, Milly's victory is what merely sympathetic readers do to narratives; they objectify a text, but they cannot really make it their own. For "sympathy," as the characters realize, does not alone suffice. At an uneasy moment, when the truth of Milly's disease risks embarrassing exposure and Merton's "secret"—"an allusion to himself conjoined with Kate"—is also hinted, Merton tries to recover and assures Milly that she'll find everyone "ready to surround you with sympathy." Milly objects to the word, which Merton concedes is "doubtless a pale word," and suggests that "What we *shall* feel for you will be much nearer to worship," a construction Milly accepts (20:84). Not surprisingly, "sympathy" virtually disappears from the novel after this point, as a word and a value. What replaces "sympathy" in Kate and Merton's response to Milly is the refinement of appreciation, a change that also signals the disintegration of their "subjective community," as James calls their union.

James's sense of "appreciation" is that faculty of immersion that includes and supersedes sympathy as a category of response. For James, "appreciation," insofar as it is "close" or "analytic," brings sympathy together with curiosity, allows the critic to "appropriate" something as "one's own" as a process of conversion rather than Hawthorne's sense of violation. James conceives of it as the creative value the critic must embrace, one that fully responds to what authors think they are doing, and the critical perception that writers must bring to what they imagine, a "fusion of horizons."[44] The appreciating critic must also understand what an author "appreciates"—the value of a writer's "report," a value that is aesthetic and perhaps economic. In this, a writer's representation can be further understood as a painter's art, James says in the preface to *The Princess*. After he lauds "bewilderment" as the condition essential to the fictive representation of "persons either tragically or comically embroiled with life," James explains how one should render the confusion caused by secrets and characteristically compares his endeavor to the painter's. The painter's "affair" is the "reflected," not the "immediate" "field of life," the realm not of "application" but of *"appreciation,"* in the same light as Hawthorne found Thompson's work analogous to his own. James then likens this enterprise to his "report as a story-teller": "My report of people's experience . . . is essentially my appreciation of it." He can take small "interest" in his characters, "save through that admirable process." "As soon as I begin to appreciate simplification is imperilled." One needs to appreciate in order to become "intimate" with one's creations, "and I can't appreciate save by intimacy, any more than I can report save by a projected light." Only then can he animate his characters and represent the "exposed and entangled state" of "experience," which is but "our apprehension and our measure of what happens to us as social creatures," the report of which "has to be based on that apprehension" (EW, 1091–92).

James represents a moment of appreciation as a key, and for many readers the central, moment in the narrative, Milly's viewing of the Bronzino portrait, in which the painter must have appreciated his subject as fully as James imagines himself to appreciate Milly. While others are quick to see the likeness, Milly is reluctant to recognize herself immediately in this portrayal of her own otherness, the American girl who is also a "dead, dead, dead" Florentine noblewoman. Rather than responding by sympathy, Milly emphasizes her differences only to admit, with bewilderment, that "One never really knows one's self." She confesses an uncertainty about her powers of judging that also expresses her uncertainty of self, one that bespeaks her uneasiness in appropriating the image as her own. This bewilderment is compounded when Milly grows confused at the way Merton looks at Kate, an uncertainty she means to settle by asking Kate to accompany her on the visit to Sir Luke, and thus initiates, as many readers have observed, the novel's competing plots of transformation.[45]

Although Milly may not know herself, James certainly knew her prototype, his beloved cousin Minny Temple, the memory of whom he considers the very source of the novel. In *Notes of a Son and Brother*, he undertakes to describe her, in "all the breadth of her sympathy and her courage": "She was really to remain, for our appreciation, the supreme case of a taste for life as life, as personal living; of an endlessly active and yet somehow a careless, illusionless, a sublimely forewarned curiosity about it."[46] In naming these qualities for "appreciation," James indicates how directly these terms of response bear on *The Wings of the Dove* as a text and in his characterizing of Milly's response to the Bronzino, just as we see how related they are to James's rhetoric of secrecy.

■ Appreciation, as the immersing sympathy that allows for appropriation, is the note on which James closes his tribute to Hawthorne in *The American Scene* (1905). Actually, he conceives of the entire project as the occasion for such "appreciations." He imagines himself to "vibrate with more curiosity" than most visitors to his homeland, so ready is he to grasp the secrets that America may finally yield to him, but these "properties of the social air" challenge him as both an observer and writer: "I became aware soon enough . . . that these elements of the human subject, the results of these attempted appreciations of life itself, would prove too numerous" to be treated readily, but "artistically concerned as I had been all my days with the human subject, with appreciations of life itself, and with the consequent question of literary representation," James finds himself "led on and on."[47] The vast array of the "human scene" will spur him to write more and more, he conjectures, just as the impressions he can represent prompt him to see more and more, especially in his relation to Hawthorne.

This sense of episodes multiplying their implications before his eyes and then again at his desk is vividly represented in his visit to Salem. His tour of Hawthorne's native town is frustrated, from the first, when he asks for directions to the House of the Seven Gables, and the immigrant he stops cannot, in "frank ignorance," tell him the way. James, of course, is dismayed, since his intention was "in all good faith, in artless sympathy and piety," to "search again, precisely, for the New England homogeneous" and for the "renewal" of his youthful impression of Salem, the America he most intimately associates with Hawthorne. Not only does the immigrant's glare remind him that New England is no longer "homogeneous," but his inability to find the fabled house disappoints his desire to pay Hawthorne an homage. In addition, James's purpose of renewing his earlier vision can be construed as his desire to confirm the wisdom of his decision, of so many years before, to absent himself, now to see for himself how little or much the American scene would create a novelistic landscape, a "fund of suggestion." His "pilgrimage" to Seven Gables, then, concentrates these various purposes—of resuming his relation to Hawthorne, returning to an American literary past, and perhaps justifying his own.

James admits to being "essentially shaken" by his failure, a disorientation mitigated only slightly—and all too ironically—when he meets a "civil Englishman," who in "all kindness and sympathy" leads the tourist to the "Grosvenor Square" of Salem. Even here, James is balked: "I could only feel, even while doing it every justice, that the place was not what my imagination counted upon." Try as he does to see the "social value" in several Salem houses, he finds their prospect too "blankly serene" to appreciate fully: "Their high bland foreheads . . . with no musty secrets in the eaves—yes, not one, in spite of the 'speciality' of the Seven Gables . . . —clarify too much perhaps the expressive mask, the look of experience" (AS, 267–68).

James's sojourn, from the first "alien snub" to the "dreadful anticlimax" of his view of the Seven Gables, seems a complete disaster, his hopes of renewing impressions and enlivening his sympathies defeated. The errand to Salem is saved, however, when he meets "a dear little harsh, intelligent, sympathetic American boy" who seems to have "understood everything" about James's visit. James comes to think of the boy as the "very genius of the place." It is psychologically appropriate that James finds this guide, since his vision of Hawthorne has always been colored by his youthful enthusiasm. The boy even becomes a doppelganger for James's adolescent spirit, one who appears uncannily, having "dropped straight from the hard sky for my benefit (I hadn't seen him emerge from elsewhere)" (AS, 270). James and the boy form "so close an alliance," since the boy was "exactly what I wanted—a presence . . . old enough, native and intimate enough, to reach back and understand." The "boy was so completely a master of his subject" that making his acquaintance by itself was "alone worth the journey." That mastery and the boy's sympathy prod James to go further in his appreciation than merely to see the dreary paltriness of the "shapeless object" called the Seven Gables. The boy calls forth to

James's memory how vivid *Seven Gables* was, and is, to his imagination. James may even have remembered that as a twenty-six-year-old story writer he once vowed, to his brother, that "I mean to write as good a novel one of these days (perhaps) as the House of the Seven Gables."[48]

So forcefully does James recollect that "admirable book" through the boy's sympathetic and "most knowing tips" that James imaginatively restores the house. Rather than settle for the sight of this "vague domiciliary presence," James throws off the "poor illusion" of seeking a literal relation between the "accomplished thing" and "those other equivocal things that we inflate our ignorance with seeing it suggested by." Thus he sees how the novel makes the house seem but a "low acquaintance," repudiating it "like a ladder kicked back from the wall." At this "break of light," James is led to a final appreciation where, in a striking passage, he describes how he has misprized Hawthorne throughout his career, how he has mistaken his appropriation of Hawthorne for the earlier writer's real genius.

> Hawthorne's ladder at Salem . . . has now quite gone, and we but tread the air if we attempt to set our critical feet on its steps and its rounds, learning thus as we do, and with infinite interest as I think, how merely "subjective" in us are our discoveries about genius. Endless are its ways of besetting and eluding, of meeting and mocking us. When there are appearances that might have nourished it we see it as swallowing them all; yet we see it as equally gorged when there are no appearances at all . . . and we recognize ruefully that we are forever condemned to know it only after the fact. (*AS*, 271–72)

This place, and its historical, literary, and personal associations, encourage James to ponder not how Salem "nurtured" his precursor but how "subjective"—how little sympathetic—he has been in reading Hawthorne, how James has subjectively turned him into the younger writer's own vision and for his own purposes.[49] He acknowledges that his misreading of Hawthorne has been for himself, ever since 1872 (two years after the letter to his brother), when James all too dismissively reviewed Hawthorne's *French and Ital-*

ian Notebooks, through the critical biography, the library introduction, and the Centenary letter. Now James realizes what "genius" makes of "appearances," even when they are meager and, as
James used to describe them, "thin." Under the influence of the
"sympathetic" and "harsh" little boy whose mastery of his subject
shows James how little he has mastered his subject of his American
literary past and his American master, James "ruefully" sees his
mistake. The example of Hawthorne's genius now seems to "beset" him after he may have supposed he had thrown it off; to
"mock" him after he may have thought he had conquered its
threat; to "meet" him after he may have believed he had surpassed
it; to "elude" him after he may have convinced himself that he had
seized it. By the close, James realizes how much Hawthorne, in all
of his elusiveness and achievement, continues to teach him, in an
image meant finally to objectify Hawthorne's core of secrecy.

Hawthorne's primary lesson for James is recounted in *Notes of a
Son and Brother* (1913), when in a well-remarked passage, James
fuses together his memories of learning, on his twenty-second
birthday, of Lincoln's death and, eleven months before, of Hawthorne's. The "interpenetration" of these two recollections seems
to James incalculably rich, but in ways he prefers not to explore.
Instead, he is moved to recall that happier time when, in his youth,
throughout a summer, he read Hawthorne's fiction, taking in "at
one straight draught the full sweet sense of our fine romancer's
work" (*NSB,* 478). The result of that experience is James's placing
Hawthorne's novels and tales "somewhere on a shelf unvisited by
harsh inquiry"; for wasn't the best charm of a relation with the
works . . . somehow to stand in *between* them and harsh inquiry"?
(*NSB,* 479). That James feels obliged to repeat this phrase makes
the novelist-critic see that his reluctance to criticize is a "fatuity of
patronage," one at which "freedom of appreciation" might look
askance. His desire to protect Hawthorne from "harsh inquiry" is
also, in some respects, to defend himself, not merely from the
rueful recognition that the "harsh" little boy, for all his intelligence and sympathy, has led him to see, but also from acknowledging the lesson Hawthorne imparts to the aspiring novelist. That
instruction is recalled when he remembers how, some years later

in Rome, an acquaintance who seemed the "clearest case of Cosmopolitan culture" made harsh inquiries about *The Marble Faun.* James remembers how he would have liked to defend Hawthorne but was too timid, through an argument that also helps to explain why he would bring together as one his memories of the president and the novelist: Hawthorne's "work was all charged with *tone,*" which gave it "an extraordinary value in an air in which absolutely nobody's else was or has shown since any aptitude for being." This "full and rare tone" was "in its beauty—for me at least—ever so appreciably American" (*NSB,* 480).

This "tone" even suggests to the young James that a career as a novelist is possible, for it resonates with the uses to which "American matter could be put by an American hand." The "consummation" Hawthorne achieved involves the "happiest moral," that "an American could be an artist," "quite in fact as if Hawthorne had become one just by being American *enough.*" For James, being "appreciably American" means the "felicity of how [Hawthorne] missed nothing, suspected nothing, that the ambient air didn't affect him as containing," a receptiveness to secrets and an invitation to sympathy that make Hawthorne "at once so clear and so entire."

NOTES

INTRODUCTION

1. James R. Mellow, *Nathaniel Hawthorne in His Times* (Boston: Houghton Mifflin, 1980), 588–89.
2. Philip Young, *Hawthorne's Secret* (Boston: Godine, 1984). See also Gloria C. Ehrlich, *Family Themes and Hawthorne's Fiction: The Tenacious Web* (New Brunswick: Rutgers University Press, 1984).
3. Among the most distinguished and influential of these works is Frederick Crews, *The Sins of the Fathers: Hawthorne's Psychological Themes* (New York: Oxford University Press, 1966). Of new studies, see especially Michael Colacurio, *The Province of Piety* (Cambridge: Harvard University Press, 1984).
4. William Empson, *The Structure of Complex Words* (London: Chatto and Windus, 1951).
5. See especially Frank Kermode, *The Genesis of Secrecy: On the Interpretation of Narrative* (Cambridge: Harvard University Press, 1979). Kermode's book has proved particularly useful in testing my ideas in chapters 2 and 4. More recently, he has further detailed his argument in an essay, "Secrets and Narrative Sequence," *Critical Inquiry* 7 (Autumn 1980): 83–101. See also Gerald L. Bruns, "Secrecy and Understanding," *Inventions: Writing, Textuality, and Understanding in Literary History* (New Haven: Yale University Press, 1982), 17–43.
6. Fredric Jameson, *The Political Unconscious: Narrative as a Socially Symbolic Art* (Ithaca: Cornell University Press, 1981), 17–103.
7. So fundamental is the secret to psychoanalytic theory that it seems oddly wrong that Freud makes only a handful of explicit references to the secret, unless one considers how his enterprise is, in large part, devoted to the systematic analysis of secret-keeping and -telling.

8. D. A. Miller, *Narrative and Its Discontents* (Princeton: Princeton University Press, 1981), ix–xiv.

9. Any study of sympathy in Hawthorne is indebted to Roy R. Male, "Hawthorne and the Concept of Sympathy," *PMLA* 68 (1953): 138–49. Also see Albert J. Guerard, "Paradoxical Sympathies," in *The Triumph of the Novel: Dickens, Dostoevsky, Faulkner* (New York: Oxford University Press, 1976), 48–68.

10. A. N. Kaul, *The American Vision: Actual and Ideal Society in Nineteenth-Century Fiction* (New Haven and London: Yale University Press, 1963), 139–213. Harold Kaplan, *Democratic Humanism and American Literature* (Chicago and London: University of Chicago Press, 1972), 152–56.

11. *Love Letters of Nathaniel Hawthorne*, 2 vols. (1907; reprint, Chicago: Society of Dofobs, 1972), 2:79–80.

12. *Love Letters of Nathaniel Hawthorne* 2:78.

13. Like Hawthorne, Emerson also identified the reader as "friend" in his use of the conventional address. Moreover, "the poet" is "only half himself," as all of us are, in our "study to utter our painful secret." "The Poet," in *Selections from Ralph Waldo Emerson*, ed. Stephen E. Whicher (Boston: Houghton Mifflin, 1957), 222–41, esp. 223.

14. James M. Cox suggests this possibility in his "Emerson and Hawthorne," *Virginia Quarterly Review* 45 (1969): 88–107.

15. Studies of Hawthorne's debts in valuing sympathy include John Stafford's "Sympathy Comes to America," in *Themes and Directions in American Literature: Essays in Honor of Leon Howard*, ed. Ray B. Browne and Donald Pizer (Lafayette, Indiana: Purdue University Studies, 1969), 24–37. On Hawthorne and Smith, see Lester H. Hunt's excellent study in the history of the idea of sympathy, "*The Scarlet Letter:* Hawthorne's Theory of Moral Sentiments," *Philosophy and Literature* 8, no. 1 (April 1984): 75–88. Hawthorne's familiarity with Carlyle is documented in Marion L. Kesselring, *Hawthorne's Reading, 1828–1850* (New York: New York Public Library, 1949), 46. Hawthorne withdrew volumes of Carlyle in July of 1848. See also René Wellek, *A History of Modern Criticism, 1750–1950*, 5 vols. "Thomas Carlyle," in *The Age of Transition* (New Haven: Yale University Press, 1965), 3:92–110. See especially pp. 97–98: "The critic's aim is 'transposition in the author's point of vision . . . till he sees the world with [the author's] eyes, feels as [the author] felt and judges as [the author] judged.'"

16. See especially Max Scheler, *The Nature of Sympathy*, trans. Peter Heath and introd. W. Stark (London: Routledge and Kegan Paul, 1954). See also Hans-Georg Gadamer on Schliermacher's project of a universal hermeneutics, in *Truth and Method*, trans. G. Barden and J. Cumming (New York: Seaburg Press, 1975), 162–65.

17. Mark Twain, *Adventures of Huckleberry Finn* (Boston: Houghton Mifflin, 1958), 20.

18. Henry James, *Hawthorne* (Ithaca: Cornell University Press, 1956), 95.

19. On intimacy between writer and reader, see Edgar Dryden, *Nathaniel Hawthorne: The Poetics of Enchantment* (Ithaca: Cornell University Press, 1977).
20. Richard Sennett, *The Fall of Public Man: On the Social Psychology of Capitalism* (New York: reprint, Vintage, 1978), 3–27, esp. 21.

ONE. SECRETS AND SYMPATHY IN *THE SCARLET LETTER*

1. Henry Nash Smith also distinguishes this passage and its relevance for "the politics of romance" in *Democracy and the Novel: Popular Resistance to Classic American Writers* (New York: Oxford University Press, 1978), 28–30. See Sacvan Bercovitch, *American Jeremiad* (Madison, Wis.: University of Wisconsin Press, 1978), 205–8. Cf. Michael D. Bell, *Hawthorne and the Historical Romance of New England* (Princeton: Princeton University Press, 1971), 144, for the "ironic context of the Election Sermon."
2. Nathaniel Hawthorne, *The Scarlet Letter*, Centenary Edition (Columbus: Ohio State University Press, 1963), 1:243–44. All references will be cited in parentheses in the text.
3. Letter to James T. Fields, 2 January 1850, in George Parsons Lathrop, *A Study of Hawthorne* (Boston: Osgood, 1876; reprint, Scholarly Press, 1970), 213. Two notable attempts to read the novel for its humor are James G. Janssen, "Dimmesdale's 'Lurid Playfulness,'" *American Transcendental Quarterly* 1 (1969): 30–34, and Edward J. Stone, "Of Lambence and Hawthorne's Hell Fire," *Nathaniel Hawthorne Journal* (1976), 196–204.
4. Of the essays that connect *The Scarlet Letter* to Hawthorne's personal experience, Frank MacShane's "The House of the Dead: Hawthorne's 'Custom-House' and *The Scarlet Letter*" most nearly anticipates my own. MacShane argues that "While there is no evidence that Hawthorne felt guilty about his role in the Custom House, there are so many parallels between his account of his stay there and the novel about guilt for which it serves as a preface, that it is possible that Hawthorne unconsciously projected his own feelings into his account of the trials of Hester Prynne and Arthur Dimmesdale," *New England Quarterly* 35 (1962): 93–101. More recently, in John T. Irwin, *American Hieroglyphics: The Symbol of the Egyptian Hieroglyphics in the American Renaissance* (New Haven: Yale University Press, 1980), 274–84; Paul John Eakin, "Hawthorne's Imagination and the Structure of 'The Custom-House,'" *American Literature* 43 (1971): 346–58; James M. Cox "*The Scarlet Letter*: Through the Old Manse and the Custom House," *Virginia Quarterly Review* 51 (1975): 432–48.
5. A complementary psychological study is John Franzosa, "A Psychoanalysis of Hawthorne's Style," *Genre* 15, no. 3 (Fall 1981): 383–409.
6. See D. A. Miller, *Narrative and Its Discontents*, 3, 154–56.
7. *The Sociology of Georg Simmel*, trans., ed., and introd. Kurt H. Wolff (London: Free Press of Collier-Macmillan Limited, 1950), 334.

8. William C. Spengemann, *The Forms of Autobiography: Episodes in the History of a Literary Genre* (New Haven: Yale University Press, 1980), 132–65, esp. 137.

9. See Stephen Toulmin, "The Inwardness of Mental Life," *Critical Inquiry* 6, no. 1 (Autumn 1979); 1–16, for a critical assessment of the "familiar metaphysical Great Divide" between public and private self: "Secrecy or disguise . . . represents only one variety of inwardness among many others," Toulmin argues, to suggest the interaction between private experience and public expression.

10. I am indebted to Stephen Nissenbaum, "The Firing of Nathaniel Hawthorne," *Essex Institute Historical Collections* 114 (April 1978): 57–86, for much of the subsequent discussion of Hawthorne's dismissal.

11. Nissenbaum, 80–81.

12. Nissenbaum, 85.

13. "The Custom-House," 3.

14. Cf. Jean Normand, *Nathaniel Hawthorne: An Approach to an Analysis of Artistic Creation*, trans. Derek Coltman (Cleveland: Case Western Reserve University Press, 1970), 61–62. The controversy may have worked to awaken the memory of earlier traumas in Hawthorne's life, an adult ordeal in which a person reenacts the shock and reactions a child suffers. One risks making too much of this signal event, yet it is also important not to underestimate its impact. For a contrasting view to Nissenbaum's, and my use of his argument, see Arlin Turner, *Nathaniel Hawthorne, A Biography* (New York: Oxford University Press, 1980).

15. For a very intelligent treatment of this experience and its relation to Hawthorne's value for sympathy, see David Leverenz, "Mrs. Hawthorne's Headache: Reading *The Scarlet Letter*," *Nineteenth-Century Fiction* 37, no. 4 (March 1983): 552–75.

16. Cf. Nina Baym, "Nathaniel Hawthorne and His Mother: A Biographical Speculation," *American Literature* 54, no. 1 (March 1982): 1–27, esp. 19–20.

17. Letter to Horace Mann, 8 August 1849; cited in Turner, *Nathaniel Hawthorne*, 186.

18. Sigmund Freud, *The Complete Psychological Works*, Standard Edition, ed. and trans. James Strachey (London: Hogarth, 1953–54), 11:96, 21:157.

19. Julian Hawthorne, *Hawthorne and His Wife: A Biography*, 2 vols. (Boston: Houghton Mifflin, 1884), 1:340.

20. Letter to James T. Fields, 6 March 1851; cited in Turner, *Nathaniel Hawthorne*, 225.

21. Sigmund Freud, *Jokes and Their Relation to the Unconscious*, trans. and ed. James Strachey (New York: Norton, 1963), 129–32.

22. *The American Notebooks*, The Centenary Edition, ed. Claude M. Simpson, (Columbus: Ohio State University Press, 1972), 8:254. Of course, the references could have been immediately consecutive.

23. Eric J. Sundquist, *Home as Found: Authority and Genealogy in Nineteenth-*

Century American Literature (Baltimore: Johns Hopkins University Press, 1979), 98.

24. Tony Tanner, *Adultery in the Novel: Contract and Transgression* (Baltimore: Johns Hopkins University Press, 1979), esp. 11–18.

25. See esp. Michael Colacurcio, "Footsteps of Ann Hutchinson: The Context of *The Scarlet Letter*," *ELH* 39 (1972): 459–64; Michael D. Bell, *Hawthorne and the Historical Romance of New England* (Princeton: Princeton University Press, 1971), 126–46. See also Nina Baym's chapter on *The Scarlet Letter* in *The Shape of Hawthorne's Career* (Ithaca: Cornell University Press, 1976). For a discussion of Hawthorne's historical sources, see Charles Ryskamp, "New England Sources of *The Scarlet Letter*," *American Literature* 31 (1959): 257–72. Cf. David H. Flaherty, *Privacy in Colonial New England* (Charlottesville: University Press of Virginia, 1972).

26. Simmel, 331–32.

27. Harold Kaplan, *Democratic Humanism and American Literature*, 153. Cf. Wilson Carey McWilliams, "Nathaniel Hawthorne: The Citizen," in *The Idea of Fraternity in America* (Berkeley: University of California Press, 1973), 301–27.

28. A thematics of this kind of vision will be taken up in my chapter on *The Blithedale Romance*.

29. Roy R. Male, "Hawthorne and the Concept of Sympathy," 139.

30. Quoted in George Frederick Drinka, M.D., *The Birth of Neurosis: Myth, Malady, and the Victorians* (New York: Simon and Schuster, 1984), 169–70.

31. Cf. Franzosa, "A Psychoanalysis of Hawthorne's Style." Franzosa rightly identifies the interest of secrecy in Hawthorne's rhetoric but does not connect it to the functions Hawthorne ascribes to sympathy. Also see Irwin, *American Hieroglyphics*, 269–73.

32. Peter Brooks, *Reading for the Plot: Design and Intention in Narrative* (New York: Knopf, 1984), 10.

33. See John Carlos Rowe, *Through the Custom-House: Nineteenth-Century American Fiction and Modern Theory* (Baltimore: Johns Hopkins University Press, 1982), 8–9, on the issue of traces and Derridean "différance."

34. "Hawthorne in Our Time," in *Beyond Culture: Essays on Literature and Learning* (New York: Viking, 1965), 179–208.

35. Richard Brodhead, *Hawthorne, Melville, and the Novel* (Chicago: University Press of Chicago, 1976), 68.

36. Nissenbaum, 80–81.

37. Freud, *Jokes*, 232–33.

38. Freud, "Humour" (1927), in *Complete Psychological Works* 21:162–63.

39. Baym, *The Shape of Hawthorne's Career*, 123–51, esp. 139.

40. See Freud, *Complete Psychological Works* 4:245–46, 288. Secrecy, Freud suggests in one of his few specific references to the subject, is often represented in dreams by "a lot of strangers" staring at a victim.

41. Yvor Winters, *In Defense of Reason* (Chicago: Swallow Press, n.d.), 172.

42. Brodhead, 68.

43. Angus Fletcher, *Allegory: The Theory of a Symbolic Mode* (Ithaca: Cornell University Press, 1964), 301. See 279–303.

44. Stephen Mailloux makes this point convincingly in reference to "Rappaccini's Daughter," in his *Interpretive Conventions: The Reader in the Study of American Fiction* (Ithaca: Cornell University Press, 1982), 72–91, esp. 87–88.

45. F. O. Matthiessen, *American Renaissance: Art and Expression in the Age of Emerson and Whitman* (1941; reprint, New York: Oxford University Press, 1968), 277, 276.

46. Brodhead, 68.

47. David Levin, *In Defense of Historical Literature: Essays on American History, Autobiography, Drama, and Fiction* (New York: Hill and Wang, 1967), 112.

48. Freud, *Jokes*, 152.

49. Nissenbaum, 85.

50. Simmel, 330.

51. Simmel, 333–34.

52. I borrow the term *replication* from Brodhead's reading of Pearl's imitative powers, especially as she appears at brook-side. In *Rediscovering Hawthorne* (Princeton: Princeton University Press, 1977), Kenneth Dauber very interestingly observes that *The Scarlet Letter* is " 'The Custom-House' writ large" and provocatively suggests that for Hawthorne, "all creation begins in duplication" (97). See "A 'Typical Illusion,' " 87–118.

53. Trilling, 203.

54. On the relation between *The Scarlet Letter* and *The House of the Seven Gables*, see Evan Carton, *The Rhetoric of American Romance: Dialectic and Identity in Emerson, Dickinson, Poe, and Hawthorne* (Baltimore: Johns Hopkins University Press, 1985), 216–18.

TWO. *THE HOUSE OF THE SEVEN GABLES*
AND THE SECRET OF ROMANCE

1. On the question of plot as a formal principle of criticizing antebellum fiction, see Nina Baym, *Novels, Readers, and Reviewers* (Ithaca: Cornell University Press, 1984), 63–81. On Hawthorne, specifically, see 66, 77; on narration in Hawthorne, see 92–93, 132–33.

2. Anonymous, "Nathaniel Hawthorne" (*Dublin University Magazine*, October 1855); reprinted in *The Recognition of Nathaniel Hawthorne: Selected Criticism Since 1828*, ed. B. Bernard Cohen (Ann Arbor: University of Michigan Press, 1969), 71–75, esp. 72.

3. Henry T. Tuckerman, "Nathaniel Hawthorne" (*Southern Literary Messenger*, June 1851); reprinted in *The Recognition of Nathaniel Hawthorne*, 55–63, esp. 60.

4. Letter to James T. Fields; cited in Arlin Turner, *Nathaniel Hawthorne, A Biography* (New York: Oxford University Press, 1980), 224.

5. Among the critics who have found the ending appropriate are Francis Battaglia—*PMLA* 82 (1967): 570–90; *SNNTS* 2 (1970): 468–73—who reads the novel for its organic harmony and John Gatta—"Progress and Providence in *The House of the Seven Gables*," *American Literature* 50 (1978): 37–48. See also Sheldon Liebman, "Point of View in *The House of the Seven Gables*," *ESQ* 19 (1973): 203–12.

6. Walter Benn Michaels, "Romance and Real Estate," in *The American Renaissance Reconsidered*, ed. Michaels and Pease (Baltimore: Johns Hopkins University Press, 1985), 156–82, esp. 164.

7. Letter to James T. Fields; cited in *Hawthorne: The Critical Heritage*, ed. J. Donald Crowley (New York: Barnes and Noble, 1970), 197; E. P. Whipple, *Graham's Magazine* (May 1851); reprinted in *Hawthorne: The Critical Heritage*, 197–201, esp. 197.

8. Letter to Fields, 3 November 1950, cited in Turner, *Nathaniel Hawthorne*, 223. Hawthorne writes: "Sometimes, when tired of it, it strikes me that the whole is an absurdity, from beginning to end; but the fact is, in writing a romance, a man is always—or always ought to be—*careening* on the *utmost* verge of a precipitous *absurdity*, and the skill lies in coming as close as possible, without actually tumbling over."

9. Preface to *The House of the Seven Gables*, Centenary Edition (Columbus: Ohio State University Press, 1963), 2:2. All future references will be cited in parentheses in the text.

10. Tzvetan Todorov, "The Secret of Narrative," *The Poetics of Prose*, trans. Richard Howard (Ithaca: Cornell University Press, 1977), 143–78, esp. 147.

11. Kenneth Dauber discusses the inertness of the novel's middle in *Rediscovering Hawthorne* (Princeton: Princeton University Press, 1977), 118–48; Frederick Crews describes the novel's ending as impotence deriving from the guilt of murdering the father-surrogate. See his *The Sins of the Fathers: Hawthorne's Psychological Themes* (New York: Oxford University Press, 1966), 171–93.

12. Cf. Freud's essay, "A Child is being Beaten: A Contribution to the Study of the Origin of Sexual Perversions" (1919), in *The Complete Psychological Works*, Standard Edition, ed. and trans. James Strachey (London: Hogarth, 1953–54), 17: 174–204.

13. Teresa De Lauretis, "Desire in Narrative," *Alice Doesn't: Feminism, Semiotics, Cinema* (Bloomington: Indiana University Press, 1982), 103–57, esp. 120.

14. For a study of the novel as a gothic parody, see Judith A. Gustafson, "Parody and *The House of the Seven Gables*," *Nathaniel Hawthorne Journal* (1976), 294–302; see also Maurice Charney, "Hawthorne and the Gothic Style," *NEQ* 34 (1961): 36–49; Terence Martin, "Hawthorne and Poe," *Kenyon Review* 28 (1966): 194–209.

15. David Downing, "Beyond Convention: The Dynamics of Imagery and Response in Hawthorne's Early Sense of Evil," *American Literature* 51 (1980): 463–77, esp. 468.

16. *The American Notebooks*, Centenary Edition, ed. Claude M. Simpson (Columbus: Ohio State University Press, 1972), 8: 491; see also 497–99.

17. Taylor Stoehr, *Hawthorne's Mad Scientists: Pseudoscience and Social Science in Nineteenth-Century Life and Letters* (Hamden, Conn.: Archon Books, 1978), 83–102.

18. See Turner, *Nathaniel Hawthorne*, 225.

19. *Mosses from an Old Manse*, Centenary Edition (Columbus: Ohio State University Press, 1974), 10:167.

20. See Susan Sontag, *On Photography* (New York: Farrar, Straus and Giroux, 1977), esp. chapter 1 for nineteenth-century views on photography as an art of transformation.

21. Leslie Fiedler, *Love and Death in the American Novel*, rev. ed. (1966; reprint, New York: Stein and Day, 1975), 224.

22. Cf. Geoffrey H. Hartman, "Words and Wounds," *Saving the Text: Literature/Derrida/Philosophy* (Baltimore: Johns Hopkins University Press, 1981), 118–57, esp. 142–43.

23. On the question of sympathy and response, see *The Rambler*, no. 60, 13 October 1750, in *The Yale Edition of the Works of Samuel Johnson*, ed. W. J. Bate and Albrecht B. Strauss (New Haven: Yale University Press, 1969), 3:318–23, esp. 319.

24. Frank Kermode, "Secrets and Narrative Sequence," *Critical Inquiry* 7 (1980), 87–88.

25. Laurence B. Holland, "Authority, Power, and Form: Some American Texts," *The Yearbook of English Studies*, no. 8, ed. G. K. Hunter and C. J. Rawson (London: Modern Humanities Research Association, 1978), 10.

26. It is possible to conjecture that Holgrave is also speaking for Hawthorne here and that the novel's plot is being reformulated even as Hawthorne is comparing this section of the narrative. The activity of telling stories brings this "secret" to light. Cf. Brook Thomas, "*The House of the Seven Gables:* Reading the Romance of America," *PMLA* 97, no. 2 (March 1982): 195–211, esp. 201, 209.

27. Joel Porte discusses this scene to a very similar effect in *The Romance in America* (Middletown, Conn.: Wesleyan University Press, 1969), 114–25. Although his study is not concerned with secrecy, many of his points anticipate my own. Kenneth Burke describes the relations among secrecy, killing, and order in *A Rhetoric of Motives* (1950; reprint, Berkeley: University of California Press, 1969), 260–67.

28. Freud, "Civilization and Its Discontents" (1930) in *Complete Psychological Works* 21:79–81.

29. The classic formulation of the question of father-figures and ambivalence is found in Freud, "The Ego and the Id" (1923), in *Complete Psychological Works*

19:3–68, esp. 28–39. For a general Lacanian consideration of this issue, see *The Fictional Father*, ed. and introd. Robert Con Davis (Amherst: University of Massachusetts Press, 1981), 1–26.

30. "Creative Writers and Day-Dreaming" (1908), in *Complete Psychological Works* 9:144–54, esp. 151. For an overview of the critical uses to which this essay has been put, see Elizabeth Wright, *Psychoanalytic Criticism: Theory in Practice* (London: Methuen, 1984), 27–29, 63–68.

31. Freud, "Creative Writers and Day-Dreaming," in *Complete Psychological Works* 9:152.

32. See Walter Benjamin, "The Storyteller," in *Illuminations*, ed. and introd. Hannah Arendt (New York: Schocken, 1969), 83–109, esp. 97–98.

33. Freud's tenet of "working-through" is elaborated in "Beyond the Pleasure Principle," in *Complete Psychological Works* 18:1–65. See also Peter Brooks's application of these principles in his "Repetition, Repression, and Return: *Great Expectations* and the Study of Plot," *New Literary History* 11, no. 3 (Summer 1980): 503–26.

34. See Freud's essay, "Remembering, Repeating and Working-Through" (Further Recommendations on the Technique of Psycho-Analysis 3), in *Complete Psychological Works* 12:145–56.

35. See esp. Joel Kehler, "House, Home, and Hawthorne's Psychology of Habitation," *ESQ* 21 (1975): 142–53; Samuel Scoville, "Hawthorne's Houses and Hidden Treasure," *ESQ* 19 (1973): 61–73; Edgar Dryden, "Hawthorne's 'Castles in the Air,'" *ELH* 38 (1971): 294–317.

36. See Cohen, *The Recognition*, 69–70. An anonymous essay from *The American Whig Review*, 16 (November 1852): 417–24, epitomizes this aspect of response. Also see Baym, "Morality and Moral Tendency," in *Novels, Readers, and Reviewers*, on the general subject of "healthy" novelists, 173–95. On *Seven Gables*, in particular, Baym quotes a review from *Peterson's* (June 1851): "The fault of the book, indeed of all Hawthorne's books in a moral aspect, is the sombre coloring which pervades them, and which leaves an effect more or less morbid on even healthy minds. The only really lovable character in the book is Phoebe" (177).

37. In a letter read to the B'nai B'rith, Freud writes of being widely ostracized as a result of his postulations and expresses his gratitude to these members of the Jewish community who accepted him: "It happened that in the years from 1895 onwards I was subjected to two powerful impressions which combined to produce the same effect on me. On the one hand, I had gained my first insight into the depths of the life of the human instincts; I had seen some things that were sobering and even, at first, frightening. On the other hand, the announcement of my unpleasing discourses had as its result the severance of the greater part of my human contacts; I felt as though I were despised and universally shunned. In my loneliness I was seized with a longing to find a circle of picked men of high character who would receive me in a friendly spirit in spite of my temerity. Your

society was pointed out to me as the place where such men were to be found." "Address to the Society of B'Nai B'rith" (1941[1926]) 20:273–74.
38. See Freud's discussion of ambivalence in "Instincts and their Vicissitudes," in *Complete Psychological Works* 14:117–40.
39. Hartman, *Saving the Text*, 142–43.

THREE. *THE BLITHEDALE ROMANCE:* SECRETS, SOCIETY, AND REFORM

1. William Hedges, "Hawthorne's *Blithedale:* The Function of the Narrator," *Nineteenth-Century Fiction* 14 (1960): 303–16; James H. Justus, "Hawthorne's Coverdale: Character and Art in *The Blithedale Romance,*" *American Literature* 47 (1975): 21–36; Kent Bales, "*The Blithedale Romance:* Coverdale's 'Mean and Subversive Egotism,'" *Bucknell Review* 21 (1973): 60–82; Irwin Stock, "Hawthorne's Portrait of the Artist: A Defense of *The Blithedale Romance, Novel* 11, no. 2 (Winter 1978): 144–56. See also David Minter, *The Interpreted Design as a Structural Principle in American Prose* (New Haven and London: Yale University Press, 1969), Joel Porte, *The Romance in America* (Middletown, Conn.: Wesleyan University Press, 1969), 125–37. Bales and Porte most nearly anticipate my reading of the novel. The best Freudian study remains Crews, 194–212. See also John Dolis, "Hawthorne's Metonymic Gaze: Image and Object," *American Literature* 56, no. 3 (October 1984): 362–78.
2. "The American Scholar," *The Portable Emerson*, 38. For an interesting analysis of the relation between Emerson and Hawthorne, see James Cox, "Emerson and Hawthorne," *Virginia Quarterly Review* 45 (1969): 87–107. Also see Gustaaf Van Cromphaut, "Emerson, Hawthorne, and *The Blithedale Romance,*" *Georgia Review* 25 (1972): 471–82.
3. *The Blithedale Romance* and *Fanshawe*, Centenary Edition (Columbus: Ohio State University Press, 1964), 3, 160. All future references will be cited in parentheses in the text.
4. Richard Poirier, *A World Elsewhere: The Places of Style in American Literature* (1966; reprint, New York: Oxford University Press, 1973), 93–143.
5. Henry James, "Preface to *The Princess Casamassima,*" *The Art of the Novel*, introd. R. P. Blackmur (New York: Scribner's 1934), 77–78. For the conventional assessment and commentary, consider Robert Emmet Long, *The Great Succession: Henry James and the Legacy of Hawthorne* (Pittsburgh: University of Pittsburgh Press, 1979), esp. 117–57.
6. Mark Seltzer, *Henry James and the Art of Politics* (Ithaca: Cornell University Press, 1984), 26–58.
7. Richard Sennett, *The Fall of Public Man*, esp. chapter 8. "Personality in Public," 150–94. See also Kent Bales, "*The Blithedale Romance:* Coverdale's 'Mean and Subversive Egotism'" and "Allegory and the Radical Romantic Ethic of *The Blithedale Romance,*" *American Literature* 46 (1974): 41–53; Nicholas Cana-

day, "Community and Identity at Blithedale," *South Atlantic Quarterly* 71 (1972): 30–39; Carl Dennis, "*The Blithedale Romance* and the Problem of Self-Integration," *Texas Studies in Language and Literature* 15 (1972): 93–110; John Hirsh, "The Politics of Blithedale: The Dilemma of the Self," *Studies in Romanticism* 11 (1971): 138–46.

8. *Love Letters of Nathaniel Hawthorne*, 2 vols. (1907; reprint, Chicago, Society of Dofobs, 1972), 2:62. For a philosophic treatment of secrets in public life, see Sissela Bok, *Secrets: On the Ethics of Concealment and Revelation* (New York: Pantheon, 1982), esp. 3–14, 29–44.

9. *Love Letters* 2:64–65.

10. Freud, " 'The Uncanny,' " in *The Complete Psychological Works*, Standard Edition, ed. and trans. James Strachey (London: Hogarth, 1953–54, 18:217–52.

11. Geoffrey Hartman, "I. A. Richards and the Dream of Communication," *The Fate of Reading and Other Essays* (Chicago: University of Chicago Press, 1975), 35.

12. For an assessment of the critical discussion, see Louis Auchincloss, "A Study of Form and Point of View," *Nathaniel Hawthorne Journal* (1972), 53–58; also see Ellen E. Morgan, "The Veiled Lady: The Secret Love of Miles Coverdale," *Nathaniel Hawthorne Journal* (1971), 169–81.

13. Philip Rahv, "The Dark Lady of Salem," *Essays on Literature and Politics, 1932–1972,* ed. Arabel J. Porter and Andrew J. Dvosin (Boston: Houghton Mifflin, 1978), 43–62. Cf. Frederick Crews, *The Sins of the Fathers: Hawthorne's Psychological Themes* (New York: Oxford University Press, 1966) 202–5. Neither Crews nor Rahv sufficiently accounts for the historical convention of the split between the dark- and fair-haired heroines. Also consider Allan Gardner Lloyd Smith, *Eve Tempted: Writing and Sexuality in Hawthorne's Fiction* (Totowa, N.J.: Barnes and Noble, 1983), 73–90.

14. See Frank Kermode on the suppression of secrets, "Secrets and Narrative Sequence": "In the kinds of narrative upon which we conventionally place a higher value, the case against propriety is much stronger; there is much more material that is less manifestly under the control of authority, less easily subordinated to 'clearness and effect,' more palpably the enemy of order, of interpretative consensus, of message. It represents a fortunate collapse of authority (authors have authority, property rights; but they poach their own game and thereby set a precedent to all interpreters)." *Critical Inquiry* 7 (Autumn 1980): 87.

15. Richard D. Rust, "Coverdale's Confession, A Key to Meaning in *The Blithedale Romance*," in *Literature and Ideas in America: Essays in Memory of Harry Hayden Clark*, ed. Robert Falk (Athens: Ohio University Press), 96–110.

16. Richard Sennett, *The Fall of Public Man: On the Social Psychology of Capitalism* (New York: reprint, Vintage, 1978), 153.

17. Leo Bersani, *A Future for Astyanax: Character and Desire in Literature* (Boston: Little Brown, 1976), 77–79.

18. Sennett ascribes a particular relevance to the relation between city life and the *theatrium mundi*. See "The Stage Tells a Truth the Street No Longer Tells," 174–76.

19. Mark Holloway, *Heavens on Earth: Utopian Communities in America 1680–1880* (London: Turnstile Press, 1951), 127–30, esp. 129.

20. Evan Carton, *The Rhetoric of American Romance: Dialectic and Identity in Emerson, Dickinson, Poe, and Hawthorne* (Baltimore: Johns Hopkins University Press, 1985), 228–52, esp. 231. This excellent study of the novel came to my attention too late for me to make proper use of the several affinities between our discussions: e.g., "Hawthorne's text insistently effects the entanglement of sympathy and violation in human intercourse rather than representing them as alternatives" (238).

21. On the general question of belatedness, see John Carlos Rowe, *Through the Custom-House: Nineteenth-Century American Fiction and Modern Theory* (Baltimore: Johns Hopkins University Press, 1982), 20.

22. Emerson, "New England Reformers," *The Portable Emerson*, ed. Mark Van Doren (New York: Viking, 1946), 111.

23. See John P. McWilliams, Jr., *Hawthorne, Melville, and the American character: A looking-glass business* (Cambridge: Cambridge University Press, 1984), 115–23, esp. 119.

24. Sennett, *Fall of Public Man*, 176. Perhaps the most important qualification to make in applying Sennett's argument to *Blithedale* is that Hawthorne lacks the kind of Marxist taxonomy that makes Balzac so attractive to Sennett's investigation of the public and private self; but consider Sennett's discussion, based on Donald Fanger, *Dostoevsky and Romantic Realism*: "the novelist concentrates on the details of personal daily life because each of these, if picked over, and apart, and turned around from every angle, will reveal not just the person's character or even personality in a myriad of different guises, but will give up a secret, which is that of a picture of the whole society. All of society is miniaturized in every small concrete manifestation of life, but the novelist and the reader of novels must force themselves to strain every faculty, to invest more feeling in details than they could ever logically warrant, in order to prise out this secret" (156–57).

25. Cf. John Carlos Rowe: "In *The Blithedale Romance*, the imagination neither mediates between the mind and its objects nor serves as a simple alternative to the imperial world" (57). "The Metaphysics of Imagination: Narrative Consciousness in Hawthorne's *The Blithedale Romance*," *Through the Custom-House*, 52–90.

26. Howard Kerr, *Mediums, and Spirit-Rappers, and Roaring Radicals: Spiritualism in American Literature, 1850–1900* (Urbana: University of Illinois Press, 1978), 11.

27. Of course, "hold intercourse" need not be construed sexually, nor do I mean to suggest that Hawthorne uses the phrase with this connotation. The case for

Priscilla as prostitute is made persuasively in Allan and Barbara Lefcowitz, "Some Rents in the Veil: New Light on Priscilla and Zenobia in *The Blithedale Romance*," *Nineteenth-Century Fiction* 21 (1969): 263–76. See also Louis J. Kern, *An Ordered Love: Sex Roles and Sexuality in Victorian Utopias—the Shakers, the Mormons, and the Oneida Community* (Chapel Hill: University of North Carolina Press, 1981), 225; for a discussion of mesmerism and sexuality, see Maria Tater, *Spellbound* (Princeton: Princeton University Press, 1978), 205–6, 227.

28. See René Girard, "'Triangular' Desire," *Deceit, Desire and the Novel: Self and Other in Literary Structure,* trans. Y. Freccero (Baltimore: Johns Hopkins University Press, 1965), 1–53, esp. 7–8. Also consider Girard's remark, "At a certain depth there is no difference between our own secret and the secret of Others," 298. For further elaboration, see "Strategies of Madness—Nietzsche, Wagner, and Dostoevski," *"To Double Business Bound": Essays on Literature, Mimesis, and Anthropology* (Baltimore: Johns Hopkins University Press, 1978), 61–83.

29. Emerson, "New England Reformers," 120.

30. Perhaps the best discussion to date of the historical relation between the feminist movement and the novel appears in Taylor Stoehr, *Hawthorne's Mad Scientists: Pseudoscience and Social Science in Nineteenth-Century Life and Letters* (Hamden, Conn.: Archon Books, 1978), 183–224. Stoehr also considers spiritualism and philanthropy in his instructive account. See also "Feminism and Femininity in *The Blithedale Romance*," by Terence J. Matheson, in *Nathaniel Hawthorne Journal* (1976), 215–27; Nina Baym, *The Shape of Hawthorne's Career* (Ithaca: Cornell University Press, 1976), 184–205.

31. "Man the Reformer," *The Portable Emerson*, ed. Van Doren, 85.

32. "New England Reformers," 132.

33. Ibid., 127–28.

34. Sigmund Freud, *Jokes and Their Relation to the Unconscious,* trans. and ed. James Strachey (New York: Norton, 1963), 108.

35. Ibid., 109–10.

FOUR. *THE MARBLE FAUN:* SYMPATHY AND THE SECRET OF ART

1. *The Marble Faun: Or, The Romance of Monte Beni,* Centenary Edition (Columbus: Ohio State University Press, 1968), 4:464. All future references will be cited in parentheses in the text.

2. This chapter addresses the thematics rather than the theory of reception. "Sympathy" is so crucial to Romantic hermeneutics that it is implicitly an issue for such theorists as Heidegger, Jauss, Gadamer, Iser, et al. Throughout, I have been guided by many of the principles raised in Paul Ricoeur, *Hermeneutics and the Human Sciences,* ed. and trans. John B. Thompson (Cambridge: Cambridge University Press, 1981).

3. Kenneth Dauber, "The Novelist as Critic," *Rediscovering Hawthorne* (Prince-

ton: Princeton University Press, 1977), 193–220, esp. 194–95. Dauber's emphasis throughout this argument in some ways anticipates my own, but to a deconstructive purpose: "Writer and reader join in a criticism of Hawthorne's work," 194. More light is shed, I think, by Ricoeur, "Appropriation," *Hermeneutics and the Human Sciences*, 182–93.

4. For comparative purposes, see Janice Carlisle, "The Bonds of Reading: Mid-Century Aims and Ideals," *The Sense of an Audience: Dickens, Thackeray, and George Eliot at Mid-Century* (Athens: University of Georgia Press, 1981), 12–63, on the kinds of social and aesthetic references Hawthorne's Victorian counterparts were secure in assuming. See also Steven Mailloux, *Interpretive Conventions* (Ithaca: Cornell University Press, 1982), 136–38, for a theoretical consideration of reading conventions and historical communities.

5. Of the many treatments of the Beatrice Cenci theme in the novel, the most helpful have been Frederick Crews, "Subterranean Reminiscences," *The Sins of the Fathers* (New York: Oxford University Press, 1966), 213–40; Joel Porte, "Saints and Assassins," *The Romance in America* (Middletown, Conn.: Wesleyan University Press, 1969), 137–51; Jay Bochner, "Life in a Picture Gallery: *The Portrait of a Lady* and *The Marble Faun*," *Texas Studies in Language and Literature* 11 (1972): 761–77.

6. *The French and Italian Notebooks*, ed. Thomas Woodson, Centenary Edition (Columbus: Ohio State University Press, 1980), 14:520. All future references will be cited as *F&IN* in parentheses in the text.

7. Porte, *Romance in America*, 144.

8. Cf. Robert Weimann, *Structure and Society in Literary History: Studies in the History and Theory of Historical Criticism* (1976; expanded ed., Baltimore: Johns Hopkins University Press, 1984), 133, 134.

9. *The Act of Reading: A Theory of Aesthetic Response* (Baltimore: Johns Hopkins University Press, 1978), 6–7.

10. For an explanation of how readers inevitably adhere to historical norms, see Ralph Cohen, "Historical Knowledge and Literary Understanding," *Papers on Language and Literature* 14 (1978): 227–48, esp. 229. Of the transaction between a literary work and the reader, Cohen writes: "A reader belongs to a historical ambience, and his literary hypotheses derive from interactions with a norm of which he himself cannot be fully conscious. Not fully conscious because, however self-aware he may be, he is living in the midst of a norm that can only be adequately perceived after it has been supplanted. The interpreter can overlook but he cannot deny that the work has a generic past identified by rhetorically inherited devices; whatever analysis he undertakes will presuppose—with his awareness or not—that there exists a relationship historically developed among particular conventions of construction and language. To identify a writer's figure or figures in the carpet, the interpreter must commit himself to some hypothesis about identity, about repetition, about the relation of the self to artistic expression. And a cultural definition is a necessary part of this literary

self." James's discussion of the secret appears in *The Notebooks of Henry James,* ed. F. O. Matthiessen and K. Murdock (New York: Braziller, 1955), 20–24, 229–30.

11. For a Lacanian reading of experience as the image of a tapestry, see *The Language of the Self,* trans. Anthony Wilden (Baltimore: Johns Hopkins University Press, 1968), 98 n. 9.

12. Gary Scrimgeour, "*The Marble Faun:* Hawthorne's Faery Land," *American Literature* 36 (1964): 271–87, esp. 272–73.

13. Murray Krieger, "*The Marble Faun* and the International Theme," *The Play and the Place of Criticism* (Baltimore: Johns Hopkins University Press, 1967), 79–90, esp. 85.

14. See David Levin, "Hawthorne's Romances: The Value of Puritan History," *In Defense of Historical Literature* (New York: Hill and Wang, 1967), 98–117. Michael Colacurcio, "Depravity, History, and the Hawthorne Problem," *The Province of Piety: Moral History in Hawthorne's Early Tales* (Cambridge: Harvard University Press, 1984), 5–36.

15. Dryden, "The Limits of Romance: A Reading of *The Marble Faun,*" in *Individual and Community: Variations on a Theme in American Literature,* ed. Kenneth H. Baldwin and David K. Irby (Durham, N.C.: Duke University Press, 1975), 17–48, esp. 42–43.

16. The notion of mood ought not to be confused with pure subjectivity. John Caldwell Stubbs sees subjectivity as lending the novel its peculiar power: "The world Hawthorne creates in *The Marble Faun* is unique for its time. It is a work given coherence by a subjective, dreaming mind. It depends for its success on our accepting the process of this mind, as it turns and gropes toward a realization of the Adamic myth, as the main strength of the work," *The Pursuit of Form: A Study of Hawthorne and the Romance* (Urbana: University of Illinois Press, 1970), 154. See also Robert Lowell's "Hawthorne" in *Hawthorne Centenary Essays,* ed. Roy Harvey Pearce (Columbus: Ohio State University Press, 1964), 4, a poem in which Lowell sees the writer as "bent down, brooding, brooding," an image Dauber finds important: "It is the process of brooding, not what is brooded upon, that is of interest," Dauber, *Rediscovering Hawthorne,* 199. How Dauber separates the activity from the occasion is less certain.

17. In a provocative and very different vein, Roy R. Male writes that "observing the fluid dialectic between literal and figurative is the way into and out of his stylistic labyrinth." "This dialectic is a dynamic and continuous process in which the recognition of either literal or figurative meanings depends radically on our recognition, at nearly the same time, of the one, the other, or both." "Hawthorne's Literal Figures," in *Ruined Eden of the Present: Hawthorne, Melville, and Poe, Essays in Honor of Darrel Abel,* ed. G. R. Thompson and Virgil L. Lokke (West Lafayette, Ind.: Purdue University Press, 1981), 84–85. Male's note refers to Michael McCanles, "The Literal and the Metaphorical: Dialectic or Interchange," *PMLA* 91 (1976): 279–90.

18. Scrimgeour, "*The Marble Faun:* Hawthorne's Faery Land," 272–73. He continues: "To make the same point another way, Hawthorne's choice of art objects is banal from the viewpoint of art but exceptionally fit for communication with the reader" 273. See also Harry Levin, "Statues from Italy: *The Marble Faun,*" in *Hawthorne Centenary Essays,* 103–17.

19. Cf. Mailloux, *Interpretive Conventions,* 90–92.

20. Cf. Nicolaus Mills, *American and English Fiction in the Nineteenth Century: An Antigenre Critique and Comparison* (Bloomington: Indiana University Press, 1973), 52–71. See also Robert Falk, *The Victorian Mode in American Fiction, 1865–1885* (East Lansing: Michigan State University Press, 1964), passim.

21. See Ricoeur, *Hermeneutics and the Human Sciences,* 190–93.

22. Krieger, "*The Marble Faun* and the International Theme," 85.

23. Dryden, "The Limits of Romance," 40.

24. For Dryden, Hawthorne shifts his interest from an interpretation of the Faun of Praxiteles to "the problem of interpretation itself" (38); for Dauber, "Neither imposing himself on the work nor being imposed on by it, he keeps up the attitude of Lowell's brooding only to enlist the reader in a communal process. The transformation into plot of such an attitude produces mystery, but a mystery that remains impenetrable . . ." (200).

25. See James R. Mellow, *Nathaniel Hawthorne in His Times* (Boston: Houghton Mifflin, 1980): "The more fruitful implications lie in some conscious or unconscious connection with Mrs. Henry Field, the former governess in the Duc de Choiseul-Praslin household. When Henry Bright . . . asked if Miriam had been patterned after Henriette Deulzy-Desportes, Hawthorne had (somewhat ambiguously) admitted, 'Well, I daresay she was. . . . I knew I had some dim recollection of some crime'" (522; see also 323).

26. Julian Hawthorne, *Hawthorne and His Wife: A Biography,* 2 vols. (Boston: Houghton Mifflin, 1884), 1:358–59.

27. Kermode, "Secrets and Narrative Sequence," *Critical Inquiry* 7 (Autumn 1980) 87–88.

28. Porte, *Romance in America,* 149–50. Porte's note is to Dorothy Waples's pioneer essay on Freudian elements in the novel.

29. Jonathan Auerbach, "Executing the Model: Painting, Sculpture, and Romance-Writing in Hawthorne's *The Marble Faun,*" *ELH* 47 (1980): 103–20. Auerbach writes, "The Model's destruction not only sheds light on the creative activity of painting and sculpture which takes place within the novel, but also illuminates Hawthorne's own creative act, the process of plotting the romance itself. By transforming the metaphor 'to execute a model' into the central event of the novel, Hawthorne turns his romance into a self-interpreting confession that compels the reader to participate in the fiction" (103).

30. See George Levine, *The Realistic Imagination: English Fiction from Frankenstein to Lady Chatterly* (Chicago: University of Chicago Press, 1981). Levine uses the Frankenstein story to show how its continuities throughout the cen-

tury establish realistic fiction's primary interest in domesticating the monstrous element of the self.

FIVE. HAWTHORNE'S JAMES AND THE POWER OF SYMPATHY

1. *Our Old Home* and *English Note-books*, 2 vols. (Boston: Houghton Mifflin, 1984), 1:564. The entry is dated 12 April 1855.
2. *The American Claimant Manuscripts*, ed. Edward H. Davidson et al. Centenary Edition (Columbus: Ohio State University Press, 1977), 12:475.
3. The most complete summary of Hawthorne's decline is found in Edward H. Davidson, *Hawthorne's Last Phase* (New Haven: Yale University Press, 1949). Also see his historical commentary (with Claude Simpson) in *The American Claimant Manuscripts*, 491–521.
4. Julian Hawthorne, *Hawthorne and His Wife: A Biography*, 2 vols. (Boston: Houghton Mifflin, 1884), 1:358–59.
5. Yvor Winters, "Maule's Curse, or Hawthorne and the Problem of Allegory," *In Defense of Reason* (Chicago: Swallow Press, n.d.), 3d ed., 172.
6. Davidson, *Hawthorne's Last Phase*, 150.
7. Nina Baym, *The Shape of Hawthorne's Career* (Ithaca: Cornell University Press, 1976), 226.
8. See Richard Brodhead, *The School of Hawthorne* (New York: Oxford University Press, 1986), 67–70, for a consideration of Hawthorne's last years.
9. For a balanced view of Lovell's Fight, see David Levin, "Modern Misjudgements of Racial Imperialism in Hawthorne and Parkman," *Yearbook of English Studies* 13 (1983): 145–58.
10. *The Snow-Image and Uncollected Tales*, Centenary Edition (Columbus: Ohio State University Press, 1974), 11:52.
11. *Roderick Hudson*, in *The Novels and Tales of Henry James*, 24 vols. (New York: Scribner's, 1909), New York Edition, 1:293. In the original version, Mallet merely says that "Without flattering myself, I may say I'm sympathetic."
12. *Hawthorne*, in *Essays on Literature: American and English Writers*, ed. Leon Edel, Library of America (New York: Viking, 1984), 352. Hereafter cited as *EL*.
13. *The Comic Tradition in America*, ed. and introd. Louis D. Rubin, Jr. (New Brunswick, N.J.: Rutgers University Press, 1973), 8–9.
14. T. S. Eliot first observed the affinity between Hawthorne and James in their treatment of relations between people and how both emphasize the interest of reaction. "The Hawthorne Aspect," in *The Question of Henry James*, ed. F. W. Dupee (New York: Holt, 1945), 112–19, esp. 116.
15. Hyatt H. Waggoner, *The Presence of Hawthorne* (Baton Rouge: Louisiana State University Press, 1979), 143–61; Brodhead, *The School of Hawthorne*, 104–200. Brodhead's excellent study was published too recently for me to make full use of his argument, but it is clear that his book stands as the most substantial examination, to date, of the relation between these two writers.

16. Of the many studies devoted to Hawthorne and James, see Robert Emmet Long, *The Great Succession: Henry James and the Legacy of Hawthorne* (Pittsburgh, University of Pittsburgh Press, 1979). Also see Peter Buitenhuis, *The Grasping Imagination: The American Writings of Henry James* (Toronto: University of Toronto Press, 1970), 38–44. Some of the most provocative and illuminating remarks on the writers are to be found in Laurence Holland, *The Expense of Vision: Essays on the Craft of Henry James* (Baltimore: Johns Hopkins University Press, 1964, reprint, 1982), 20–27.

17. The best psychoanalytic study of this relation is John Carlos Rowe's erudite essay, "James's *Hawthorne* and the American Anxiety of Influence," *The Theoretical Dimensions of Henry James* (Madison: University of Wisconsin Press, 1984), 30–57.

18. Preface to *The Princess Casamassima*, in *European Writers and The Prefaces*, ed. Leon Edel, Library of America (New York: Viking, 1984), 1102. Hereafter cited as *EW*.

19. Laurence Holland first notices the likeness of James's construction in the preface to *The Princess* and his earlier characterization of Hawthorne in *The Expense of Vision*, 72.

20. Preface to *The American* in *EW*, 1062–63.

21. Letter to Charles Eliot Norton, 16 January 1872, *The Letters of Henry James*, 4 vols. (Cambridge: Harvard University Press, 1974–84), 1:250.

22. For an illuminating account of the "personal affections" in *The Princess Casamassima*, see Michael Anesko, *"Friction with the Market"* (New York: Oxford University Press, 1986), 101–18.

23. "The Science of Criticism," *EL*, 95–99, esp. 98.

24. For an opposite reading, see Tzvetan Todorov, "The Secret of Narrative," in *The Poetics of Prose*, trans. Richard Howard (Ithaca: Cornell University Press, 1977), 143–78. Todorov makes the point that James's life "is perfectly insignificant (like any presence): his work, an essential absence, asserts itself all the more powerfully" (178).

25. Preface to *The Lesson of the Master* in *EW*, 1234–36.

26. *The Notebooks of Henry James* (New York: Braziller, 1955), 220–21.

27. James went to work on the story at once, pausing only to record notes for two other works: the conversation recounted to him between Howells and Jonathan Sturges, in which the older man bids the young one to live all one can, which became *The Ambassadors*, and another, which never took recognizable shape, where a man escapes an unhappy marriage into a life of reading, until his wife returns. *The Notebooks*, 224–28.

28. Surprisingly, for all the speculation about the relation between James's life and fiction, no critical study exists that examines these four stories and the debacle of the theater. Yet no less a reader than Ford Madox Ford observed the importance of embarrassment for James. Ford writes that James was "our first Anglo-

Saxon writer to perceive that this life of ours is an affair of terminations and embarrassments. . . . Mr. James must have known too many shrinkings, embarrassments, and fine shades to render them without remorse; . . . Mr. James, then, never got over the crudities of merely living." Ford Madox Hueffer, "A Haughty and Proud Generation," *The Yale Review* 11 (1922): 706–7.

29. Rachel Salmon, "A Marriage of Opposites: Henry James's 'The Figure in the Carpet' and the Problem of Ambiguity," *ELH* 47 (1980): 788–803. See also William Goetz, *Henry James and the Darkest Absyss of Romance* (Baton Rouge: Louisiana State University Press, 1986), 166–72.

30. "The Figure in the Carpet," in *The Novels and Tales of Henry James*, 24 vols. (New York: Scribner's, 1909), New York Edition, 15:233.

31. See William Veeder, "Image as Argument: Henry James and the Style of Criticism," *The Henry James Review* 11 (Spring 1985): 172–81. Veeder also notes the interest of "sympathy" as a critical response, 175.

32. On the question of objective and subjective categories, see Paul Ricoeur, *Hermeneutics and the Human Sciences* (Cambridge: Cambridge University Press, 1981), 50. Ricoeur's treatment of "distanciation" as the key to breaking down the "dichotomous character" of interpretation—the split between objective and subjective principles—is akin to the Jamesian sense of "appreciation," 90–92. Cf. Steven Mailloux's positing of an "intersubjective model" of interpretation, in "Literary Theory and Psychological Reading Models," *Interpretive Conventions* (Ithaca: Cornell University Press, 1982), 19–39.

33. Letter to H. G. Wells, 21 September 1913, in *The Letters of Henry James* 5:686–87. For the broader implications of James's sense of reading, see Walter Benn Michaels, "Writers Reading: James and Eliot," *MLN* 91 (October 1976): 827–49, esp. 828–29. Also see Goetz, *Henry James and the Darkest Abyss of Romance*, 90–92.

34. Ruth Bernard Yeazell, "Talking in James," *Language and Knowledge in the Late Novels of Henry James* (Chicago: University of Chicago Press, 1976), 64–99.

35. Broadhead, *The School of Hawthorne*, 178.

36. "Nathaniel Hawthorne," *EL*, 458–68, esp. 459.

37. "The Art of Fiction," *EL*, 53.

38. "Letter to the Hon. Robert S. Rantoul," *EL*, 468–74, esp. 471.

39. Nicola Bradbury, *The Later Novels of Henry James* (Oxford: Clarendon Press, 1979), 1. Also see Leo Bersani, "The Jamesian Lie," *A Future for Astyanax* (Boston: Little Brown, 1976), 128–55.

40. For a comparison between *The Marble Faun* and *The Wings of the Dove*, see Marius Bewley, *The Complex Fate* (New York: Gordian Press, 1967), 31–54.

41. *The Wings of the Dove*, vols. 19 and 20 of *The Novels and Tales of Henry James*, 24 vols. (New York: Scribner's, 1909), New York Edition. Future references will be to book and chapter.

42. Among Hawthorne's plots, we can observe that Hester moves from object to

subject, while Coverdale reverses this progress. In *The Marble Faun*, the "trans-formations" entail Hilda's transition from object to subject, while Kenyon, like Holgrave in *Seven Gables*, learns to scale down his subjectivity.

43. For a study of the aestheticizing of the self in *Wings of the Dove*, see Ross Posnock, "James, Browning, and The Theatrical Self," *Henry James and the Problem of Robert Browning* (Athens: University of Georgia Press, 1985), 105–39, esp. 126–31. For a Lacanian treatment on the question of self as object, see Donna Przybylowicz, *Desire and Repression: The Dialectic of Self and Other in the Late Works of Henry James* (Tuscaloosa: University of Alabama Press, 1986), 1–38. Przybylowicz eschews discussion of *Wings*.

44. Cf. Ricoeur on Gadamer, *Hermeneutics and the Human Sciences*, 61–62.

45. Of the voluminous criticism on this question, see especially John Goode, " 'The pervasive mystery of style': *The Wings of the Dove*," in *The Air of Reality: New Essays on Henry James*, ed. John Goode (London: Methuen, 1972), 244–99, esp. 293–97.

46. *Notes of a Son and Brother*, in *Henry James Autobiography*, ed. and introd. Frederick W. Dupee (New York: Criterion, 1956), 283. Hereafter cited in text as *NSB*.

47. *The American Scene*, introd. Leon Edel (Bloomington: Indiana University Press, 1969), xxv–vi, 265–72. Hereafter cited in text as *AS*.

48. Letter to William James, 13 February 1870, in *The Letters of Henry James* 1:205.

49. For Leon Edel, this passage suggests how the "entire visit" left James "wondering how this place had nurtured Hawthorne," in *Henry James, The Master: 1901–1916* (New York: Avon, 1972, reprint, 1978), 250.

INDEX